NOTES
ON
ECCLESIOLOGY

Notes
on
Ecclesiology

by
Thomas E. Peck

With a new introduction
by C. N. Willborn
and
a biographical sketch of the author
by C. R. Vaughan.

Presbyterian Press
Taylors, SC

© 2005
Presbyterian Press
Greenville Presbyterian Theological Seminary
P.O. Box 770
Taylors, SC 29687
bookstore@gpts.edu

Printed in the United States of America

ISBN: 1-931639-07-8

Notes on Ecclesiology was originally published in Richmond, VA by the Presbyterian Committee of Publication in 1892.

Introduction

The nineteenth century was a fertile period for the development and explication of the doctrine of the Church. In Scotland, William Cunningham (1805-61) wrote numerous articles on the Church, which were gathered and published in 1863 as *Discussions on Church Principles.* This noteworthy volume was, according to the editors, concerned with the "character of a spiritual society," (iii). Cunningham was following in the footsteps of honored Scottish fathers in the faith, such as Andrew Melville and George Gillespie. In *Aaron's Rod Blossoming*, Gillespie provided the Church with a marvelously biblical defense of that all important distinction   of the two-fold kingdom of Christ—one a general kingdom, over which Christ rules with the Father and Spirit, and the other a spiritual kingdom, over which Christ has been given sole Kingship.   Thus, as John Brown of Haddington (1722-87) argued a century later, "Christ's spiritual kingdom is of a spiritual nature....Everything pertaining to the kingdom is spiritual," (*Systematic Theology,* 311).

Zeal for the doctrine of the Church was not limited to Scotland, for in the United States a number of men were expending much energy to expound a robust ecclesiology, one soundly biblical and God-honoring. The early Princetonian Samuel Miller (1769-1850) wrote a manual for presbyteries, a work on baptism, and, of course, his fine work on the ruling elder, which remains in print today. About the same period, the Associate Reformed Church gave North America John Mason (1770-1829), who carried on an active ministry as pastor, educator, and publisher. The pastor from New York City provided the Church a fine general work on ecclesiology entitled *Essays on the Church of God,* a work which was both appreciated and influential on both sides of the Mason-Dixon Line.

One of those men influenced by Mason's ecclesiology was Thomas Ephraim Peck (1822-93). Peck was born in Columbia, South Carolina and reared by a good and godly mother, Sarah Parke Peck who was prematurely widowed when young Thomas was but ten years of age. After graduating from South Carolina College (now University of South Carolina), Peck entered upon studies at Columbia Seminary but had to withdraw due to serious illness. In the end, he prepared for the ministry by studying privately with his former college professor and a Presbyterian minister, James Henley Thornwell. After holding pastorates in South Carolina and Baltimore, Maryland, he joined the faculty of Union Seminary, Virginia in 1860 where he served the Presbyterian Church faithfully as Professor of Ecclesiastical History and Church Government for more than twenty years. In 1883, the mature and respected Peck succeeded Robert Lewis Dabney (who departed for Texas and the founding of the University of Texas) as Professor of Systematic Theology.

Peck's earliest contributions reflect his debt to men like Mason and Thornwell and their emphasis on the biblico-theological *loci* of ecclesiology. He argued successfully for the restoration of a long neglected "divinely appointed ordinance of public worship," namely, *the collect.* The collection of tithes and offerings is hardly to be found absent from an evangelical worship service in our time, but in the day of Peck it laid buried deep in the recesses of history. Due to a wonderful paper originally published in pamphlet form in 1854 and later in his *Miscellanies,*[1] the Church was awakened to this element of public worship and is better for it.

His efforts to re-establish *the collect* in the worship of Christ's Church stand hand-in-hand with his commitment to restore to the visible Church her divinely prescribed fiscal and temporal agent—the deacon. Here Peck is taking up a cause of his mentor, James Thornwell and in chapter nineteen of this reprint, Peck is at his very best in setting forth the biblical office of deacon. It was the superlative churchman's desire that the office would finally be restored to such a biblical degree that widows would find their proper ecclesiastical protection and provision, the sick and lonely would find repair in the Church, the spiritual message would be to the whole man, soul *and* body, and so the reproach of the world removed from the Church and greater honor bestowed upon the King of the Church.

These efforts served as a catalyst for more extensive work on the diaconate from another disciple of Thornwell and fellow South Carolinian, John L. Girardeau. Through the labors principally of Peck and Girardeau a more complete office of deacon was adopted by the Presbyterian Church in the United States as seen in subsequent revisions to the Book of Church Order (1879-1938) in the Presbyterian Church in the United States (Southern Presbyterian Church).

The present reprint, *Notes on Ecclesiology,* contains Peck's mature thought on the doctrine of the church, which includes his essay on the diaconate. We may lament with C. R. Vaughn that Professor Peck did not write more for public consumption, his *Notes,* the reader will find, pro-

---

[1] "Address on the Subject of Systematic Beneficence," in *Writings of Thomas E. Peck* (1895-97; reprint, Carlisle, PA: Banner of Truth Trust, 1999), 1:130-45.

vides a solid presentation and defense of divine right (*jus divinum*) Presbyterianism. Peck believed that Christ so loved His Church that He provided her with clear details in the nature and manner of church governance. Christ, Peck believed, did not leave His people as orphans in this world, but gave her the best of care through the offices, ordinances, sacraments, and worship of the Church. The biblical doctrine of the Church, the spiritual society of God, is set forth in this little volume in a logical and warm fashion by a master interpreter of Holy Scripture.

The present reprint on ecclesiology includes a brief biographical sketch of the author by Clement R. Vaughn, a colleague in the Union Seminary, which lends further insight into the man and his ministry. It is indeed an opportune time for this fine volume to be made available and it is the hope of this writer and the publisher that the Church will avail herself of this fine biblical study. No words can commend enough Thomas Peck's *Notes on Ecclesiology*. May God bless the distribution of this work to a new generation; then the Church will be stronger and more beautiful for having received refreshing from Her Covenant Head. SDG!

C. N. Willborn
Associate Professor of Church History and Biblical Theology
Greenville Presbyterian Theological Seminary
Taylors, SC

The biographical sketch of Thomas E. Peck that follows originally appeared in the March-April issue (5:225-242) of the *Union Seminary Magazine* in 1894.

BIOGRAPHICAL SKETCH OF DR. T. E. PECK.[1]

By Rev. C. R. Vaughan, D. D.

D R. PECK was born in Columbia, South Carolina, on the 29th of January, 1822. He was the son of Ephraim Peck, a native of Connecticut, and Sarah Bannister Parke, daughter of Thomas Parke, LL. D., professor of the classic languages in the College of South Carolina. His father, a man of delicate constitution, had come south for his health, and opened a small mercantile establishment in Columbia. After a few years' residence he united with the First Presbyterian Church, and developed a strongly marked and active Christian character. On the 4th of January, 1821, he intermarried with a daughter of Professor Parke, and after a married life of somewhat over eleven years died, leaving four living children, two sons and two daughters. Thomas, the oldest child, was ten years old at the time, and William, the youngest, just two months old. The daughters, Mary Susan and Ann Catharine, grew to womanhood and married, the first, Rev. Samuel H. Hay, the second, Rev. Lucius Simonton. After the death of her husband Mrs. Peck lived with her father until his death in 1840. She opened a school for small children, and soon her school-room was full. For many years she pursued this business for the support of her children. Mrs. Peck was a remarkable woman—strong-minded, cheerful, a devoted Christian, resolute, active and persevering. Prematurely widowed, yet content with her

---

[1] Dr. Vaughan prepared this sketch for the *Union Seminary Magazine.* It appeared first in that periodical in the March-April No. of 1894.

iii

lot, the brave young mother fought her battle for her children with consummate energy and with unfaltering faith in a covenant-keeping God. Her reward was rich, even in this world, and in the noble character and career of her oldest son her reward was richest. Living in the home of his grandfather, the early days of Thomas Peck were spent in the atmosphere of a college. His traits were early formed into a scholastic type. His preparatory training was conducted in the academy of the town then under charge of John Daniel, an efficient and faithful teacher. He was ready for college before he had completed his fourteenth year. At that early age he entered on his collegiate course, took the regular curriculum, and graduated with great distinction in the eighteenth year of his age. In the year 1838 he was brought into connection with the person who was destined to exert the controlling influence on his mental and spiritual character. Dr. James H. Thornwell entered the college on his first professorship at that time. The young professor and his congenial pupil were soon attracted to each other, and the web of destiny began to weave between them. A strong personal attachment sprang up. Dr. Thornwell was a frequent and welcome visitor at the home of his pupil as well as a most influential power over him in the class-room. Under this fortunate connection young Peck was brought to the obedience of the Christian faith. This occurred in his junior year, but he made no open profession of his faith until after his graduation. During his college career his grandfather, Dr. Parke, served as librarian and treasurer of the institution, and his grandson was associated with him in the discharge of both offices during the intervals in his studies. After the death of his grandfather young Peck was continued in the office of librarian. There is nothing known of the mental processes by which he was led to the conviction that it was his duty to enter the ministry. It was probably under the same influence which had led him to the acceptance of the gospel. After his mind was made up he entered the Seminary, but before two weeks had passed he was suddenly seized with an attack of sickness, and was forbidden by his physician to resume his studies for six months after his recovery. Singular to say, he never re-entered the Seminary. Continuing in the position of librarian to the college, he commenced the study of theology under the guidance of his friend, the young Professor of Metaphysics. All his theological training was from him. It is a singular circumstance that, living in a stone's throw of a theological seminary, he should never have sought its advantages. He had, undoubtedly, an extraordinary substitute in the great talents and strong personal friendship of an extraordinary man. At that time both of them had doubts of the advantages of a seminary training; nor were Dr. Peck's views on the subject entirely settled until he was called himself to the work of teaching in such a school. By his own experience of both methods of ministerial training, he finally became satisfied of the superior value of the seminary system, except the cloistered life of the student. He at length obtained licensure and entered on his work. His first engagement was in Fairfield district where he preached to the churches of Salem and Jackson, the latter now Lebanon Church. While thus engaged his friend, Dr. Thornwell, received a call to the Second Church of Baltimore, just vacated by the resignation of Dr. Robert J. Breckenridge. This call was accepted. But the College and State of South Carolina generally were opposed to his going, and insisted on the rigor of the law, which required a year's notice to be given before a professor could resign. With the consent of the church in Baltimore, Dr. Thornwell sent Mr. Peck to fill the place until he could be honorably released. This policy ultimately resulted in Thornwell's remaining in Columbia, but the movement proved decisive in the case of his young friend. A church was in course of erection on Broadway Street in Baltimore for the accommodation of a colony from the Second Church. The building being completed and a church organized, Mr. Peck was called as pastor, and entered on the charge in 1846. The congregation was never large, and there was little prospect of encouraging growth. The population of that part of the city was chiefly composed of Methodists and Romanists; and for several years the fine abilities and faithful preaching of the young pastor contended in vain with the surrounding difficulties. His style of preaching, though of a high order, was not popular in the sense which draws people without any partialities to his system of belief to attend on the services of a minister. His labor was not altogether in vain. The congregation grew steadily, though slowly, and the thorough training of a teacher so clear and effective moulded many a valuable servant of the kingdom who afterwards became the strong helper of other churches.

In the year 1857, on the retirement of a warm personal friend from the charge of the First Presbyterian Church of Lynchburg, Virginia, Mr. Peck was unanimously called to the pastoral office, without ever having been seen or heard by any member of the congregation. With his peculiar views such a call came with peculiar force. He at once visited the church, and on a survey of the ground announced his willingness to accept the call if the church, having now seen and heard him, saw proper to confirm their invitation. His presence and the taste of his quality intensified the purpose of the people into eagerness; the call was renewed and promptly accepted, unless the Presbytery of Baltimore interposed to prevent. That body, which had been content to let him struggle on in this difficult position, without any special sympathy, at once roused to the apprehension of losing him. The Central Church, just vacated by the resignation of Dr. Stuart Robinson, immediately extended a call to him. The two proposals came before the Presbytery at once, and the body decided in favor of the church in Baltimore. Mr.

Peck, suppressing his personal preferences, assumed the care of a large and important field in the same city in which he had spent twelve years of discouraging work.

After he had been actively engaged for several years as pastor in the Broadway charge, Mr. Peck was married to Miss Ellen C. Richardson, the daughter of Scotch parents, and a staunch Presbyterian. The marriage proved singularly fortunate. No two people were ever better suited to each other. The strong character and sterling piety of the wife was just suited to the strong character and sterling graces of the husband; and during a married life of nearly forty years each proved the best earthly blessing of the other. Seven daughters were born to them—four in Baltimore and three at Hampden-Sidney. Three of these died in infancy, and one in the very bloom of womanhood.

After Mr. Peck had been in charge of the Central Church some twelve or eighteen months, in the year 1859, he was elected to the chair of Ecclesiastical History and Church Government in Union Theological Seminary in Virginia. The call was promptly declined, for the reason that he had been so short a time in the Central Church he did not suppose he had fulfilled the divine will in putting him into that field. But during the ensuing winter his health began to fail; he was becoming fully satisfied that preaching in so large an audience room was injuring him, and when the call to the Seminary was renewed in the spring of 1860, he accepted it. He reached his new post on the 7th of April, 1860, and entered on the happier life, and the long term of over thirty-three years of honored and useful service, which was terminated by his death on the 2nd of October, 1893. His health had been steadily failing for a year or two before his death, but his work was unflinchingly done up to the close of the term in the spring of that year. But the welcome vacation brought no relief to the subtle disease that was preying upon him. He steadily grew worse, and on the opening of the fall term he was unable to meet his classes. The work of the Seminary had just gotten under way when it was interrupted by the tidings that the venerable and beloved instructor in the theological department had passed into the peace of God. He had not completed his seventy-third year. On the afternoon of the next day the funeral services, held in the College Church, were attended by a large assembly, composed of the entire population of the village of Hampden-Sidney, the officers and students of both institutions, and delegates from the surrounding congregations. The demonstration of respect and sorrow was as marked as were the claims of the dead to receive it. All the family of the deceased who were in this country, except his aged mother, were in attendance and shared in the amazement of the whole assembly in hearing the voice of the widowed wife mingling bravely in the song of praise which greeted the advancement of the good man into his high estate. The quiet history of a quiet life is easily told. The task of making a just estimate of the talents and character of a remarkable man now remains to be done, and presents a work of much greater difficulty.

The personal character of Dr. Peck was strongly and beautifully marked. Its leading quality was an absolute and inflexible integrity. Even in his boyhood he was grave and thoughtful beyond his years, though now and then the underlying traits of a different sort would show themselves in outbreaks of joyous merriment. He was not fond of society ; he was not fond of sport; his habits were studious; his mind was more engaged with books and serious reflection than with the employments which are commonly suited to the boyish age. As he grew older these tendencies strengthened. Under the care of his faithful teacher, John Daniel, he made steady and rapid progress. His fidelity in the discharge of his duties made him the favorite pupil of his master. Always obedient, always faithful to his appointed tasks, a strong personal attachment sprang up between them. He was fully prepared for college before he had completed his fourteenth year. He at once entered on his collegiate career, but, unfortunately, was placed in the freshman class when he ought to have been placed in a higher position, where his energies would have been suitably taxed. He found the tasks of the freshman course so easy and familiar, his well-formed habits, not yet confirmed and hardened, gave way to a carelessness which finally brought on him a touch of censure. But only a touch was needed, and from that time his energies were so well directed that he graduated with great distinction. During his tenure of the librarian's office, he made good use of his opportunities for personal improvement, and after Dr. Thornwell's appearance on the scene, and especially after the entry of divine grace into his heart, his character soon took on the colors which marked it to the end of his days. The natural gravity of his temperament, and the natural bent of his intellect to a thorough and accurate apprehension of whatever subject engaged his attention, developed a character of intense integrity, sober, steadfast, staunch in principle, tinged with something of the severity which strong convictions will always impart, and is often mistaken for the severity of personal disposition. So far was this from being true of Dr. Peck, that underneath this grave earnestness and elevation of moral conviction glowed the fire of a generous enthusiasm, warm affections, and what seemed to be so incongruous as not to be suspected, a keen sense of humor, a lively wit, and strong sensibilities to the charms of home, to the value of friendship, to the love of country, and to the love of race. The most marked trait of his character, mental and moral, was his devotion to principle. His intellect always sought the central principle of a subject; his heart was always open to the naked force of obligation. Conformity to the will of his chosen Lord was the leading trait of his religious character. Obedience to the law of right, full adjustment of character, feeling and conduct to the demands of

truth in every sphere, and especially in the sphere of revelation, were the objects which regulated all his energies. He
would do what he thought was right, no matter if he stood
alone against overwhelming odds, no matter whom it hurt,
no matter whom it offended. He was repeatedly tried in this
way during his connection with the Presbytery of Baltimore.
He more than once voted alone against the whole body, and
the event almost invariably justified his resistance to the
prevailing current. His convictions of the obligations of
right were inexorable. This resolute fidelity sometimes
puzzled the lovers of expediency, and their politic sup-
pleness shrank under the severity of convictions which they
could not understand. Yet there was not an atom of pride
or selfishness in it; it was the sole datum of an integrity
that never flinched from responsibility, or tampered with its
own convictions of truth and rightness. His views of himself
were profoundly humble. He saw the evils of his own heart
with a distinctness and a deep sensibility which scourged his
self-esteem into complete abnegation. All these exhibits of
stern fidelity were the fruit of his deep insight into the obligation of truth and duty. If there ever lived in this world a
man of high and staunch principle, it was the subject of this
sketch. Of the stuff martyrs are made of, he was all compact. His ideal of Christian character was framed on the
words of our Lord, "*If ye love me, keep my commandments.*"
His conscience was tender and imperative in its ascendency.
His affections glowed under his steadfast demeanor like the
white heat of anthracite. It is often the case—and he was a
typical instance—that under the grave and steadfast character of a Calvinist, so often misunderstood, there glows the
sweetest and tenderest affections, the liveliest sensibilities to
poetic beauty, to the charms of wit, and even a frolicsome
humor. Dr. Peck was full of these seemingly incongruous
qualities. His affections were strong and naturally received
what they gave. His family were devotedly fond of him; his

students loved him; his friends were strongly attached to him. His laughter was so full of intense merriment it was irresistibly contagious. His own wit was as bright as his enjoyment of the wit of others. It seemed a singular expression of character to see this grave, earnest mind abandon itself to a hilarity so free and joyous. His feelings were all deep and energetic, and in their higher moods would sometimes flow over into his preaching until the vigorous logic and the stately march of his periods would glow like a chain of steel in the fire of a furnace. In the earlier years of his religious history, he was subject to occasional fits of depression, but in later years these passed away. This is the common experience of men of unusual talents. They stand on the threshold of the great arena eager for the competition and thirsting for success, yet uncertain of themselves; their abilities untested; and the strong impulses to action checked and fretted with the doubt whether the venture will prove a source of satisfaction or distress. In many cases this stage of the mental development produces moodiness and irritation; discontent with self breeds suspicion of others; and the manifestations of character become unpromising and perilous. In Dr. Peck's case there was nothing of this; the firm texture of his mind, and his strong hold on the principles of religion, held down such effects of depressed feeling, and left him only to the grief it created, and to the silence of a steady endurance. As he passed on, and the development of his intellect and his growth in grace expanded into maturity, his steadfast nature, with its underlying currents of lively and affectionate sensibility, grew equable in their habitual manifestations. His work, whatever it was, was always well and faithfully done, according to the law of his own exact and veracious conception of duty.

As a thinker, Dr. Peck was peculiar in some respects. His intellect was thoroughly developed under the boundary lines of his own gifts. Its leading characteristic was the power of analysis; and this faculty was under the control of a feeling of obligation to truth which determined the utmost thoroughness and exactness, both in his processes and his conclusions. He struck straight for the central principle in every subject of his investigation, and vigorously followed the logical lines of its development. In his sermons, in the briefs of his lectures, in all his work, this character of completeness and precision of outline, this thoroughness of analysis, was conspicuous. His logical expositions rung clear in every link. This trait seems to have been characteristic from the beginning to the end of his career. It appears in a marked degree in one of his trial pieces for licensure now before us. It appears in a still more striking form in his *Ecclesiology*, the little work which embodies the mature results of long years of professional exertion in the class-room. Occasionally this vigorous pursuit of thoroughness subjected him to disadvantage in his public preaching. He was at times apparently over-trained, made stale by over-exertion, to use a phrase from the scientific discipline of modern athletics, and there would be a noticeable lapse of faculty due to weariness from the strong wrestle with his deep compacted analysis. But as a general rule, it brought him into the pulpit or the chair of his lecture-room with a mind full of well-digested thought. He left little room for impulse, for sudden inspiration, for flashes of feeling or fancy. His mastery of the art of mental composition was complete in a rare degree, and when he was called upon to use his well-wrought material he was ready to respond. Not very often, and yet not very rarely, his feelings would kindle, not by flashes but by steady increase, into an intense glowing animation, and interpenetrate the strong-linked cable of his argument until it was hot with passionate emotion. But usually it came forth in a clear, well-sustained and strong stream of calm thought, bearing on the purpose in view with pointed logical power. Dr. Peck was no speculative genius, careering over the fields on either side of his line of march, and pushing on mere tentative expeditions. His mind was not inventive, but didactic—trained to exposition, not to discovery. His fidelity to his task as the teacher of a great fixed creed, his love of positive truth, his conscientious obligation to present no mere probability as authoritative reality kept him back from all mere tentative excursions. This stern integrity made him the invaluable teacher, not less than the high-toned Christian man that he was. But as an expositor of truth, as an exegete of Scripture, as a philosophic student of history, he was probably without a rival in his day. Clear as a brilliant day, his well-hammered expositions left the feeling on his audiences in the public assembly and on his classes that he had reached and was building on the bottom rock of his subject. The only fault of his teaching was the natural tendency in the class of minds to which he belonged to push his logic to extremes, and with less regard to the effect of circumstances in modifying conclusions than is necessary in some cases. His place as *a teacher* will be hard to fill.

This supremacy of the analytic faculty obscured faculties of less prominence though existing in no unseemly disproportion to it. His imaginative faculty was vigorous, but was seldom allowed to show itself in those forms in which alone it is popularly recognized. It made itself apparent in his clear and often stately style, in the general hues and colors sometimes thrown over his topics, and in the definite outlines impressed on his narrative of facts. It seldom appeared in the mere ornament of his diction; still less frequently in positive trope and figure, or imaginative analogies.

As a preacher, Dr. Peck justly took a high rank. His manner was ordinarily quiet; he used little gesture; there was no dramatic power. But from the full fountain of a full mind flowed a steady stream of clear-cut and continuous argument, brightened now and then with a diffused coloring of imaginative conception and infused with a spirit of habit-

ual earnestness, which now and then deepened into passionate fervor, and rose into the region of a positive and high
eloquence. Occasionally a flash of sarcasm would bite in
the impression of the truth with extraordinary power. Generally there was an entire mastery of himself; occasionally
he would be caught up in the torrent of his emotions, and
the entire audience would follow with breathless interest a
discourse protracted far beyond the modest limit ordinarily
placed on his discussions. A scene like this in his earlier
life is still remembered in the Buffalo congregation, when he
preached for an hour and a half on the anticipation of heaven,
during which he came down from the pulpit and walked back
and forth before the people with his eyes streaming with
tears and his lips trembling under the torrent of his pathetic
conceptions. A similar scene in some respects occurred in a
sermon delivered in Farmville during the war. Such exhibi-
tions, however, were rare. The prevailing type of his preaching was just what the commission of the gospel requires of
every gospel minister, "*Go teach all nations.*" Dr. Peck's
preaching was didactic and eminently instructive; its staple
was clear exposition; it was aimed to develop as clearly and
fully as possible the mind of the Spirit. The convincing
power of his statements was wonderful, and constituted one
of the charms of his preaching. His exegesis of Scripture
was exact and full; and when he had hewed the truth out of
the mine, his analysis of its significance bore the stamp of
that thoroughness and exactness which was the leading trait
of his thinking. His enforcement of the truth on the heart
and conscience bore the marks of the deep earnestness of his
convictions. His style, both in speaking and writing, under-
went a change as he passed from youth to age, although even
to the last, when roused in preaching, the stately march of
his periods renewed the musical vigor of his earlier discussions. The longer sentences which distinguished his style at
first grew compact and often curt in his later work. The ex-

pression of collateral connections in his ideas was cut down; all modifications which interrupted the straight progress of the main thought were pruned away. He struck straight from the shoulder; every word not essential to carry the thought was ruled out. His style grew sententious and terse, almost curt. The thought stood revealed in itself and in its relation to the end in view, with no room for question of its meaning or its intent. This development no doubt was due to the training of the class-room, and the necessity for precision and clearness in his instruction of his classes. But it was at the same time a development along the line of the leading trait of his intellect, and probably would have made its appearance if he had continued to teach only from the pulpit. His manner of speaking also changed; there was little variety in his emphasis in passing from sentence to sentence, but the supreme power of his clear thinking was unabated to the end.

Dr. Peck was eminently a biblical preacher. He understood that his commission was to preach the word, to teach whatsoever the Master had said. His faithful and reverent spirit abhorred the prostitution of the Christian pulpit into a rostrum from which all sorts of subjects were discussed, and the instruction of the people made subordinate to their amusement. In this matter his example and his instructions were faithfully exerted to impress correct conceptions of gospel preaching on the students under his care. As long as such men are moulding the character of the rising ministry, the church has at least one valuable guarantee that it will not lack for ministers who need not be ashamed of their work.

As a teacher, Dr. Peck carried the same traits of thoroughness and exactness into the class-room. His explanations were always clear, distinct in outline and thoroughly digested in the analysis of the body of the subject. His procedure was the old common-sense Socratic method of question and answer, following the statements of the text-book closely, and thus discovering the fidelity with which the student had mastered it. Where he agreed fully with the text his concurrent expositions were brief. When he differed with the text his expositions of his own views were extended and carefully made. Occasionally he would resort to what was the favorite method of Dr. Baxter and Dr. Thornwell. After requiring the statement and proof of a point from the student, each of those great dialecticians would assume the defence of the opposing error, thus revealing the lines of attack on the truth and requiring the learner to expose the error and defend the truth. Then, in the close of the wrestle, the teacher would expound clearly the whole ground covered, display the error in the antagonist reasoning, and show the strength of the supports of the truth. As a general rule, Dr. Peck was content with a fair statement of the opposing position, and then with a direct exposure of the infirmity of its defences. His manner to the students was always kindly, not demonstratively sympathetic, though his sympathies were always true and strong, and whenever an appeal was made to them it was always so met as to make a repetition far easier than the original application. He was hardly ever severe in censure; a silence that was as vocal as words and more impressive was his method of rebuke, and a few grave words of kindly warning were the only approach to discipline. He was so revered by his classes nothing more was needed. He was solicitous to evoke the powers of the student, and used an effective degree of effort for the purpose, but had no extraordinary aptitude for this species of influence. His great merit lay in the unrivalled clearness of his expositions of the truth and its opposing error. There was no excuse for any student leaving the class-room with any incompetent conceptions. If he paid due attention he could not fail to carry away just views of the subject.

As a writer, the traits of style which distinguished his preaching appeared in his written discussions. Whenever

he did write for the public press the work was valuable; but
it was a fault with him, as it is with other gifted men, that he
published so little. He has left behind him but few completely written sermons, but a great mass of notes and
sketches from which it may be possible to make a valuable
contribution to the literature of the church, and to leave
something more than his living influence to attest the qualities
of a most noble servant of the Master, and to extend the influence of his noble gifts. We earnestly hope this may be
done. Dr. Peck published one small volume containing the
notes of his lectures on Ecclesiology. It is packed from beginning to end with the rich results of his study, and lends
emphasis to the regret that he published no more. Occupying for years the chair of Ecclesiastical History and Church
Government, he was fully competent to have given many a
valuable lesson to the church and the world from his thorough
mastery of the story of the visible kingdom of our Lord.
Occupying for years the chair of Theology, he was fully competent to have added to the treasures of the church in the
exposition and defence of her creed. His actual publications,
besides the little volume just mentioned, are limited to a few
review articles, a few sermons, and a few articles in the
Baltimore Critic, of which he was at one time joint-editor
with Stuart Robinson. It is due to the memory of Dr. Peck
that this deficiency be made up out of his posthumous writings if it can be done.

There is one great service rendered by him which is not
generally known and in some respects perhaps the greatest
he ever rendered. He is to be credited with restoring to the
church that principle of her creed which is now recognized,
that giving is an ordinance of worship. It is assuredly a remarkable fact that principles and even public offices, distinctly set forth and solemnly covenanted to be observed in
the written creed of a church, may not only pass out of use,
but actually out of knowledge. The office of the deacon and

the principle that giving is an ordinance of public worship are samples of this fact in the history of the Presbyterian Church in this country, and we believe also in the history of the same church in the British Islands and on the continent of Europe. When the work of missions at home and in foreign parts fairly begun in this country, the only recognized method of raising the necessary funds was by means of agents sent round to visit the churches. The very end and purpose of the organized church was this very enterprise of spreading the gospel and providing the men and means to do it through her own established instrumentalities. Yet this great leading end of the church had completely died out of the knowledge and practice of the church; and when, under the stress of the difficulties created by this extraordinary condition of things, Dr. John Holt Rice offered a resolution in the General Assembly of the Presbyterian denomination that the church of Christ was by its very nature a missionary society, he was construed as making an unauthorized innovation. The reason of this state of things was this: The missionary movement was begun and directed by the Congregational churches of New England. The organic weakness of that system compelled the formation of societies outside of the church to carry on the work. The very terms of the apostolic commission and charter of the church required this work to be carried on by the church itself and not by any outside organization whatever. But the Presbyterian Church, blind as a bat to the fundamental object of her own existence, took up the work of missions in coöperation with these Congregational societies. It nearly resulted in her ruin. In the course of time and events, however, her eyes were opened; but when she essayed to withdraw from this anomalous connection, and go into the discharge of her fundamental and plain duty, she was openly resisted. She was charged with bad faith. Her right to establish her own missions was denied. She was held bound by a temporary alliance with those who had no sympathy with her principles, rather than by the command of her Head. The extraordinary conflict which ensued explained the extraordinary resolution of Dr. Rice, which to us seems as superfluous as a formal declaration that it is the business of a bank to do a banking business, or of a college that it is designed for educational purposes. The old school of Presbyterians, having opened their eyes, clung firmly to the discovered line of their duty. They withdrew from their anomalous entanglement and commenced their own work. But they were still in the dark as to the principles which regulated the subject, and years were to elapse before they succeeded in embodying their creed in their practice. They continued to raise the funds for missions by travelling agents. They seemed utterly unable to rise to the conception, simple and obtrusively obvious as it is, that the revenues could be raised under the pastors and other officers of each church. The system of agencies, however, worked so badly and was fruitful of so much mischief to the pastors and churches, thoughtful men began to turn to the teachings of the Bible, the creed and common sense, and soon the divinely-given and distinctly covenanted principles which regulated the subject began to emerge. That great man and staunch Presbyterian, Robert J. Breckenridge, then a pastor in Baltimore, and editor of the *Baltimore Literary and Evangelical Magazine* began to teach what he had discovered in the creed as drawn from the Bible. He found that the office representing the revenue and charitable side of the church had utterly perished out of the very knowledge of the church that such an officer was a part of her organization. Out of nine hundred churches then under the General Assembly only *nine* had deacons. It is now fully recognized that the organization of a Presbyterian church is as incomplete without deacons as a human face is without a nose. It is now recognized that the office of deacon is as much, and even more distinctly, an office of divine appointment as the office of ruling elder.

These principles, though as truly in the covenanted creed of the church then as they are now, had sunken out of view; and it is no wonder that the church had lost sight of the revenue principles of the kingdom when the revenue officers of the kingdom had been abolished. Under the able vindication of Breckenridge and the coadjutors who at once flocked around him, the office of the deacon was restored to the place the Lord of the kingdom had given it, and an immense impulse was given to the revenue and work of the church. For all the benefits of this restoration, thanks are due, under God, to Robert Breckenridge.

But all was not yet recognized that the Bible and the solemnly covenanted standards of the Presbyterian Church demanded. The revenue officers of the kingdom were found, but not the principles and rules for raising the revenue. Under the discoveries of Breckenridge the travelling agents were abolished, and the raising of the revenue was recognized as a regular part of the work of every organized church under the orders of its own government in the elders, and by the executive agency of its own financial officers, the deacons. But the system worked under friction; collections were looked upon under purely business aspects; they were not considered as expressions of religious feelings, or as having any sanctifying purpose. The rectifying principle for all this incompetent conception of the subject had long ago been drawn from the Scriptures and embodied in the Standards. They taught that giving was a divinely-appointed ordinance of public worship; that it sustained the same relation to the sanctification of the worshipper that, prayer, or praise, or sacrament sustained; that its benefits were conditioned by the spirit in which the ordinance was used, just as every other ordinance was conditioned. It was a principle of extraordinary power, and bore upon personal and spiritual benefits to the user of the ordinance of great value. looking not merely to the resources of the kingdom, but to the personal sanctification and comfort of the worshipper. This is now the universally recognized doctrine and practice of the church. Yet it lay long forgotten in the creed which every minister and elder of the church formally adopts at their ordination, and which the whole church glories in calling its own. That it was discovered and brought out to exert its vast and beneficent influence, we trust for ages to come, we owe under God to Dr. Thomas E. Peck. He was the first to find it in the creed and first to bring it back to the knowledge and obedience of the church. He did it in a paper, short, but crammed full of such irresistible evidence that it passed promptly when presented to the Presbytery of Baltimore, and began its march to the ascendency it now maintains. Dr. Peck's titles to the esteem and gratitude of the church are many; but no service but one—his training of the ministry for several years—rendered by him compares in importance with this.

There is another development of the deacon's office required by the plain and positive demand of the Standards and the word of God which remains to be accomplished. The financial side of the deacon's office, important as it is, bears no proportion to the importance of its chief significance. The deacon's office represents that side of the Christian church by which it confronts the temporal evils of human life. It is also our Lord's appointment to secure the protection of his widows, his orphans, and his dependent poor within his kingdom. When it is advanced, as it will be finally, from its theoretical position in the creed to that practical development in every Christian church which it was designed to secure, it will add immeasurably to the safety of God's helpless servants, to the well-being of the sick and friendless stranger, to the honor of the church, and to the glory of her benignant head. It will extinguish the reproach on evangelical Protestant Christianity that it is solely concerned for the spiritual welfare of mankind, and makes no provision for their temporal wants. It will strip Rome of one of her boasted superiorities and do justice to the kingdom of Christ. God speed the day.

Dr. Peck's domestic character and relations remains to be analyzed. In his family relations he was most happy. He was reverenced and dearly loved by all its members. A most affectionate and faithful father, his children never once seemed to think of such a thing as going contrary to his wishes. His sway was that of absolute confidence in his wisdom, rectitude, and affection. a confidence interpenetrated and colored by the warmest personal love. The sunnier elements of his nature broke from the restraints of his habitual gravity more freely and frequently under the shadow of his own roof-tree than anywhere else. In times of public trial and personal affliction, he was the calmest and quietest of men. The secret of his peace was his deep, unfailing confidence in God. During the war, when the pressure on the people at home for the means of sustenance had become stringent and universal, the writer of this sketch, then living some forty or forty-five miles distant, happened to meet some one from the neighborhood of the Seminary and inquired how the professors were getting on. "Well," said he, "Dr. Dabney is fighting the Yankees, Dr. Smith is hunting for provisions, and Dr. Peck is trusting in God." He felt the calamity involved in the overthrow of the liberties and rights of self-government of the Southern people as every good man in the Confederacy felt it, but he bore it in silence and went on with his work. In his domestic afflictions, and in the final long struggle with the disorder that ended his life, the same steadiness and absolute submission was his prevalent feeling. The words were frequently on his lips, "It is the Lord, let him do what seemeth him good." His last hours were sunken into insensibility, and he passed into the visions of the eternal peace without a sign of his parting.

A brave and strong standard-bearer has fallen at his post,

faithful to the last. An example of fidelity to the truth, regardless of the judgments of men and only mindful of the
will of the Master of Assemblies, has been left to those who
come after him. A most accomplished advocate and defender of the faith has left his work to be taken up by another. A noble character has left its record on earth and
gone to its reward in heaven. The tears of natural grief are
mingled with the upturned and smiling eyes which follow
with joyful confidence the good man's ascent into the region
of endless rest.

> "Avaunt; to-night my heart is light;
>   No dirge will I upraise;
> But waft the saint upon his flight
>   With a pæan of God's praise.
> Let no bell toll, lest his glad soul,
>   Amid its hallowed mirth,
> Should catch the note as it doth float
>   Up from the accursed earth.
> From grief and groan to a golden throne
>   His favored soul is riven;
> From grief and groan to a golden throne
>   Beside the King of Heaven."
>
> —*From Poe's Lenore Unpaganized.*

Dr. Peck left a family of a remarkable character in more
than one respect. One of the most remarkable members of
it is his aged mother, who, in her ninety-third year, survives
her oldest as well as her youngest child. Infirm, but in
sound health and with faculties unimpaired, the venerable
saint bears her bereavement with cheerful trust in a long-
tried and trusted Saviour. She waits without impatience and
with serene hope her own summons to cross the river of the
bitter water and rest in the shade of the trees on the farther
side. Mrs. Peck, the widowed wife of the dead soldier of
Christ, bears her loss with a serenity of hope and confidence
not seen once in a thousand cases of similar bereavement.
Her steadfast and brave faith in the glorious assurances of
the Christian gospel so completely overshadowed her perso-

nal loss in the heart-felt realization of the glory into which her husband had entered that she had no room for thoughts of self or the losses of her home and children. She said she was so taken up with the thought of his delight that when the funeral assembly was called on to close the funeral service with a song of praise to God, her own voice mingled with clear and decisive expression in the ascending harmony. For the first time in the life of every one present this strange and noble triumph of faith and hope was witnessed—a freshly widowed Christian wife with unfaltering tones praising God for his goodness to her dead.

Dr. Peck leaves three living daughters out of the seven that were given him : Sarah, the wife of Rev. James Edward Booker, pastor of the Hebron church, Virginia, in Augusta county; Ellen, wife of Rev. Alexander Sprunt, pastor at Rock Hill, South Carolina; and Sophie. wife of Rev. James R. Graham, Jr., missionary in China. Several grandchildren give reasonable assurance that his blood will continue to run in the veins of the living on earth for years to come. Meanwhile he rests in the vision of God, and will be fully content when his body, as well as his soul, awakes in the likeness of his Lord.

ECCLESIOLOGY.

NOTES

ON

ECCLESIOLOGY.

BY

T. E. PECK, D. D., LL. D.,

PROFESSOR IN UNION THEOLOGICAL SEMINARY.

RICHMOND, VA.
PRESBYTERIAN COMMITTEE OF PUBLICATION.
1892.

PREFATORY NOTE.

THE most of these "Notes" were printed in 1880 by the students of Union Theological Seminary in Virginia, exclusively for their own use. They are now published for the first time. About fifty pages have been added, the additional matter consisting of the expansion of the hints on "Apostolical Succession" and of a short chapter on "The Deacon's Office."

THE AUTHOR.

CONTENTS.

6   CONTENTS.

ECCLESIOLOGY.

INTRODUCTORY.

THE scientific theologians of Germany have arranged the cycle of sacred knowledge under five leading categories, viz.: 1, " *Theology*," the science of God. 2, *Anthropology*, the science of man in relation to God. 3, *Soteriology*, the science of salvation. 4, *Ecclesiology*, the science of the church. 5, *Eschatology*, or the science of "the last things." The term *Theology*, in this classification, you will notice, is used in a narrow sense for a particular branch of theology, commonly so-called; and is concerned with discussions touching the Being and Personality of God, and embraces, as a sub-division, " *Christology*," or the doctrine of the Person of Christ, the God-man. It includes also the doctrine concerning the creation and government of the world, and the doctrine of angels and dæmons. (See Hagenbach's *History of Doctrines*; Robinson on the Church.) " *Anthropology*," or the science of man, treats of such questions as the origin of the soul, liberty and immortality, the fall, sin, &c. *Soteriology*, or the science of salvation, embraces, chiefly, the doctrines of redemption and atonement, justification, and, in short, the priestly work of Christ in all its relations to the curse of the law, and to human guilt and condemnation, and the work of the Holy Ghost. (*Hagenbach ut sup. cit.*)

Now, such a classification implies in the history of doctrine, these three things: 1, That *Ecclesiology* is a branch of theology in the wide sense. 2, That it comes after the first three, in a natural or logical method. 3, That it comes after the first three in an historical order.

(1), Ecclesiology belongs to theology. The doctrine of the church belongs to the things which have been revealed of God, and are, therefore, objects of faith. Accordingly, we find this doctrine in the very earliest symbol of the Christian church, the "Apostle's Creed," standing in the same relation to the "credo" as the other articles, and in the same order, with respect to the doctrines concerning the Father, the Son, and the Holy Ghost, which we find in the classification we are considering. So also, in nearly all the larger creeds and confessions of a later date. The 25th chapter of our own "Confession of Faith," is entitled "Of the Church."

(2), The doctrine of the church, in a rational or logical order, falls to be considered after theology, anthropology, and soteriology, for the very obvious reason that the church is the great and last result contemplated by the revelation concerning God, man, and salvation. It is the highest end, next to the glory of God, of all the counsels and all the works of the Father, Son, and Holy Ghost. Chosen by the Father, redeemed by the Son, sanctified by the Spirit, and finally presented a "glorious church," without spot or wrinkle, or any such thing, the Bride, the Lamb's wife, shall be hailed by principalities and powers in heavenly places, as the highest and noblest display of the manifold wisdom of God (Eph. iii. 9, 10); as far transcending in glory the old creation, over which the morning-stars sang together and all the sons of God shouted for joy, as the second Adam, who is a quickening Spirit, transcends in glory the first Adam, who was but a living soul.

Meanwhile, during this dispensation of testimony and of trial, it is the office of the church, as the pillar and buttress of the truth, to bear witness of the great truths which are comprehended under the terms Theology, Anthropology, and Soteriology. She is not only the object of the working of that Triune God of whom theology treats, and the subject of that sin and salvation of which anthropology and soteriology treat, but to her have been committed the lively oracles which alone determine the faith of mankind upon all these classes of truths, and through her are these truths to be published to the race. The contents of the message are to be pondered first, then the nature of the messenger. This is the rational order.

(3), It is also the order of history. It is worthy of note that "the history of the church since the apostles seems to have been a development in succession of these four in their order. "Theology" had its full development during the controversies concerning the nature of the Godhead, which closed with the labors of Athanasius; "Anthropology," during the Pelagian controversy, closing with the labors of Augustine. Next, after a thousand years of repose and silence in the church, was developed Soteriology, through the labors of Luther and Calvin, proclaiming salvation as by grace through faith; leaving the fourth (Ecclesiology) yet to be developed." (*Robinson on the Church*, pp. 27, 28.) This is certainly striking, though absolute accuracy would, perhaps, require the statement to be modified and limited.

In harmony with this idea, that the development of Ecclesiology may be reserved for the last, perhaps our own times, is the fact that many of the most obtrusive tendencies of speculation, socialistic, political, philosophical, in the nineteenth century appear in discussions about the principle of *fellowship*, the principle upon which the church is constituted. I may instance "Communism," "St. Simonianism," &c., in social philosophy; the principles of "sodality" and "solidarity," in political philosophy; and the principle of "catholicity" used as the criterion of certitude in philosophy properly so-called. (See *Trench's Hulsean Lect.*, VIII., p. 125; *Morell's Philosophy of Religion; Morell on Phil. Tendencies of the Age*, L. 4th.) Indeed, it is not unlikely that two of the three frog-like, unclean spirits which John tells us (Rev. xvi. 13) proceed out of the mouths of the dragon, the beast, and the false prophet, "infidelity" and "formalism," may form a coalition upon the principle of catholicity (*quod semper, quod ubique, quod ab omnibus*) for one final, desperate assault upon the church of God, (see *Presb. Critic*, Vol. I., p. 291–'2), envied, like Abel of old, for her possession of the absolute truth, certitude and assurance.

However this may be, there can be no doubt that the question of the church is, in our day and in our own branch of the church, one of the most conspicuous; and there is little doubt that assertions are made in regard to the nature and functions of the church, in some of these discussions, which, if accepted and believed, must be fatal to the soul.

These facts constitute an ample vindication of the importance of the studies upon which we are about to enter as well as of the appropriateness of the place assigned to them in the Seminary Curriculum.

II.

TERMS AND DENOMINATIONS.

"CHURCH." This word, and German *kirche*, Saxon *circe*, and Scotch *kirk*, are derived, probably, from the Greek κυριακος, or το κυριακον, that which belongeth to the Lord. "As a house of God is called a Basilica, *i. e., regia a Rege*, so also it is named *Kyrica, i. e., Dominica a Domino* (κυριος)" says an old author (quoted in *Gieseler's C. H.*, § I.) It appears from *Ulfilas* that, in general, the Greek names of Christian things were adopted among the Goths. The Greek origin of the word is confirmed also by its being found not only in all the German dialects, (Swedish *kyrka*,

Danish *kirke*, etc.,) but also in those of the Sclavonian nations who were converted by the Greeks (Polish *cerkiew*, Russian *herkow*, Bohemian *cyrkew*.) (See note to the section in *Gieseler ut supra*.)

"Synagogue." This word is used in the LXX. often, as well as in the New Testament. It is put for any kind of an assembly, whether sacred or civil (Exod. xii. 3, 19; Num. xvi. 2), nay, even in a bad sense, for a profane and impious assembly (Psa. xxvi. 5); sometimes for the place of meeting (Luke vii. 5), in which the Jews were accustomed to assemble to hear the law, offer prayers and perform other offices of devotion beside those which were to be performed in the temple. Thence the so frequent mention of synagogues in the New Testament, the origin of which, according to some, was in the time of Moses (Acts xv. 21); according to others in the time of the captivity, when they were deprived of the temple services. Hence, the "synagogue" has come to denote the Jewish church, in like manner as "the church" has been applied to the Christian church.

"Ecclesia" is a Gentile, as synagogue is a Jewish, denomination (*Turretin*, Vol. III., pp. 7, 8). Hence, in the Epistle of James (ii. 2), which is addressed to Jewish Christians, the assembly of worshippers is called the synagogue; but the churches under the gospel being composed for the most part of Gentile converts, the term *ecclesia* is most commonly used (*Turretin ut supra— Witsius, Exercit. Sac. in Symbolum*, xxiv. p. 451, *Amstelod*, 1697).

The Greek εκκλησια answers precisely to the *kahal* and *gheda* and *moid* of the Old Testament, all these terms signifying *an assembly*, especially one convened by invitation or appointment. (*Mason's Essays on the Church*, No. 1, Works, Vol. IV. p. 3). "That this is their generic sense," says Dr. Mason, "no scholar will deny; nor that their particular applications are ultimately resolvable into it. Hence it is evident, from the terms themselves, nothing can be concluded as to the nature or extent of the assembly which they denote. Whenever either of the two former occurs in the Old Testament, or the other in the new, you are sure of an *assembly*, but of nothing more. What that assembly is, and whom it comprehends, you must learn from the *connection* of the term and the subject of the writer." A few instances will exemplify the remark :

In the Old Testament, *kahal** is applied : To the *whole mass* of the people (Exod. xii. 6) ; to a *portion* of the people, who came upon Hezekiah's invitation to keep the passover (2 Chron. xxx. 24) ; to the *army* of Pharaoh (Ezek. xvii. 17) ; to an *indefinite multitude* (Gen. xxviii. 3) ; to the society of Simeon and Levi (Gen. xlix. 6) So also *gheda* is applied : to the *whole* nation of Israel (Exod. xvi. 22) ; to the *particular* company of Korah, Dathan and Abiram (Num. xvi. 16) ; to the assembly of the *just*, as opposed to the *wicked* (Psa. i. 5) ; to the *judicatory*, before whom crimes were tried (Num. xxxv. 12, 24, comp. with Deut. xix. 12, 17, 18). In like manner εκκλησια, in the New Testament, is applied : To the *whole body* of the redeemed (Eph. v. 24, 27) ; to the *whole body* of professing Christians, whether more or less extensive, as in the apostolic salutations and inscriptions of the Epistles ; to a *small association* of Christians meeting together in a private house (Col. iv. 15, Phil. i. 2) ; to a civil assembly *lawfully* convened (Acts xix. 39) ; to a body of persons *irregularly* convened (Acts xix. 32). In application to the church, note the following meanings: 1st, The church invisible. 2d, The church visible, in the sense of a single congregation worshipping statedly in

---

* It is only this word which the LXX. render by εκκλησια ; though they sometimes use συναγωγη to represent it. In Psa. xxvi. 12 ; lxviii. 27, a cognate word in the plural is rendered by the plural of *ecclesia*. The three Hebrew words seem to be used indiscriminately in Num. x. 1–7, still it may be a question whether the assembly of vs. 7 is the same as that of vs. 3, or rather with the select assembly of chiefs in vs. 4.

one place. 3rd, Separate congregations united under one government, (Church of Jerusalem). 4th, The church visible, vaguely and indefinitely so called—the whole body of professing Christians, without reference to external organic unity (Confession of Faith, Chap. XXV. Art. I.; compare "Jews"). 5th. The church representative, the church court.

"Πανηγυρις," (Heb. xii. 23) which has a signification somewhat different from the *ecclesia*. When the people among the Greeks were convoked for the purpose of deliberating and determining concerning matters pertaining to the republic, the assembly, as we have already noted, was called *ecclesia*. But when, as in the Panathenæa, they were invited to some festive spectacle, then the assembly was called Πανηγυρις, and an oration delivered on such an occasion was called Πανηγυρικος λογος. An assembly of the faithful, therefore, convened to act upon things pertaining to the kingdom of God, *i. e.*, spiritual and heavenly things, may be called *ecclesia*, but inasmuch as they are invited and admitted to the greatest spectacle in the universe, the glory of God shining in the face of Jesus Christ, the assembly may be called πανηγυρις. (See *Witsius ut Sup.*)

III.

DEFINITIONS AND DESCRIPTIONS.

The church may be defined, "a society of faithful or believing men, called by God, through the word, out of the whole human race, to the communion of the covenant of grace in Christ." (*Witsius ut sup.*, 24, sec. 6.) The different members of this definition must be explained in their order:

1st. It is a *society*. This implies not only that the individuals composing it are *many* (1 Cor. x. 17); but as we are taught in this text, and in 1 Cor. xii. 14, many joined together organically, so as to make *one body*.

Society implies a community of nature and of ends. Instance in the family and in the state, which, like the church, have been instituted by God. The same is true, to a certain extent, even of voluntary associations. The members are "fellows," at least with respect to the ends for which the association is instituted. This idea of community of nature, feeling, interests, etc., is expressed emphatically in the common illustration drawn from the human body. (See 1 Cor xii.; Eph. iv. 4, &c.) If one member suffers or rejoices, the other members suffer or rejoice with it. The functions discharged by one member are discharged for the good of all. Each is interested in all and all in each. The notion of a body, however, implies also (see Eph. iv. 16) organization, a constitution of the parts or members in certain relations to each other and to the whole, and especially a common relation or union to a head, a directing power which shall give unity to the operations of all the parts. Of the body, the church, Christ is the head. This view of the nature of society shows the absurdity of all theories of the church which make connection with the church the means of regeneration. This is equivalent to saying that a man must become a member of society in order to be a human being; that the atmosphere creates the lungs, or that the light makes the eye. The truth is, that a man becomes a Christian and a member of the church at the same time by the same act of God; but in the order of nature he must become a Christian first.

The same idea of society is conveyed in other images of Scripture besides that of a body. For instance, the images of a tree (Rom. xi.), a fold under one shepherd (John x.), a city or state (Phil. iii. 20, with Eph. ii. 19). See *Potter on Church Government*, Chap I.; *Mason's Plea for Communion*, at the beginning.

2d. It is a society of *men*. The angels are our fellow-servants (Rev. xix. 10), having the same Master; they are children of the same great family (Job. i. 6;

xxxviii. 7), and partakers of the same blessedness, which consists in communion with God, whence we are said "to come to an innumerable company of angels" (Heb. xii. 22). Yet they are what they are in a different mode and by a different title, not redeemed by Christ, not called by the gospel, not born again of the Spirit, not partakers of the covenant of grace, which are the highest privileges of the church, and its characteristic marks. (See Heb. ii. 16). *Witsius ut supra*, 24, sec. 5.

3rd. It is a society of *believing* men. As I have already stated in the course on History, the word and the life of the church constitute its *form* or formal nature; and faith is the first and most prominent exponent of the life. Now, faith cometh by hearing and hearing by the word of God. The word comes promiscuously to all, but is not believed by all. Faith makes the difference among them. The faithful have a new life. Faith is mixed with the word (Heb. iv. 2), and a Christian is the result, and the church is composed of Christians. The object of faith is substantially the same in all ages, and, therefore, faith is substantially the same; and, therefore, the church is substantially the same in all ages. (See Acts ii. 41–47; Heb. iii. 5, 6; iv. 1, &c.)

4th. It is a society of *holy* men. This is virtually included in the last, but deserves an articulate statement. (1 Peter ii. 9; 1 Cor. i. 2, and other inscriptions to the Epistles). (See *Witsius ut sup*).

5th. It is a society *called of God* (Gal. i. 6 *et al*). God is said to be the caller (Rom. ix. 11). Hence the church is the church of the living God (1 Tim. iii. 15). Hence the church is, in one sense, a voluntary society, and in another sense it is not. The call of God is a command, as well as an invitation to every man who hears it, to come out and be separate from the world which lies in wickedness. If he is destitute of faith, he is bound to seek it, and if he seek it not, he is lost.

On the other hand, no man is coerced to become a member of the church. God makes his people willing in the day of his power. The κλητοι are called sweetly as well as powerfully by the Spirit, *enabled* and *persuaded* to receive Christ as he is offered to them in the gospel. As before man, the church is a voluntary society; for in the whole matter God has left the conscience free from the commandments of men.

God is a sovereign in calling (Rom. ix. 11). Many are called but few are chosen (Matt. xx). This is implied in the very term " Ecclesia."

6th. It is a society called of God *by the word*. Hence where there is no word, there is no church. (See under third head, " believing men ;" see 1 Cor. i. 21). This word is law and gospel.

7th. The church is called *out of the whole human race*; first, the Israelites (Psa. cxlvii. 19, 20); then the Gentiles (Isa. lv. 5; Acts xv. 14.)

8th. The *end* of this calling is *communion with Christ in the covenant of grace* (Prov. ix. 4, 5; Isa. lv. 2, 3; 1 Cor. i. 9 *et al.*.

9th. The church is *one*. This follows from all that has been said.

IV.

DISTINCTION OF CHURCH EXTERNAL AND INTERNAL.

It is to be noted, however, that there is a two-fold form, or if you prefer the expression, state and condition of the church ; the one *internal* and *mystical*, in which God alone judges with certainty concerning its members; the other *external* and *visible*, in which man is also the judge. To refer to the definition of the church already given, we may note :

1st. That there is a *two-fold calling :* the one external by the *word* (Matt. xx. 16) ; the other *internal*, by the *Spirit* (Rom. viii. 30).

2d. A *two-fold faith* answering to this calling: the one *common*, found even in reprobates, by which, assenting to the truth of the gospel, they experience some transient joy (Acts viii. 13; Matt. xiii. 20, &c.; Mark vi. 20; Heb. vi. 4, &c.); the other *saving*, "the faith of God's elect" (Tit. i. 1), "faith unfeigned" (1 Tim. i. 5), "faith working by love" (Gal. v. 5).

3d. A *two-fold holiness:* the one *relative, external, federal*, consisting in the segregation from the communion of the impure and the profane (Ezra ix. 2). In this sense the Israelites are called "the holy seed." See also Rom. xi. 16. Such a holiness is recognized also in the New Testament. (See 1 Cor. vi. 1, 2; 1 Cor. vii. 14). The other is *absolute, internal, real*, the property of those who are born again, a conformity to God and an image of his holiness (Psa. xciii. 5; 1 Pet. i. 15, 16).

4th. A *two-fold communion in the covenant:* the one *external* in the signs of the covenant, belonging to the infant offspring of parents in the covenant (Gen. xvii. 7; Acts ii. 39), and to adults who make a credible profession of their faith, though they possess it not (John xv. 2, 6); the other, an *internal, spiritual*, saving communion in the things signified, such as remission of sins, the law written upon the heart, etc. (Heb. viii. 10–12). Compare the distinctions in Romans ii. 28, 29, which may be analogically transferred to Christianity. (*Witsius, Ex.* 24, § 11.)

Hence the two-fold form or condition of the church, the one *visible*, depending upon the profession of faith and the observance of worship; the other *spiritual* and *invisible*, which, owing its origin to the eternal election of God, reaches its consummation by a living faith and holiness. (See 1 John ii. 19.)

With this distinction correspond very nearly the definitions commonly given, and given in our *Confession of Faith*, Chap. XXV.)

The *church invisible* is thus defined: See Sec. 1.— "The Church," &c. Note that the invisible church catholic, according to this definition, differs from the *internal, mystical, spiritual* church of which we have been speaking only in this, that it includes *all* the elect of all ages, past and future, while the latter includes only those who at any given period are actually justified and sanctified. (See the scriptural references in the *Confession*.) The invisible church catholic may be considered either *universally* and καθόλου, with respect to the whole multitude of the faithful which constitute it, of whatever time or place they may be; or *particularly* and καταμερος, and now, concerning that which reigns with Christ in heaven, and now concerning that which labors and sojourns in the world and is distributed in particular churches. (*Turretin*, Sec. 7, Quest. 2, Lect. 18, Vol. III. p. 9.)

Note, that the church invisible is not *practically* recognized at all by the Church of Rome; they make a distinction between the church militant and the church triumphant. The church militant, which is also visible, is the Roman Catholic, out of which there is no possibility of salvation. To this church they ascribe all the attributes of the true or invisible church, unity, catholicity, holiness, indefectibility, etc., and thus make merchandize of souls. The great champion of Rome, in the sixteenth century, Bellarmine, thus defines the church (See *Turretin ut sup.*): "*Coetum hominum, ejusdem Christianae fidei professione, et eorundem sacramentorum communione colligatum, sub regimine legitimorum pastorum, ac praecipue unius Christi in terris vicarii, Pontificis Romani,*"—a definition not drawn from the Scriptures, but made to serve a turn.

THE CHURCH VISIBLE is thus defined in our *Confession of Faith*, Chap. XXV. Sec. 2: "The Visible Church, &c." *Turretin* gives a definition in some respects more complete, or at least more explicit. It is as follows (18, 2, 10, p. 10): "*Societas hominum praeconio evangelii vocatorum ad unius fidei professionem, eorundem sacrorum communionem, et ejusdem ordinis observationem.*"

Before I proceed to consider the contents of these definitions of the church visible, I will say a word on its relation to the church invisible, in addition to what has already been said when considering the general doctrine of the church. This relation is suggested by the etymon of the term "*ecclesia*," and is contained in the notion of a vocation, or rather an evocation (ἐκ-καλεῖν), a calling out of the mass of the human race. Both are referred, the church visible and the church invisible, to the sovereign purpose of God; of which the whole process of salvation is an evolution. That purpose was a purpose to save, "not merely myriads of men as *individual men*, but myriads of sinners as composing a mediatorial body, of which the Mediator shall be the head; a mediatorial kingdom whose government shall be on his shoulders forever; a church, the Lamb's bride, of which he shall be the husband, a bride whose beautiful portrait was graven upon the palms of his hands and whose walls were continually before him, when in the counsels of eternity he undertook her redemption. "Christ did not undertake from eternity the office of a prophet merely, nor the office of a priest merely, but as the result of all and the reward of all, to found a *community*, to organize a *government*, and administer therein as a perpetual *king*." (*Robinson on the Church*, pp. 38, 39, and Appendix to *Discourses on Redemption*, note to Dis. IV.) Now in the manifestation and fulfilment of this purpose in *time*, "the ideal ἐκλεκτοί of the covenant of redemption became the actual κλητοί. Inasmuch as they are called by an external clesis of the Word, they are gathered in successive generations to constitute the *ecclesia* on earth. In as far as they are called also by the internal clesis of the Spirit, they are gathered to constitute the invisible *ecclesia*, the full and complete actual of the eternal ideal. For whilst, indeed, the effectual call of the Spirit can alone fulfil the promise of the eternal covenant to Messiah, yet, as that call is

2

externally through the word and the visible ordinances, the very process of calling and preparing the elect of God creates the visible church in the very image of the invisible, and it is in this visible body that the Mediator carries on his administration, works by his Spirit, etc., and it is by this body that he carries on his purposes of mercy toward a world lying in wickedness." (*Robinson*, pp. 41, 42.) See also *Robinson's "Discourses on Redemption,"* pp. 455 *et seq.*

V.

GENERAL DESCRIPTION OF THE CHURCH VISIBLE.

See the definitions given in No. IV. Many of the features of the visible church are common to it with the church invisible, and have been described in preceding numbers, III., IV. It is a society, an organized society, a society of men, a society called of God, a society called by the word, called out of the whole human race, a society subject to the authority of Christ as its head.

The characteristic features of the church visible, those which make it visible, are, according to the definitions:

1st. A credible profession of faith and holiness, and not real faith and holiness, as the term of membership and communion on the part of adults.

2d. The right of infants, children of such credible professors, to the initiating sign and seal of the covenant, recognizing them members of the church, in somewhat the same manner as minors in civil society are members of the state.

3d. Certain sacred rites and forms of worship, through which this credible profession is made, and the covenant state of infants recognized.

4th. A certain "order" or government, or system of discipline, in the hands of church officers, called of God and chosen by the people.

5th. The possession and use of oracles, ministry, ordinances, for the ingathering of the elect and their sanctification; in other words, for the completion of the mystical body of Christ, the church invisible. (See *Confession of Faith*, Chap. XXV., Sec. III.) Out of the church visible there is "no ordinary possibility of salvation." (*Ibid.*, Sec. II.)

6th. Catholicity. I mention this as a distinctive feature of the church visible, although it belongs also to the church invisible, for the reason that the term catholic is used in several different senses: (1), In the widest sense, embracing all differences of places, times, persons, and states, and denoting the whole family of God, in heaven and earth, militant and triumphant, past, present, and future. In this sense it is properly applied only to the church invisible. (2), In a narrower sense, for the church under the gospel, in opposition to the church under the law; and this in regard to places, persons, and times. (*a*), *Places*. Christian church no longer restricted to one place of worship. (John iv. 21, 23; 1 Tim. ii. 8.) (*b*), *Persons*. Christian church has no respect to differences of family, rank, nation, etc. Neither Jew nor Greek, male nor female, etc. (Rom. x. 12; Acts x. 35; Col. iii. 11; Apoc. v. 9.) (*c*), *Times*. The Christian church must continue till the consummation of the ages. In the sense thus explained, the term catholic is also applied to the whole church on earth, in opposition to "particular churches," existing in certain places or at certain times. (3), In an abusive sense, as equivalent to "*orthodox*." Commonly so used by the Fathers after Augustine, to denote a particular church which maintained its communion with the church universal, and had not been separated from it by heresy or schism. Thus, the "Catholic church in Smyrna," "in Alexandria," etc. This use of the term seems to have become common during, and in consequence of, the discussions about the Montanists, Donatists, Novatians, and other catharic of early times. Unfortunately, however, catholicity was made to depend upon official succession, instead of the succession of the truth; and this stupendous error led, in the course of time, to Popery. (See on the word Catholic, *Witsius, ut sup.* xxiv. 20; *Turretin*, L. xviii., q. 6, Vol. III., p. 27, 28; *Pearson on the Creed*, Art. IX.; *Suicer's Thesau. sub verb.*)

It is in the second of the senses above given that our Confession uses the word of the church visible. "All those throughout the world."

7th. Unity. Same remark about this term as the last. The true idea of unity in the church visible will be explained when we come to consider the Presbyterian system, in opposition to Popery and Independency.

So much for the general features of the church visible. Many of these will be described more fully hereafter, as they are connected with the proofs of the existence of such a church, and with the mode in which it is maintained and perpetuated.

VI.

PROOFS OF THE EXISTENCE OF A CHURCH VISIBLE.

1st. To say nothing of the dim traces of such a body in the garden of Eden, to be discerned in the skins with which our first parents were clothed, (implying that the animals slain had been slain in sacrifice, and that the form of public worship, by which a *profession of faith* in the promise of God was made, had been already instituted); nor to insist upon the clearer traces of it in the history of Cain and Abel; (*public worship and profession of faith*, Gen. iv. 4, with Heb. xi. 4; —*stated times* of worship, vs. 3, "at the end of days;" —*a stated place*, marked by some insignia of God's presence, a foreshadowing of the tabernacle and the temple, vs. 16, and compare 14, "from thy face shall I be hid;" *excommunication*, vs. 14, compare with vs. 12,

16—*apostasy from a religious profession*, vs. 16); nor upon the additional trace of such a body in the times of Enos, when "men began to call themselves by the name of the Lord," Gen. iv. 26—or, as it is explained afterwards in the history, vi. 2, "sons of God," in opposition, probably, to the apostate posterity of Cain, who were called "sons of men," or, as we say, "men of the world,"—see Gen. iv. 17, 19, 22, and compare Psa. xvii. 14 ; iv. 6 ; nor again in the times of Noah (when, in consequence of the intermarriage of the "sons of God" with the "daughters of men," or the members of the true church with apostates—see Gen vi. 1, &c., and compare Num. xxv. 1, &c.; Ezra. ix. 2, Neh. xiii. 26, 27 ; universal apostasy was the result); nor upon the manifest tracks of a patriarchal church, before the covenant of circumcision with Abraham, (see the history, specially the account of Melchisedek, Gen. xiv. 18, &c.; Heb. vii.); not to insist upon any of these, the visible church becomes conspicuous from the time of the ecclesiastical covenant with Abraham, down through the whole history of his descendants in the line of Jacob, to the advent of the Messiah. This church, or "kahal Jehovah," embraced all who had the token of the covenant in their flesh, whether regenerated or not, whether in or out of Judea (Acts ii. 5). Now, if such a church existed before the advent of Messiah—a church founded upon faith (or the credible profession thereof), in the promise of salvation, with solemn ordinances of worship, by which that profession was made and constantly renewed ; a church embracing the infant offspring of such professors, and possessing a sign and seal by which this status of infants was recognized ; a church with a government and discipline in the hands of men appointed of God, and in general with a ministry, oracles and ordinances, for the edification of the true worshippers ; a church, too, as will appear hereafter, catholic in its constitution and design, though not so in fact to any great extent under

the law; if such a church existed then, what has became
of it ?   Its ceremonial form has been abolished, but it
has not ceased to be the church on that account, any
more than the creature in its chrysalis condition ceases
to be when it passes into the higher and freer sphere
of the gorgeous butterfly.   Nor does it cease to be because the people who pre-eminently enjoyed its privileges at first have been deprived of them; any more
than the olive tree has ceased to be because the
natural branches have been broken off and wild ones
have been grafted in.   He who denies the existence of
a visible church since the advent of Christ, is bound
to show that the church before Christ has been abolished, both in law and fact.   (See *Mason*, Vol. IV.,
pp. 5–8 ; Essay I.)

2d.   " The Old Testament scriptures proceed on the
supposition that the visible church state, co-extensive
with the Redeemer's kingdom on earth, was *not* to cease
at the introduction of the gospel dispensation." (*Mason
ut sup.*, p. 8, &c.)

(1), There are numerous predictions concerning the
church, and numerous promises to her in her public
capacity, which are still unfulfilled, and can never be
fulfilled, if her visible unity be not asserted.   See
Isa. lxvi. 12, 22 ; xlix. 23 ; lx. 3, 5.   Now, upon the
principle that " God is not the God of the dead, but
of the living " (Matt. xxii.), the church must continue
to exist in order to receive the fulfilment of these
promises.   (*Mason*, IV., p. 8, &c.)

(2), The nature of many of these promises implies
that the narrow ceremonial trammels by which it was
confined should be done away.   The promises, therefore, imply at once perpetuity and change, and consequently, that the change is not inconsistent, much
less incompatible, with perpetuity.

Note (*a*) that these promises contemplate the church
as *one ;* (*b*) that this unity is not ascribed to her as
composed of the elect alone.   The church is not rep-

resented as consisting of a multitude of independent associations, but as a great *whole*; and further, as a *visible* body, her "light" visible, the "brightness of her rising" attracting the "kings," etc. (See also Isa. liv. 1, 2, for a description implying the same thing.)

Note the difference between the *unity* and the *oneness* (or *oneliness*) of the church. The papists indentify them; the Protestants predicate *unity* of the church invisible; *oneness* of the church visible. See *Litton Church of Christ*, p. 1, chap. 1, sec. 1, (American Edition, pp. 268, ff.) for this *unity*; p. 1, chap. 1, sec. 2, pp. 335, ff.) for the *oneness*. It is in this last sense that Mason here calls the church *one*.

3rd. "The language of the New Testament implies that an external visible church state was not abolished with the law of Moses." (*Mason*, IV., 11, &c.)

"The writers of the New Testament never go about to *prove* that there is a visible church catholic; far less do they speak of it as *originating* in the evangelical dispensation; but they assume its existence as a point which no Christian in their days ever thought of disputing." The doctrine of the one visible church is interwoven with the texture of their language. (Acts vii. 38: ii. 47; viii. 3: 1 Cor. xii. 28, &c.; Rom. xvi. 23; 1 Cor. x. 32; xv. 9, &c., &c.) The church to which the Lord added daily such as should be saved, was not the body of the elect, for no addition can be made to them; nor a single congregation, unless God had no more people to be saved in Jerusalem than, together with mere professors, were sufficient for one pastoral charge. Nor is it to be imagined that Saul confined his persecutions to a single congregation, nor that he was able to pick out the elect. Nor will a sober man allege that God has set no officers but in one congregation, or that they have no functions toward any but His elect; or that all whom He hath set are themselves of the number; nor yet that "offence" can never be given to any but the elect," . . . "The

phrases referred to (in the above cited passages) being
utterly inapplicable either to a single congregation, or
to the body of the redeemed, must designate another
and different society, which can be no other than what
we have called the visible church catholic. Too extensive for partial assemblies, too notorious for any
secret election of men, and yet a church—*the* church—
it is *general, external,* and but ONE."

The phraseology of the New Testament on this subject, as on many others, is borrowed from that of the
old. "Ecclesia" is the same as "kahal," and the
Seventy constantly use the former to render the latter.
The Jews, then, would understand by "ecclesia Theou,"
the "kahal Jehovah." The Gentiles would (the Greeks,
I mean), understand "ecclesia" by itself, but would
know nothing of "ecclesia Theou" without looking
into the Jewish scriptures, the Old Testament. The
word "church" is like the word "Christ" in this respect. "Neither the nature of the church, nor the
office of her head, is to be understood without an appeal to the same scriptures. Consequently that very
rule which expounds the "Christ of God" as signifying
one who was qualified by the Father's appointment
and by the measureless communication of the divine
Spirit to be a Saviour for men, will oblige us to expound the "church of God" as signifying that great
visible society which professes his name. (See Mason,
pp. 14–17.)

4th. "The account which the New Testament gives
of the church confirms the doctrine of the visible
unity." (*Mason ut supra*, p. 17, &c.)

(1), One of the commonest appellations is "the kingdom of heaven:" *one*, because *the*, not *a*, kingdom. The
parable of the "wheat and tares" teaches that it is VISI-
BLE as well as *one*. (Here read pp. 18, etc., in proof
that the parable designates the church, and not civil
society). So also the parable of the "net" and the
"virgins." These parables of course cannot describe

the body of the elect; and it would be absurd to limit
them to a single congregation. Ergo, &c.

(2), The image of a "body" in 1 Cor. xii. It plainly
signifies a *whole.* Then *what* whole? Not the church
at Corinth, far less a particular congregation, unless
the commission of the apostles and the use of all spiritual gifts extend no further. Not the church of the
elect, for there are no "schisms" in that body as such.
Nor can it be affirmed, but at the expense of all fact and
consistency, that God hath set no officers except in the
church of His redeemed. For upon that supposition
no church officer could ever exercise his office toward
any non-elected man; the pastoral relation could never
be fixed without knowing beforehand who are the elect
of God, or else no person, however blasphemous and
abominable, could be kept out of a church, because
such "blasphemer" and "injurious" may possibly be a
"chosen vessel." The body, then, here described, must
be the visible church catholic. (See *Mason ut supra.*)

It may be further noted that this body is represented,
here and in Eph. iv., as endowed with sundry gifts,
means of salvation and edification, "ministry, oracles
and ordinances." These means of salvation are *external* and *visible;* a visible Bible, a visible ministry, visible worship, sacraments, discipline, etc.; and if the
church and the ordinances committed to her are not
of opposite natures, the fact that the ordinances have
a solid external existence is proof that the church has
also. Indeed, if the New Testament church is not the
same great society which God formerly erected for the
praise of His glory, and to which he committed the
ancient oracles (Rom. iii. 2), then these oracles form
no part of the trust committed to the church of the New
Testament, and belong not to the rule of her faith,
which is contrary to the whole drift of Scripture teaching in regard to the relation between the Old and New
Testaments. (*Mason, ut supra.*)

Finally, the general principle of the church visible

is so inseparable from the Christian style and doctrine, that its most strenuous opposers are unconsciously admitting it every hour of their lives. They
talk habitually of the "church," the "faith of the
church," the "worship of the church," "God's dealings
with his church," and a thousand things of like import; and they mean by "church," in such phrases,
something different from "the elect," and from a "particular "congregation;" and that something, if they will
analize it, will turn out to be the visible church catholic,
or the "aggregate body of those who profess the true
religion, all making up *one* society, of which the Bible is
the statute-book, Jesus Christ the head, and a covenant
relation the uniting bond. (*Mason*, p. 26.)

VII.

First Organization of the Church Visible.

I noticed at the beginning of No. VI. the traces of
the church in the times before Abraham. But, until
the time of the father of the faithful, it cannot be said
to have been formally organized upon the principle of
visible unity. Until Abraham's time no separation had
been made between the family and the church (as there
had been virtually between the church and the state);
now the line is drawn within the family itself, part being in the church, and part out of it. The account of
this organization is to be looked for among the trans-
actions of that memorable period which elapsed between the call of Abraham in Ur of the Chaldees, and
the birth of Isaac. On the first of these occasions Jehovah gave him a double promise: (1), A numerous
progeny and great personal prosperity (Gen. xii. 2, 3).
(2). That he should be the medium of conveying extensive blessings to the world (vs. 3). And to these
promises may be referred all the communications
which God subsequently made to him. Called up at
different times, explained, expounded and confirmed,

each one of them became the basis of an appropriate covenant.

1st. The first promise is repeated (Gen. xii. 7), with an engagement to bestow upon the progeny of Abraham the land of Canaan, which was afterwards (xiii. 14–17) confirmed in the most ample terms. And again, in the declining years of Abraham, the Lord came to him in a vision, and having cheered him with this gracious assurance, "I am thy shield, and thy exceeding great reward," (xv. 1); the promise was renewed and solemnly ratified as a *covenant* (vs. 8–21). The promise of a posterity having been thus sealed, never occurs again by itself.

2d. Fourteen years after the date of this event, God appeared again to Abraham, and made *another covenant* with him. I should prefer to say that there were *two stages of the covenant*, rather than *two covenants*: one stage in which Abraham appears as the mere recipient of the promise, rather than as a party (Gen. xv.); the other in which he appears as a party (Gen. xvii.) It is recorded in Gen. xvii. 1–14 (which read). What was this covenant? Not a covenant, either of works or grace, for eternal life. For Abraham had been "justified by faith without the works of the law," and had been interested in the covenant of God's grace before this. His eternal life had been secured many years. Nor was it merely a personal or domestic covenant. This, too, had been concluded long before, as has been shown. It recognizes, indeed, all that was included in the personal covenant, which it might otherwise be supposed to supersede; but it has features of its own, so peculiar, that it cannot be considered in any other light than that of a distinct engagement. For, besides the solemnity with which it was introduced, and which would hardly have preceded a mere repetition of former grants, it contained *new matter*; it constituted *new relations* and was affirmed *in an extraordinary manner*. (See *Mason*, page 33, *et seq.*) (1), *New*

Matter: "Father of many nations," meaning not at all
that he should be a literal father of many nations, but
that he should be the means of blessing to all the families of the earth, in such a manner as to become what
no other man, in the sense of the covenant, ever did
or ever can become. (See Rom. iv. 13–17; Gal. iii. 7,
8, 9, 29.) He should be the father of a spiritual seed,
as well as the father, according to the other covenant
(xv., see above) of *a natural*. Gal. iii. 6, 7, shows that
the covenant in Gen. xv. was not a promise as to the
"natural seed" only. Indeed, the frequent reference to
Gen. xv. 6 by Paul, in proof of justification by faith
alone, without works, shows that the covenant described
in that chapter was a covenant for spiritual blessings ;
and this confirms the view that there were not two
covenants, but two stages of the same covenant. (See
p. 29). (2), *New relations*: "To be a God unto thee, and
to thy seed after thee." Whatever relation is here expressed, it grew out of the covenant.

It could not be, therefore, Abraham's relation to God
as the God of his salvation, for in that sense God was
his God long before. It embraced his seed, too, and
God did not now engage to be their God with respect
to eternal life, for all that was settled in the covenant
of grace, and the privilege could not reach beyond
those who were the actual partakers of the same precious faith with Abraham. Whereas, in the sense of
this covenant, God was the God of all Abraham's seed,
without exception, under the limitations which restricted the covenant operation, first to Isaac and afterwards to Jacob, including such as should choose their
God, their faith, and their society. For he was to be
their God in *their generations*, *i. e.*, as soon as a new individual of this seed was generated, he was within the
covenant, and, according to the tenor of it, God was his
God. We conclude then, that the covenant with Abraham and his seed contemplated them, not primarily
nor immediately as of the election of grace, but as an

aggregate which it severed from the bulk of mankind, and placed in a social character under peculiar relations to the "most high God."

To define precisely the nature of this correspondence we must go a step further, and ascertain who are meant by the "seed." It cannot be the carnal descendants of Abraham exclusively, for (*a*), three large branches of that seed were actually shut out of the covenant, *i. e.*, the children of Ishmael, Esau and Keturah. (*b*), The covenant provided for the admission of others who never belonged to that seed. See Gen. xvii. 12: "Not of thy seed." This principle was also acted upon under the law of Moses, when the seed of Abraham had become a nation. Ex. xii. 48, for the stranger's right to the passover. See also Deut. xxiii. 7, 8, where the Egyptian, descending from Ham, is put on the same footing with the Edomite, descending from Abraham, (*c*), Abraham was to be the father of *many nations;* "the many nations" being equivalent to "all the families of the earth," in one form of the promise. (Comp. Rom. iv. with Gal. iii.) These "many nations" were the "seed" of him who was their "father:" the seed in the same sense in which he was the "father." But the covenant was with Abraham and his seed; therefore, these "many nations" were included in the covenant.

3d. This covenant was affirmed in an extraordinary manner, viz.: by the rite of *circumcision*. The uses of this rite were two: (1), It certified to the seed of Abraham, that the covenant with their great progenitor was in force; that they were entitled to all the benefits immediately derived from it. (2), It was a seal of "the righteousness, etc. (Rom. iv. 11), and as such certified; (*a*), that Abraham was justified by faith; (*b*), that the doctrine and the privilege of the righteousness of faith were to be perpetuated among his seed by the operation of God's covenant with him; and, therefore, that all who *believed* were children of Abraham, and

3

personally interested in the righteousness by which he was justified.

II. This covenant never has been annulled. See the argument in the third of Galatians, where the apostle shows, (1), that the Sinaitic covenant did not and could not annul it; and (2), that it was still in force, so that all who believed were Abraham's children or seed, and heirs of the promise. (vs. 29). But more particularly, it is to be noted, that according to Paul: 1st, The promise that Abraham should be the father of many nations could not be fufilled until the Gentiles were brought in, or until the Christian dispensation. (Comp. Rom. iv.) The "promise" upon which his argument turns is, "I will be a God unto thee, and to thy seed after thee." The Abrahamic covenant, therefore, is still in force. (Comp. Heb. viii. 6–13.) 2d, If not, then the *visible church, under the gospel*, is not in covenant with God; and if no covenant, no promises; if no promises, then the Christian church is worse off than the Levitical. See Isa. lix. 20–22, which is a prediction of New Testament times, but it has no meaning if there is no covenant with the Christian visible church. (Comp. Rom. xi. 26, where the apostle represents the fulfilment of the promise as still future.) But the promise, by its very terms, is given to the church, "in covenant;" her members, in constant succession, are the "seed" out of whose mouth the Spirit shall not depart; and when the Jews are restored, they will be brought into this very covenanted church, and be again recognized as a part of the seed. 3d, In arguing the rejection of the Jews, and their future restoration, and the vocation of the Gentiles, the apostle reasons upon false principles, if the Abrahamic covenant has ended. (See Rom. xi. 17-24).

Add the following: Acts ii. 38, 39, where note the following points.

1st. The sameness of the *form* (*See Introductory Lecture on History*) of the church. "The promise is

unto you," &c.   It matters not whether this promise be
that of the Messiah or the Spirit, for they go together,
and one is nothing without the *other*.   The revelation
of salvation, upon which the church is organized, is
then the same under the law and under the gospel.

2d. The constituents of the church are the same,
believers and *their children*.

3d. The differences in the church, under the two
dispensations, are these: (1), Under the gospel the
requirements for church communion are more spiritual
than under the law ("repent"), and imply a larger
gift of the Holy Ghost—("ye shall receive the gift of
the Holy Ghost.")   (2), The initiatory seal is changed:
"baptism," instead of circumcision.   (3), The church
is more catholic under the gospel, "to all that are afar
off," &c.   Some of these points will be considered more
fully hereafter.   See also Acts iii. 25, 26.

Note the mistake which was made by the Pharisees
who came to John the Baptist (Matt. iii.), and which
John removes so effectually in verse 9th, that the
Abrahamic covenant and the Sinaitic were the same;
and, therefore, that until the Abrahamic covenant expired, the Jews could not be cast off.   See and compare Gal. iii., with Heb. viii. 6-13, and Acts iii. 22-26).
Paul, as well as John the Baptist, evidently taught that
the Abrahamic covenant might survive the casting off
of the Jews.

In the foregoing account of the nature of the covenant with Abraham, it will be seen that the community
organized upon it possessed the three elements which
are essential to the constitution of such a body.   These
elements, according to Whately (*Essays on the Kingdom of Christ*, Es. 2), are officers, rules, and penalties
by which the rules are enforced: (*a*), Officers; the
church being at first "a church in the house;" all official authority was lodged in the head of the house.
(*b*), Rules; obedience to God's commandments, and
faith in his promise—both signified by the sign of cir-

cumcision. (c), Penalties; expulsion or excommunication. The officers under the Sinaitic covenant were
priests and Levites; but there can be no doubt that
the patriarchal or family church continued, even under the outward Levitical; and at a later period (after
the captivity) became more prominent than the Levitical form. In this the *elders* were the officers; and indeed, circumcision and the passover were eminently
family institutions. And the church, after the coming
of Christ, emerges once more as a church, under the
government of *elders*. The object of faith and the
moral law were the same in all the stages. The penalty
of excommunication was also the same. The visible
community was the same, therefore, through all changes
of dispensation. And the definition of this community
is the definition of the visible church. The church that
now is, therefore, was organized in the family of Abraham.

VIII.

METHOD OF PERPETUATING THE CHURCH VISIBLE.

The next question that claims our attention is the
mode in which the visible church is perpetuated, or
its privileges, the privileges of the Abrahamic covenant, transmitted. How is a succession of the "seed"
preserved? The definitiongiven of the visible church,
indicates that this is done in two ways: 1st, By a
credible profession of the true religion; 2d, By hereditary descent. Of these in their order.

1st. Under all the dispensations of the church, the
individual who was without the bounds of the covenant
previous to his being of adult age, was to be admitted
on his *personal faith* in that religion which the covenant was intended to secure. (*Mason*, No. III. p. 47.)
Till then he was to be considered an "alien," "for-
eigner," "stranger." Upon this point there is a general agreement. But as to what is implied in this personal faith there is no small diversity of views.

(1), Some contend (as for example John Locke, in his *Reasonableness of Christianity*), "that all that is necessary is a general profession of the truth; under the gospel a general profession of belief that Jesus is the Christ, the Son of God." But this is the sum of the gospel; and an intelligent reception of this proposition as the object of faith involves a reception of the whole testimony of God. See 1 Cor. xii. 3, in which passage it would be, in the last degree, absurd to say that the meaning is, "no man can pronounce the words, Jesus is the Lord, but by the Holy Ghost." See also, 1 John v. 1, 5. And if this could not be the meaning then, when Christianity was a new thing among the heathen, much less would it do now, when Christianity is learned by *rote* by millions of children.

(2), Others think that a fuller profession of faith in the doctrine of revelation should be required, without solicitude as to the question whether these doctrines have been felt in their saving, transforming power. This seems to be the principle acted upon in some branches of the Presbyterian Church, in which persons of fair moral character, who can answer the questions in the catechism, are admitted to the Lord's table— herein differing from other churches (which they accuse of popery), only in demanding more knowledge. It is a sufficient answer to this view to say, that it divorces truth from that which is its great end, godliness. Hence we find in such churches an unusually large proportion of orthodox wicked men, or at least of orthodox men, who show no spirituality. We must never forget that a bad life is a bad, if not "the worst," heresy.

(3), Others again reverse the opinion of the last, and make the profession to be one of " experience," and not at all, or very little of faith in the doctrines of God's word. I have myself seen persons join the Methodist Episcopal Church on probation, as they call it, simply by giving their hand to the minister, and nothing was said or done by which any man could tell whether the neophytes were Christians or Mahommedans as to their faith. The presumption, of course, was that they professed faith in Christ, but it was only a presumption. All which is absurd, because a man cannot be a Christian without some knowledge of Christ, (See John vi. 45; xvi. 7–15; even babes must know something, Matt. xi. 25–27); for he cannot be a Christian unless he has been *taught* by the Spirit, who witnesses of Christ. The church is the great witness bearer the pillar and ground, or buttress, of the truth, and knowledge is indispensable. A profession of faith must include the following things. (See *Mason*, p. 53.) (*a*), Acquaintance with, at least, the leading doctrines of revelation. (*b*), Some evidence of the saving power of these doctrines upon the heart. (*c*), An open, unequivocal avowal of the Redeemer's name; and (*d*), vigilance in the discharge of religious and moral duty. (*Mason*, p. 53.) And all these particulars are implied in an adult being baptized *into* the name of the Father, the Son and the Holy Ghost. Further, it must be noted that the profession of faith upon which a person is admitted to church privileges, is a credible profession. The visible church, because it is visible, and its affairs administered by men, through visible ordinances, can insist upon nothing more than a profession which *seems* to be true and sincere. It is God's prerogative to judge the heart. And even our Lord Jesus Christ, who knew what was in man, and knew that Judas Iscariot was a devil from the beginning, admitted him not only to the fellowship of the church, but even to the office of an apostle, because he would have been adjudged to be qualified for church membership and office by the measures of human judgment. The doctrine, therefore, of Montanism, Donatism, Anabaptism, etc., in regard to a church which shall consist only of the regenerate, is a dream. It is false, both in law and fact; the principle

upon which the judgment of the church is founded in
this case, is the principle upon which every association
of *men* must proceed in judging of the qualification of
its members.   The judgment must be founded upon
what *appears*, not upon what *is*.   A profession of faith
in Christ, then, which is not discredited by other traits
of character, entitles an adult to the privileges of his
church.   This is the first way of securing a succession
of the covenanted seed, and of handing down these
blessings to the end of time.   (*Mason*, as above.)

2d. The other and the principal channel of transmission is that of *hereditary descent*.   The relations and
benefits of the covenant are the birthright of every
child born of parents who are themselves of the seed—
" I will establish my covenant between me and thee, and
thy seed after thee, in their generations, for an everlasting covenant."   This is a characteristic of every public covenant which God has made with man.   Take for
example the covenant with Adam and with Noah.   Every
human creature comes into being under the full operation of both these covenants.   In virtue of the one he is
an " heir of wrath," and in virtue of the other, an heir
of promise to the whole extent of the covenanted
mercy.   He has the faithfulness of God pledged to
him, as one of Noah's covenanted seed, that the world
shall not be drowned by a second deluge, nor visited
by another calamity to exterminate his race.   Now no
imaginable reason can be assigned why, in the covenant with his visible church, the uniform and consistent God should depart from his known rule of dispensation, and violate all the natural and moral analogies
of his works and his government.   It cannot be.
There is no such violation ; there is no such departure.
(*Mason* p. 58, and read on to the end of the chapter.)

IX.

The Initiating Seal.

We have seen that the Abrahamic covenant had such a seal; that it was the "seal of the righteousness of faith"; that it certified that the Hebrew, to whom it was applied when he was eight days old, belonged to the church of God, and was entitled to all the privileges which it derived from that covenant. And further, that the right to this seal belonged not only to the literal, but to the covenanted seed, as is clear from the provision made for the circumcision of those who were "not" of the literal "seed" of Abraham. (Gen. xvii. 12, 13.) Now this covenant is still in force, as has been proved; and if the rite of circumcision had not been abrogated, it would still be the duty of professing parents to apply it to their male offspring. But circumcision has been laid aside. Has the seal which it conveyed been abolished also? If so, then it follows, (1), That there is no longer any initiatory seal for either adults or infants, for an abolished seal is abolished. (2), That the church of God is under the operation of a covenant which has no initiating seal. If it be said that baptism is such a seal, then it follows that baptism has come in the place of circumcision; and if so, then God has a visible church, in sealed covenant with himself, distinct from that church which is composed of the elect only; and as he has never made a new visible church, nor drawn back from his old engagements, that church must be the one which was organized by the Abrahamic covenant; and then it follows, further, that the application of circumcision must furnish the rule for the application of baptism, and infants are to be baptized. (*Mason*, pp. 64, 65.)

In circumcision, and indeed in any ordinance, we must distinguish between the substance and the form. The substance of the ordinance, that which properly constituted the *seal*, was the certification to the person sealed of his interest in God's covenant. The rite of circumcision was no more than the *form* in which the seal was applied. The rite may be, and was, and is yet performed without any sealing whatever. The sons of Ishmael, the modern Jews, are examples. On the other hand, the certification might have been the same and the rite different—the perforation of an ear or the amputation of a toe, etc. It cannot be argued, therefore, that because the ancient form is laid aside, that the seal and all that it certifies have been laid aside too. It would be quite as just to infer that because the form of church polity is altered the church no longer exists. If it be said that the rite and the seal, though distinguishable, are in fact inseparable, and that the latter cannot be applied except through the medium of the former, the answer is, that the objection concludes equally against the existence of a church on earth. In truth, it is a fundamental principle that forms of dispensation do not affect the substance of the things dispensed. The covenant of grace has been dispensed under *five* forms,* the Abrahamic covenant under *three*, and yet neither has been abolished. Therefore, the change in the form of the seal does not abolish it. But as circumcision has been abolished, and no one pretends that any other rite has taken its place than baptism, either baptism is that seal, or there is no initiating seal at all under the gospel. If there is no seal, then the privileges of believers are abridged, instead of enlarged, under the gospel, and in this respect the gospel covenant is not what the apostle affirms it to be—"a better covenant founded

---

* 1, Adam to Noah; 2, Noah to Abraham; 3, Abraham to Moses; 4, Moses to Christ; 5, Christ to the end. But as No. 2 is essentially the same as No. 1 (the Noachian covenant or covenant of "forbearance," embracing so far as it was singular, the whole human race, and therefore *not* "the covenant of grace,"), there have been only *four* forms of the "covenant of grace." 1, Catholic; 2 and 3, Particularistic; 4, Catholic.

upon better promises." Baptism, then, is the substitute for circumcision.

This may be argued further, (*a*), From the coincidence in the purpose and meaning of the two ordinances. They both put a mark upon their subjects as belonging to that society which God hath set apart for himself. Both signify and seal that wondrous change in the state of the sinner whereby, being justified by faith, he passes from condemnation into acceptance with God (Rom. iv. 11; vi. 3, &c.; Acts ii. 38; Col. ii. 11-14), which doctrines of pardon and acceptance are exhibited in that society alone which, under the name of his church, God hath consecrated to himself, and of which he hath appointed the circumcised and the baptized to be esteemed members. Both represent and are means of obtaining that real purity which is effected by the Spirit of Christ, and is the characteristic of all those members of his church who are justified by faith in his blood. (Deut. x. 16; xxx. 6; Acts vii. 51; Rom. vi. 4; Col. ii. 11-14.) They answer, then, the same ends; baptism being better suited to the Christian dispensation as being capable of more extensive application. (*b*), From the scriptural manner of representing circumcision and baptism where they are spoken of *together*, or where baptism is mentioned in connection with the covenant of which circumcision was the seal. For one example see Acts ii. 38, 39. For another take the passage in Col. ii. 11-14, above cited. In which note, (1), That both baptism and circumcision are represented as signs of *spiritual* mercies. It is for this reason alone that they are or can be used as *terms* to convey the idea of such mercies. (2), Circumcision was a sign of regeneration and of communion with Christ as the fountain of spiritual life. The apostle is treating of a believer's completeness in Christ. And in order to show that he means the *inward grace*, he calls it the *circumcision* made *without hands*, and to make all mistake impossible, explains his explanation by adding the "putting off the sins of the flesh *by the circumcision of Christ.*" (3), Baptism, too, is a sign of regeneration and of communion with Christ as the fountain of spiritual life. In baptism, Paul says the believer is buried with Christ, and risen with him through a divine faith. The "uncircumcision of the flesh" is a state of unregeneracy. Here, then, again, circumcision and baptism are employed by turns to denote the same thing—a believer's sanctification by union with Christ. He identifies the two ordinances as the same seal under different forms. But the two forms cannot exist at the same time, and circumcision has passed away. Therefore, baptism remains as the "circumcision of Christ," or Christian circumcision, and is expressly so called by Paul, as will be seen by comparing the last clause of verse 11 with the first of verse 12. Compare Rom. iv. 11, 12, where Abraham is called not only the "father of all them that believe," but the "father of circumcision" to them, *i. e.*, he communicates the sign and seal as well as the thing signified. Now, if it had been said that he was the "father of circumcision" to the circumcision only, it would mean that the form of the seal, as well as the seal itself, had been handed down by Abraham to his descendants with the things signified. But he is represented, also, as the father of circumcision to the uncircumcised; to those who walk in the steps of the faith which he had while yet uncircumcised; *i. e.*, these last receive the seal as well as the covenant. But circumcision has been abolished. How, then, is Abraham the "father of circumcision" to the uncircumcised? Through baptism, which has come in the place of circumcision (*Mason*), and as there is no distinction between the mode in which Abraham has handed down the sealed privileges of God's covenant to those who were and those who were not of the circumcision; and as they were made over to the former and their infant seed, they must also be made over to the latter and their infant seed. If it should be said that the baptism of infants implies the application of the seal of the righteousness of faith to multitudes who never had and never will have that righteousness, and consequently that the seal of God's covenant is often affixed to a lie, the answer is that the same difficulty lies against circumcision of infants not only, but against the administration of baptism and the Lord's supper to adults, unless we can be assured that all the recipients are true converts. But the difficulty is created by false notions of the church, and confounding the covenant of grace with the ecclesiological covenant. The seal of God's covenant does, in every instance, certify absolute truth, whether it be applied to a believer or an unbeliever, to the elect or to the reprobate. (*Mason*, p. 83.)

X.

INFANT MEMBERS.

According to the definition of the visible church in our Confession of Faith, the children of those who profess the true religion are members of it as well as their parents. This has been already proved, (*a*), From the fact that the Abrahamic covenant, which included the seed, was an ecclesiological covenant, and has never been abrogated; and consequently that the Christian church, which is founded on the Abrahamic covenant, must include the infant seed of believers. (*b*), From the fact that all the public covenants made with men before Christ—Adam's, Noah's, the Mosaic—recognized the unity of the family and the identity of the federal status of parents and children. (*c*), From the fact that baptism has come in the place of circumcision. (*d*), From the recognition of the same principle in the whole course of God's providential government. When we are asked, therefore, for a "Thus saith the Lord" for infant baptism under the New

Testament, we answer, where has God, in the New Testament, taken away from his people a privilege which they had always enjoyed? The burden of proof lies on them who deny, not on those who affirm. But we proceed to some considerations which tend to confirm the right of the infants of professors to church privileges under the gospel.

1st. If they have no such right, then God has not only departed from the analogies of former federal constitutions, and from the general analogies of his providence, but has done so to abridge the privileges of his people under the new and better covenant. And when we consider that the children of believing parents share in all the *disasters* of the visible church, its corruptions, its persecutions, its declensions, the supposition becomes monstrous that they are excluded from its privileges. It represents God not only as discriminating against his people by debarring them from a privilege, but as retaining the principle only for the infliction of calamity. (*Mason*, p. 93.)

2d. If there be no infant membership under the gospel, then the church has no authority over the children of believers, but they are to her as Turks or Pagans. She has no authority to instruct or admonish them, any more than the children of Pagans. If she had acted upon this principle she would long ago have ceased to exist. Baptists themselves do not act upon it. They feel, in spite of their own doctrine, that the children of the church do sustain a peculiar relation to it, and that the church is bound in a special manner to look after their instruction. At the same time, it must be acknowledged that they are more remiss in this duty than sects which formally recognize the ecclesiastical status of the children of the church.

3d. If there be no infant membership in the Christian church, then God has inflicted upon *believing* Jews the very curse which he threatened against the unbelieving, so far as the children are concerned. (See Acts

4

iii. 23.) Who are the "people" in this passage? Not the nation of the Jews; for they were the rebels that were to perish " from among the people," a people who were to continue in the divine protection. Not the elect; for God never " cast away his people whom he foreknew," and they who committed this crime never belonged to the elect—were never "among" them. If neither the Jewish nation nor the elect, it could be no other than that people whom he owns as his, and who are called by the collective name of his *church*. And the passage occurring in Moses is a proof of the unity and perpetuity of the visible church. What is meant by "destruction" here? Not temporal death; for that penalty was never ordained for the sin of unbelief in the Messiah. Not an exclusion from the Jewish nation, for this effect did not take place; and further, if it had, it was as likely to prove a blessing as a curse. It must mean exclusion from the communion of the visible church. This is its technical sense in the Old Testament. Now the execution of this threatening involved the casting out of the children of those on whom it was executed, and conversely the preservation in the church of the children of those who believed. If the converse does not hold good, then the children of believers were cast out, and then the threatening was executed upon believers as well as upon the rebellious. If the Jewish Christians had understood the apostles in this way, it is impossible to believe that they would not have made trouble about it. As to the spirit of the Jewish Christians, witness the commotions about circumcision as recorded in the Acts and constantly referred to in some of the Epistles. The Judaizing teachers made circumcision not only a term of communion, but of salvation; and if their doctrine had prevailed, circumcision in the Christian church must have been regulated by the Mosaic law, and this law prescribed the circumcision of infants. The only pretext upon which a compliance with this ordinance according to the law of Moses was binding upon the Gentile converts, was that the children of these converts were members of the Christian church. If they were not, the answer would have been easy. Whatever may be the duty of *adults*, there is no reason to circumcise infants, because, by the new order of things, they do not belong to the Christian community and have no concern with its "sealing ordinances." Yet no such exception was ever taken. (See Acts, xxi. 21.)

4th. If there be no infant membership in the Christian church it is hard to account for the language of God's word respecting children. (See Isa. lxv. 23; Mark x. 14; Acts ii. 39; Rom. xi. 23, 24, *et al.*)

5th. The supposition of infant membership is necessary to give any plausible interpretation of 1 Cor. vii. 14. "Holy" here cannot mean internal purity, for that children of professing parents are holy in this sense is contrary to reason, to scripture and to fact. It cannot mean "legitimate," for marriage is an institution existing from the beginning, and altogether independent of Christianity. It must mean separated and set apart to the service of God. (Lev. xx. 26.) This is evident from the contrast of "unclean"—common. Compare Acts x. 14. The terms "holy" and "unclean" or "common," were precisely the terms for those who were, or were not, respectively within the external covenant of God, and were, therefore, precisely the terms to express the relation of infants to the church visible, according as they were or were not the offspring of parents who were, one or both, members of the church visible. The only plausible objection to this view is, that if the terms "holy" and "unclean" have the meaning asserted for them, then the word "sanctified" must have the same extent of meaning; and if so, the unbelieving partner to the marriage relation must become a member of the church in consequence of the church membership of the other partner.

Answer: (1), The objection, of course, takes for

granted the impossibility of marriage producing such a change in ecclesiastical relations (which we also hold). Then it follows that the whole statement means *nothing*. It neither means "holy," in the sense of being within the external covenant, nor in the sense of internal spiritual holiness, nor in the sense of legitimacy, and there is nothing else that it can mean. It is a holiness which is neither within nor without, neither in soul, nor spirit, nor body, nor condition, nor state, nor anything else.

(2), The covenant of God never founded the privilege of church membership upon the mere fact of intermarriage with his people; but it did found it expressly upon the fact of being born of them.

(3), By a positive statute adults were not to be admitted into the church without a profession of their faith. Hence, the doctrine of Paul must be explained so as to agree with the restriction of this statute. The believing partner does "sanctify" the unbelieving; this is plainly asserted, but not so far as to make the unbelieving a member of the church; this would contravene the statute above named.

(4), The very words teach that this sanctification regards the unbelieving parent, *not for his own sake*, but as a *medium*, affecting the transmission of covenant privileges to the children of a believer. The question was, whether, in the case of one of the parties in the marriage-relation being a Pagan, and the other a Christian, the former or the latter should determine the relation of the offspring to the church, or whether neither should. The answer is, that in this case, where the argument for the children seems to be perfectly balanced by the argument against them, God has graciously inclined the scale in *favor* of his people; so that, for the purpose of conveying to their infants the privilege of being within his covenant and church, the unbelieving partner is sanctified by the believing. It must be thus or the reverse.

This passage decides the same point in another way. It assumes the principle, that where *both* parents are reputed believers, their children belong to the church as a matter of course. (*Mason*, pp. 109–118.) So that the origin, as well as the solution of the difficulty, establishes the doctrine, that by the appointment of God the infants of believing parents are born members of his church. See *Hodge's Comm. in loc.* (1 Cor. vii. 14.)

XI.

THE NOTES OR MARKS OF A TRUE CHURCH.*

1. The occasion and importance of the question.

2. What is a *mark*? How many kinds of marks? What *probable*, and what *necessary* or essential marks? About which kind is this question?

3. What essential to constitute a mark? What meant by its being *proper*? By its being *conspicuous*?

4. The state of the question—not about the marks by which a man may be probably concluded to be one of the elect, or of the church invisible, nor about the church visible, generally considered, as contradistinguished from heathenism, but about a particular church; how the true and orthodox may be discriminated from false and heretical churches; how a church in which we can be *saved* is discriminated from one in which we cannot.

5. These marks may be more or less fully stated. The word only, or the word with the addition of sacraments, discipline, holy life, etc. But they all may be referred to the word.

---

* *Nota* in Latin ; γνώρισμα in Greek. The Greeks (Aristotle) made the γν. of two sorts—the *probable* (εικοτα) and the *certain* (τεκμηρια). The question here is about the latter sort—about *properties*, not about *accidents*. See Turretin, L. 18. Q. 12. Art. 2.

The voice of God is the word; the faith of men is about the word; their life and obedience is the fruit of the word; the order of the church is from the word; the sacraments are the seals and appendices of the word, or a visible word. The word is *vexillum, sceptrum, lux, norma, et statera.*

6. A church may possess these marks more or less perfectly, but all must possess the fundamental doctrines of the gospel. Distinction between essentials and non-essentials. These doctrines must not be judged by the private opinions of doctors, but by the formularies of the body; and the word must be so preached, and the sacraments so administered, that the tendency of the whole shall be to gather in and more or less completely build up the elect of God.

7. Proofs that the *word* is a mark of a true church:

(1), From Scripture: John x. 27. The sheep hear Christ's voice; and those who make a credible profession of hearing it are to be judged in charity to be his. John viii. 31, 32. "If ye abide in my words then are ye my disciples indeed," &c.—xiv. 23. Wherever Christ dwells with the Father, there is his house and temple, but he dwells with those who keep his word. *Ergo*, Matthew xviii. 20; Acts ii. 42. Further, as the science of contraries is one, the mark by which the false is discriminated from the true is a mark by which the true may be discriminated from the false. But this is by the doctrine they teach. Isa. viii. 20; Deut. xiii. 12. Illustrate here the distinction of essentials and non-essentials. The criterion of old was the doctrine of God's unity, (Deut. xiii.); under the gospel the doctrine concerning Christ. 1 John iv. 11, &c. The sin of false teachers in both cases is *idolatry*, for God in Christ is the God of the New Testament. See also Gal. i. 8, 1 Tim. iii. 15, Eph. ii. 19, 20, and thus even to the end, Eph. iv. 11, 12, 13. Hence the removal of the candlestick is the removal of the church. Rev. ii. 5.

(2), From the Fathers: Tertullian, Chrysostom, Jerome, Ambrose, Augustine, and even Vincent of Lirens, Bellarmine, and other Roman Catholic writers; nay, " the Catholic doctrine" itself is founded upon it.   See *Turretin*, iii. pp. 78, ff.

8. But it is objected—

1. To make the Word the mark of the church, is to make the less conspicuous the mark of the more.   Answer.   The difficulty only exists under the Roman Catholic view of the relation of the two, the relation of the church and Scriptures.

2. Doctrine cannot be the mark of the church, because doctrine is either controverted or not.   Uncontroverted doctrine cannot be, because all agree upon it.   It can be, therefore, no mark of distinction, rather is it a mark of communion.   Controverted doctrine cannot be, because *sub judice lis est*, and the decision can only be made by the church, which must therefore have been determined to be a church previously, and upon independent grounds.   Answer: This, again, is a difficulty mainly on the Popish view—denial of right of private judgment; for then, what is controverted may be determined by what is agreed.   The affirmative articles may be the rule by which we may decide the negative, as the *rectum est index sui et obliqui*. Illustrate this by the fact of the apostles citing the Old Testament (and see Acts xvii. 11).   The Papists receive the same Scriptures that we do, and as truth is one, they are bound to show that what they hold beside the teaching of Scripture is in harmony with Scripture.   Particularly illustrated by the doctrine of a mediator, sacrifice and intercession.   Again: Answer by the argument *ad hominem*.   The notes which the Papists lay down are controverted.   *Ergo*, no notes.

3. The judgment of man is fallible.   If, then, human reason judges what is true doctrine, it errs.   Answer: (*a*), That fallible reason does not always err *in fact;* if otherwise, we should never know anything. (*b*), Even

if we accept the decision of an infallible church, we accept it with a fallible reason; therefore we err. Why should the infallible statements of Scripture become fallible when passing into the fallible medium of the human mind, any more than the statements of an infallible church, especially considering that Scriptures are so much plainer than the bulls of Popes?

4. The common people cannot understand Scripture, and therefore cannot know whether a church has the true mark or not. Answer: (*a*), They can understand Scripture as easily as the decrees of the church. (*b*), The contents of Scripture are two-fold, natural and supernatural. In regard to this last, all men stand on the same level: none can understand without the Spirit; with the Spirit, all can. And the doctrine which constitutes the notes of a church belong to this class— the doctrine of salvation. At any rate, the common people are better judges of those notes than of those which the papists lay down.

5. Making the Word a note is making the *form* a note; but the forms of things are recondite, whereas a note must be conspicuous. Answer: This is true of *sensible* objects, but not of *intellectual*, in which last, forms are the most conspicuous, and the form is the best note, because "*dat esse rei.*"

6. But if the form is the being of the thing, then to make the form a note is to explain the thing by the thing itself, *idem per idem.* Answer: This is done in every definition, a definition being only the statement of the genus and the specific difference, which together constitute the formal nature of a thing.

7. Every man knows the church before he knows the Scriptures; *i. e.*, the thing before the note. Answer: It is not true that he knows the church, *as a true church*, before he knows the Scriptures; and this is the knowledge in question. See *Turretin*, L. 18, q. 12, vol. iii. (Carter's ed.), p. 74, ff.

THE PRETENDED NOTES OF ROME.

[See Turretin, L. 18, q. 13.]

Among the notes of the church mentioned by Bellarmine and discussed by Turretin, the chief is that of " succession," or as it is commonly termed, " apostolic succession." A full refutation of the Papal doctrine on this subject may be found in an article in the *Southern Presbyterian Review* for July, 1872. The following is that article:

APOSTOLICAL SUCCESSION.

All branches of the Christian church hold to an apostolical succession in some sense; for without it there is no ground upon which they can claim, with the slightest color of plausibility, a divine sanction for their existence. Presbyterians, for example, hold that they have the doctrine, the polity, the worship, which were taught and ordained by the apostles. They hold that the succession is to be determined, not by history or tradition, but by a direct appeal to writings which are not only more ancient than the writings of the *Fathers*, but have, according to the confessions of these Fathers themselves, a *divine* authority—the writings of the apostles. The body which now holds the doctrine of justification without the works of the law, is, *pro tanto*, a truer successor of the church to which the Epistle to the Romans was addressed, than the church now at Rome which denies that doctrine and curses all who hold it.[1] The body which is now governed by a presbytery is a truer successor of the church of Ephesus, which was also governed by a presbytery in the days of Paul, than a church of the present day which is governed by a prelate, an officer of which

---

[1] See *Gerhard, Loc. Theolog.* Loc. 23, Chap. 11, § 5, § cxc.

the apostolic records know nothing. All this is true, *whatever the intervening history may be.**

We need not say that this is not the sense in which the term is used in this article. It is of the apostolical succession as held by the papists and their "apists" that we propose to treat, and especially of the doctrine as held by the papists, which alone can claim the merit of being intelligible or consistent. The doctrine as held by their imitators, as we may take occasion to show, is mere moonshine, having no meaning, because separated from the system of doctrine and worship of which it forms a part, and because destitute, upon its own principles, of any true historical basis.

The fundamental principle of the apostolical succession is thus stated by the Council of Trent: "Sacrifice and priesthood have been so joined together by the ordination of God, that both have existed under every dispensation. Since, therefore, the Catholic Church, under the New Testament, has received, by institution of the Lord, the holy, visible sacrifice of the Eucharist, it ought also to be confessed that there is in it a new, visible and external priesthood. Further, that this priesthood was instituted by the same Lord our Saviour, and that to the apostles and their successors in the priesthood he gave the power of consecrating, offering and administering his body and blood, as also of remitting and retaining sins, Holy Writ shows, and the tradition of the Catholic Church has always taught."†

---

* There is still another sense in which the term may be used. There has been such an *order of men as Christian ministers*, continuously from the time of the apostles to this day. This is a very different thing from the "apostolic succession" in the mouths of papists and prelatists, which is the succession, in an unbroken line, of *this or that individual minister*. "How ridiculous it would be thought," says Archbishop Whately (*Kingdom of Christ, Essay* II., § 30), "if a man laying claim to the throne of some country should attempt to establish it without producing and proving his own pedigree, merely by showing that that country had *always been under hereditary regal government!*"

† Concil. Trident. Canones et Decreta. Sess. 23, Chap. 1.

Note, then, carefully, that among the papists, apostolical succession means a succession of *priests* * in the proper sense of the word, *sacerdotes*, ἱερεῖς, officers whose business it is to offer true and proper expiatory and propitiatory sacrifices. That this is the meaning of the Council is not left to inference or conjecture. It says that there has been a priesthood under every dispensation of religion; it argues that the eucharist is a sacrifice, and therefore there must be a priesthood to offer it; in the canon corresponding with this decree, it curses all who say that the priesthood is "only an office and a naked ministry for preaching the gospel," and not a visible and external *sacerdotium;* it derives this priesthood from Christ, as the Levitical priesthood was derived from Aaron; that is, from Christ, not as the founder of the Christian Institute, but as the first in order of priests under the new law, as Aaron was the first in the order of priests under the old; and, in proof of this, referring to Heb. v. 4, 5, it makes the apostles Christ's immediate successors as priests, and the priests of Rome the successors of the apostles as priests.

The difference between their priests and the ministers of the gospel, is much wider than between the priests of the family of Aaron and the ordinary Levites who were not of that family. It cannot be too carefully borne in mind, that the question of apostolical succession is a question about the succession of *priests*, not at all of *ministers of the word*.

Note, in the second place, that the apostolical succession involves a peculiar view of the sacraments. The priests are not ministers of the word, and, of course, a sacrament is not a *verbum visibile*, as Augustine calls it; not a sign of truths conveyed by the word, and differing from the word (so far as it is a *sign*) only in the kind of language employed as a vehicle. If this

---

* The English word priest is simply "presbyter writ short."

view were allowed, the priests of the new law would be
no better than those of the old.   Their sacrifices would
be only symbols and actually convey no grace.   So
low a view of her priesthood Rome cannot tolerate.
"The power with which the Christian priesthood is
clothed," says the Catechism of the Council of Trent,
"is a heavenly power, raised above that of angels; it
has its source, not in the Levitical priesthood, but in
Christ the Lord, who was a priest, not according to
Aaron, but according to the order of Melchisedec."
So again the same Catechism: "Priests and bishops
are, as it were, the interpreters and heralds (inter-
nuncii) of God, commissioned in his name to teach
mankind the law of God and the precepts of a Christian life; they are the representatives of God upon
earth.   It is impossible, therefore, to conceive a more
exalted dignity, or functions more sacred.   Justly,
therefore, are they called, not only angels (Mal. ii. 7),
but gods (Ps. lxxxii. 6),* holding as they do the place
and power and authority of God on earth.   But the
priesthoood, at all times an elevated office, transcends
in the new law all others in dignity.   The power of
consecrating and offering the body and blood of our
Lord, and of remitting sins, with which the priesthood
of the new law is invested, is such as cannot be comprehended by the human mind, still less is it equalled
by, or assimilated to, anything on earth."

---

* Papists are not good interpreters.   This passage has no reference at
all to the Levitical priests.   It is "a brief and pregnant statement of
the responsibilities attached to the *judicial* office under the Mosaic dispensation."   The judges are frequently called "gods" in the law.   (See
Exod. xxi. 6; xxii. 8, 9, in the Hebrew *Elohim*.)   Hence vs. 6, "*I have
said*, Ye are gods."   Augustine (Enarratio in p. 81) regards Israel as a
whole as the subject of the Psalm, and vs. 6, as an address specially to
the *elect, eos qui prædestinati sunt in vitam æternam*.   The authors of
the Catechism are unfortunate in citing a passage for the purpose of
glorifying the priesthood, in which the tone throughout is one of severe
rebuke, and in which these "gods" are told they shall "die like men."
Our priesthood is one which knows no change by reason of death—one
after the power of an endless life.   (See 7th chapter of Hebrews, *passim*.)

Every priest is ordained to offer gifts and sacrifices; wherefore these priests must have somewhat to offer. The preaching of the word will not do, because any-body who knows the plan of salvation may tell it to his fellow-sinners. Singing, praying, and alms-giving will not do, for a similar reason. The two sacraments of the New Testament have been pitched upon because they are symbolical ordinances; and the meaning of a symbol is more easily perverted than the meaning of words. The ordinance of baptism has been perverted, as to its matter, by substituting a mixture of oil, spit-tle, salt, and water, for the element of water (that is, an element which *defiles* has been substituted for the ele-ment that *cleanses*); it has been perverted, as to its form, by ascribing a significance to it altogether dif-ferent from that which the New Testament ascribes to it; and it has been perverted, as to its design, by mak-ing it a physical cause of grace to the recipient in every case in which no obstruction is opposed to its operation. It is not the baptism of the New Testa-ment at all, but a ceremony totally different. It re-quires, therefore, a different kind of administrator from that minister of the word whose office it is, by the appointment of Christ, to administer *Christian* baptism.

In like manner they have perverted the ordinance of the supper. It is no longer a simple memorial of the sacrifice of Christ, which was offered *once* for all, but a true and proper offering of the body, blood, and divinity of Christ continually for the living and the dead. The matter, form, and design of this sacrament have all been so perverted, that its identity has been lost. "We therefore confess," says the Tridentine Cat-echism,* "that the sacrifice of the mass is one and the

---

* See the Cat. Trident. on the Sacrament of the Eucharist. We quote, for the most part, from the English translation made by Donovan, Pro-fessor of the Royal College, Maynooth. Balt., 1833. So also the Council itself (Sess. 22) in its Canons, Canon 2. "If any shall say

same sacrifice with that of the cross; the victim is one
and the same, Christ Jesus, who offered himself, once
only, a bloody sacrifice on the altar of the cross. The
bloody and the unbloody victim is still one and the
same, and the oblation of the cross is daily renewed in
the eucharistic sacrifice, in obedience to the command
of our Lord, 'This do for a commemoration of me.'
The Priest is also the same, Christ our Lord: the ministers who offer this sacrifice consecrate the holy mys-
teries, not in their own person, but in the person of
Christ. This the words of consecration declare: the
priest does not say, 'This is the body of Christ,' but,
'This is my body;' and thus invested with the character of Christ, he changes the substance of the bread
and wine into the substance of his real body and blood.
That the holy sacrifice of the mass, therefore, is not
only a sacrifice of praise and thanksgiving, or a commemoration of the sacrifice of the cross, but also a sacrifice of propitiation, by which God is appeased and
rendered propitious, the pastor will teach as a dogma
defined by the unerring authority of a General Council

---

that Christ in these words, 'Do this in commemoration of me,' did not
make the apostles priests, or that he did not ordain that they and other
priests should offer his own body and blood, let him be anathema."
Can. 3. "If any one say that the sacrifice of the mass is a sacrifice
only of praise and thanksgiving, or a bare commemoration of the sacrifice performed upon the cross, and not also a *propitiatory* sacrifice:
or that it profits only him who receives it, and ought not to be offered
for the living and the dead, for sins, punishments, satisfactions, and
other necessities, let him be anathema."

Bossuet, in his *Exposition de la Doctrine de l'Eglise Catholique*, which
was written for the purpose of conciliating the French Protestants,
softens the statement of the Council, or, at least, cites (in 13) the mild-
est language of Sess. 22, c. 1, and insists that the church in offering
Christ to God in this sacrament, does the same thing which is done in
the Reformed Church, except that the one affirms and the other denies the *real presence*. He denies that Rome pretends to offer any new
propitiation for the appeasing of God anew, as if he had not been sufficiently appeased by the sacrifice of the cross; or that any supplement
is made to the price of our redemption, as if it were insufficient. He
represents all as being done in the sacrament in the way of intercession
and application. Yet he expressly holds the doctrine of Trent, and
what that is we have seen.

of the church." The papists make a distinction, indeed, between the eucharist considered as a *sacrament* and the *sacrifice*,* but the distinction is of no importance in the present argument.

Further, the papists hold that all grace is conveyed through the sacraments; that "by them all true righteousness begins, or being begun is increased, or having been lost is restored."† They hold, also, that the grace is always conferred upon the recipient of the sacrament, where duly administered, unless the recipient places a bar or obstacle in the way; and the Trent Council curses all who say the contrary.‡ None, therefore, can be saved without baptism,§ and all baptized *infants* (since they can oppose no "bar") are regenerated. As the sacraments can be administered (except in certain extreme cases) only by a priest, the priests have the whole matter of salvation absolutely in their own hands.

---

*See the Roman Catechism on the Sacrament of the Eucharist. It says: "The difference between the eucharist as a sacrament and a sacrifice is very great, and is twofold. As a sacrament, it is perfected by consecration; as a sacrifice, all its efficacy consists in its oblation. When deposited in a tabernacle, or borne to the sick, it is therefore not a sacrifice, but a sacrament. As a sacrament, it is also to the worthy receiver a source of merit, and brings with it all those advantages which we have already mentioned; as a sacrifice, it is not only a source of merit, but also of satisfaction. As in his passion our Lord merited and satisfied for us, so in the oblation of this sacrifice, which is a bond of Christian unity, Christians merit the fruit of his passion, and satisfy for sin."

† *Concil. Trident, Decretum de Sacramentis, Sess.* 7, *præmium.*

‡ Canon 6, of Sess. 7. In Canon 8 all are cursed who say that the sacraments do not confer grace *ex opere operato,* but that faith alone in the divine promise is sufficient to obtain the grace.

§ Baptism is of great consequence in Rome, as it ought to be, seeing they make it the sacrament of justification. But the glory of the priesthood consists in the privilege of immolating Christ, and of judicially absolving men from their sins. Baptism may be administered even by a woman, by Jews, infidels, and heretics, in case of necessity, provided they intend to do what the church does in that act of her ministry. *Cat. Trid. on the Sacrament of Baptism.* But the eucharist, the sacrifice of the mass, and judicial absolution, can be administered only by a priest. *Con. Trid. Sess.* 14, *chapter 6 : Cat. on the Eucharist,* 72.

The power of the priest to confer grace by the sacraments is not impaired by his personal character, however foul.   He may be living in "mortal" sin ; he may, like the Pope Alexander Borgia, be mixing poison with the wine which he is about to give his friend at his own table ; nevertheless, he can confer the grace of God in the sacraments ; and, in Can. 12, Sess. 7, the *holy* Council curses all who say the contrary.   The sacraments are everything; the preaching of the word nothing, in this holy, catholic, apostolic church.

Again, as to the mode in which the priests, since the time of the apostles, become their successors Rome holds that it is by the sacrament of orders. The main points of their doctrine are: (*a*), That as Christ made the apostles priests by imparting to them the Holy Ghost and the power of judicial absolution (John xx. 22, 23), so the apostles have transmitted to their successors, the bishops of Rome, the same gifts; which bishops, in their turn, by imposition of hands, communicate the priesthood to the lower order. (*b*), That, as in the sacraments of baptism and confirmation an indelible character is imparted, so also in the sacrament of orders. By this indelible character, he who has once become a priest is always a priest; he can never again become *a* laic.* (*c*), That with this process the people have nothing at all to do.   They have no voice at all in making priests.   Canon 7, Sess. 23 of Trent.   The priesthood is a distinct *caste*.   They perpetuate the church as the apostles created it before them.

These points constitute the essence of the doctrine of orders. The apostolical succession as held in Rome is, therefore, summarily comprehended in the three assertions: (*a*), That there is a true and proper priesthood on earth, under the Christian dispensation. (*b*), That there is a true and proper sacrifice, to be continually offered. (*c*), That the succession of priests is secured by the sacrament of orders; this last point, of

---

* See Con. Trid. D. and C., Sess. 23, Can. 4.

course, involving the assertion of the succession as a
fact in history. We propose to consider these in their
order.

I. As to the priesthood under the "new law," as the
papists delight to call the gospel, we remark:

1. That scarcely any truth is more clearly revealed
in the New Testament than that of the *universal* priesthood of believers. The passages in which it is either
expressly asserted or taken for granted, are too numerous to be cited. One or two will suffice : " Ye are
a chosen generation, a royal priesthood, a holy nation,
a peculiar people." 1 Pet. ii. 9; comp. vs. 5. The papist will of course say that this description of believers
under the gospel is identical with that of Israel under
the law (Ex. xix. 5, 6); and that, as the general priestly
character of Israel was consistent, in point of fact, with
the existence of a special order of priests in the family
of Aaron ; so a special order of priests is by no means incompatible with the universal priesthood of believers
under the gospel. As an abstract proposition, this may
be conceded; but there is a very great difference between the two dispensations in point of fact. *First*,
there is no institution of a priesthood in the New Testament as there was in the Old. *Second*, there is no limi-
tation put upon the exercise of priestly functions or
privileges on the part of the priestly people under the
New Testament as there was under the Old. Let the
papists show us any chapters in the New Testament
corresponding with such as the Leviticus viii. in the
Old, and we will believe them. They have their "solemn ceremonies" in the consecration of their priests;
but they are ceremonies which the court of Rome. not
Jesus Christ, has ordained. If they say they observe
the rites ordained in Leviticus, then they confess that
their priesthood is after all the Aaronic, and not, as
they have been accustomed to boast, a priesthood after
the order of Melchisedec. Let them show us in the
New Testament any such stern prohibitions against the

people intermeddling with priestly functions as there are in the Old. So far from finding any such prohibitions, we find no discrimination at all, in regard to priestly character and function, between the ministry and the people, or (to use the language of Rome) between the *clergy* and the *laity*. It is the duty and privilege of all alike to offer *spiritual* sacrifices acceptable to God through Jesus Christ. The writer of the *Epistle to the Hebrews* exhorts his brethren, without any note of distinction, to do what the high priest alone could do, and that only once a year, under the law— "to draw near with a true heart unto God." He bases this exhortation upon the fact that they have "boldness to enter into the holiest by the blood of Jesus, by a new and living way which he hath consecrated for them, through the veil, that is to say, his flesh; and upon the fact that they have a High Priest over the house of God." Heb. x. 19-22.

2. The apostles are nowhere called priests, or represented as performing priestly functions. Considering the extent to which the institutions and technical language of the Old Testament moulded the forms of representation in the New, this fact is very noteworthy. The apostles do sometimes use the sacerdotal and sacrificial language of the Old Testament to describe their work, but it is always under conditions which show, beyond doubt, that they are speaking figuratively. Thus Paul (Rom. xv. 16) speaks of himself as "the minister (λειτουργὸν) of Jesus Christ to the Gentiles, ministering (ἱερουργοῦντα) the gospel of God, that the offering up (προσφορὰ) of the Gentiles might be acceptable, being sanctified (ἡγιασμένη) by the Holy Ghost."[*] Here observe, (*a*), That while the word λειτουργὸν has no

---

[*] The argument here is all the stronger, because, as Whately says (*Cautions for the Times*, p. 40), "Paul is actually *searching* for something in his own office, to parallel the functions of a priest"—and this is all that he can find. How differently would a Papal priest, *now* writing to the church of Rome, express himself!

strictly sacerdotal sense, being used for any public functionary (as for instance, in this very epistle, chapter xiii. 6, of the civil magistrate; comp. vs. 4, διάκονος), yet we concede that there may be a reference to its sacerdotal use in the Septuagint. (See Deut. x. 8; xvii. 12; Joel i. 9; comp. Hebrew x. 11). (*b*), That the second word, which is undoubtedly sacerdotal, is explained by the nature of the offering which is made to God, to wit, the *Gentiles*, not the *mass*. If the Gentiles are a *sacrifice* in the strict and literal sense of the term, then, of course, Paul is a *priest*, in the same sense. But the first will not be asserted, we apprehend, even by a papist. The truth is, Paul's statement amounts to this: "I am indeed a priest, but my priestly functions are exercised in preaching the glad tidings to the Gentiles, and in making an offering to God of those who are, through the word, sanctified by the Holy Ghost." If the priesthood of Rome were of this kind, no objection could be made to it. But it is altogether different. Its office is to offer a propitiatory sacrifice for the living and the dead.

We have said that the *apostles* use sacrificial language in describing their work. But Paul, we believe, is the only one of the apostles who does; and he only in the instance cited, unless Rom. xii. 1, Phil. ii. 17, 2 Tim. iv. 6, be considered instances. Peter, the "first pope," never uses it, so far as we have been able to find, in special application to the ministry. His style is, "We will give ourselves to the ministry (διακονία) of the word and to prayer." Acts vi. 4. "The elders who are among you I exhort, who am your fellow-elder and a witness of the sufferings of Christ, and also a partaker of the glory that shall be revealed; feed the flock of God which is among you, taking the oversight thereof (or, performing the office of bishops in it), not by constraint, but willingly; not for filthy lucre, but of a ready mind; neither as being lords over God's heri-

tage, * but being ensamples to the flock." 1 Pet. v. 1–3.
How strange would such words sound from the mouth
of his pretended successors! It is too plain that the
ministry of the apostles was not the same as the ministry of the papal priesthood; and that if the papal
ministers are true and proper priests, they possess a
dignity to which the apostles, with Peter at their head,
did not dream of aspiring. It is hardly necessary to say
that we hold with the apostles.

3. Not only do the apostles say that all believers are
priests, and claim no special priestly character for
themselves, but a special argument is made by one of
them to show that there can be no true and proper
priests on earth since the offering of Jesus Christ and
his passing into the heavens. The doctrine of Rome
makes utter nonsense of the Epistle to the Hebrews,
and particularly of the 7th chapter. The papists say
that their priesthood is of the order of Melchisedec;
and yet the main feature of the priesthood of Melchisedec, according to the apostle, is that it *admits of no
succession*. "They truly (the Levitical priests) were
many priests, because they were not suffered to continue by reason of death; but this man, because he
continueth ever, hath an unchangeable priesthood."
Heb. vii. 23, 24. But why quote particular verses?
Almost every verse in this chapter is a dagger which
goes to the heart of the papal theory. Nothing but
the most audacious effrontery could venture to maintain such a theory in the face of such an argument.
The papal priesthood is simply an insult, impudent
and shameless, to Christ, who alone possesses a priesthood after the order of Melchisedec. It is not only
destitute of even the shadow of evidence, but is a di-

---

* This is the only instance in which the word κλῆρος is used of *persons* in the New Testament; and yet it is the word from which the
word *clergy* comes. According to this passage, the *clergy*, or inheritance of God, is the *laity*, or flock, which is in danger of being lorded
over. See Campbell's Lect. on Eccl. History, L. 9. This is worthy of
being noted, because the distinction of clergy and laity came in with
the notion of a sacerdotal ministry in the church.

rect contradiction to the teaching of the Scriptures; and being the corner-stone of the apostolical succession, the whole structure tumbles into ruins, or, rather, is proved to be "the baseless fabric of a vision."

II. As to the next element involved in this doctrine, the power of the priesthood to offer a true and proper sacrifice, it need not detain us so long. For,

1. If there be no proper priesthood on earth, there can of course be no proper offering of sacrifice. Priesthood and sacrifice go together; together they stand or fall.

2. The only true and proper sacrifice which the papal priests pretend to offer is that of the mass; and this is a pure invention of men, instigated no doubt by the devil, that restless plotter against the glory of Christ and the salvation of his church.

It would be out of place in this discussion to enter into an elaborate argument against the sacrifice of the mass. It will be sufficient to say, (a), That the silence of the Scriptures seals its condemnation. It is altogether incredible that nothing should be said about any sacrifice in the eucharist, if that ordinance were a sacrifice, and especially if it had occupied the place in the religion of the apostles which it occupies in the religion of Rome—if it had been considered a fundamental point and necessary to the proper observance of Christian worship. The apostles give line upon line and precept upon precept in regard to things which the papists themselves would confess to be of very inferior importance, and yet say nothing about this. This silence is the more remarkable upon the papal theory, because the doctrine of the mass is, by their own confession, hard to be believed, indeed plainly contradicted even by the testimony of the senses, and therefore liable to the strongest assaults of Satan. Further, how can these Judaizers account for the fact that, while in the old law there is constant mention of priests and sacrifices, and most minute details as to both, we find nothing corresponding in the new? It is indeed an awful *mystery*, since the apostles have not even attempted to throw any light upon it.

But not too fast. The papists pretend that they do find in the New Testament a sacrificial character ascribed to the eucharist. For example, 1 Cor. x. 21 ; Heb. xiii. 10. Now, as to the first passage, it is sufficient to remark that Paul does not compare the table of the eucharist with the *altar* of the Gentiles, but the Lord's table with the *table* of demons. The table of demons is not the *altar* of the Gentiles upon which they sacrificed to their idols, but the *table* upon which, after the sacrifice had been offered, the meats were spread for a feast in honor of the idol. And even if the comparison had been one between the Lord's table and altars, the conclusion would not follow which papal logic seeks to draw; for the apostle is not concerned about the reason and nature of altar or sacrifice, but only about the communion or participation of the worshippers with it. He aims to show that the Corinthians could not with a good conscience be present at these feasts in the idol-temples, because they had been made partakers of the Lord's supper, and so had communion with Christ and professed his religion, as those who ate of the ancient victims under the law were made "partakers of the altar," that is, professed the Jewish religion.[*]

As to Heb. xiii. 10, we remark that nothing is said here about the eucharist; that the only sacrifices mentioned in the context as connected with this altar are *praise* and *alms-giving* (vs. 15, 16); that the altar is said to be Christ himself in vs. 15;[†] and in vs. 9 we have a solemn warning against just such a religion as Rome teaches—a religion of *meats* and not of *grace.*

---

[*] See Turretin, L. 19, Q. 29. Opp. 3, p. 456, Carter's Ed

[†] So Aquinas : "This altar is either the cross of Christ, or Christ himself, in whom and by whom we offer our prayers to God." Bellarmine, though not very scrupulous about the arguments he uses, does not urge this place, because many Catholics understand by altar here, Christ and the cross. See Turret. *ut supra.*

(*b*), The only other argument we shall mention against the mass is that of the Epistle to the Hebrews. The argument is of the same sort with that respecting the priesthood. As the perfection of the priesthood of Christ admits of no succession of mortal priests, so the perfection of his sacrifice admits of no repeated sacrifices. Let us quote one passage only from the Hebrews: "Nor yet that Christ should offer himself often, as the high priest entereth into the holy place every year with the blood of others; for then must he often have suffered since the foundation of the world; but now once in the end of the world hath he appeared to put away sin by the sacrifice of himself. And as it is appointed unto men once to die, but after this the judgment; so Christ was once offered to bear the sins of many; and unto them that look for him shall he appear the second time, without sin unto salvation. For the law, having a shadow of good things to come, . . . can never, with those sacrifices which they offered year by year continually, make the comers thereunto perfect. For then would they not have ceased to be offered? because that the worshippers, once purged, should have had no more conscience of sins. But in those sacrifices there is a remembrance again made of sins every year." Heb. ix. 25–28; x. 1–3. This sword of the Spirit effectually cuts the throat of the sacrifice of the mass. With respect both to the priesthood and the sacrifice, the papists have done the very thing against which the whole Epistle to the Hebrews is a warning. They have apostatized from the gospel, and have gone back to Judaism.

Having thus disposed of the second element of the doctrine of succession, we may tarry, before proceeding to the next, to say a word or two in reference to the doctrine of sacramental grace in all its forms. *First:* The whole idea of the papists and their apists, that salvation is conveyed through the sacraments rather than through the word, is utterly foreign to the thinking and language of the New Testament, which gives this prominence to the word and not to the sacraments. Take an example or two out of very many. Paul says to the Corinthians (1 Epistle i. 14–17), "I thank God I baptized none of you but Crispus and Gaius, lest any should say that I had baptized in my own name. . . . For Christ sent me *not to baptize, but to preach the gospel.*" So Peter: "Being born again, not of corruptible seed, but of incorruptible, *by the word of God,* which liveth and abideth for ever; . . . and this is the word which by the gospel is preached unto you." 1 Peter i. 23–25. And even where the sacrament is spoken of as the means of regeneration, it is almost always coupled with the word, or, if not, something is added in order to guard against the error that there is any efficacy in it *ex opere operato.* Thus in Eph. v. 26, Paul speaks of the church as sanctified and cleansed "with the washing of water *by the word.*" "Go . . . preach the gospel. . . . He that believeth *and* is baptized shall be saved." Mark xvi. So Peter, in speaking of baptism as saving us, takes care to say that he is not speaking of the outward ordinance, but the answer of a good conscience toward God. 1 Peter iii. 21.

The idea of the apostles was that the *word* was the charter of salvation, and conveyed everything that was conveyed; that the sacraments were a species of symbolical word, and *pro tanto* performed the same office as the word written or spoken; and that in addition to being *signs* or symbolical words, the sacraments were *seals* of the word as charter, ratifying the covenant contained in the word, and possessing no value whatever if detached from the word. The doctrine of Rome, that by the sacraments all grace begins, and when begun is increased, or when lost is restored, has not the shadow of a foundation in the Scriptures, or in common sense.

Second : That there is no grace given except through

the sacraments, is a doctrine still more monstrous; flatly contradicting many passages of the Scriptures. See, for example, the case of Peter in Acts x. 47, where the "first pope" argues from the fact that these heathen had received the Holy Ghost, that no man could forbid them to be baptized. And then, be it observed, he does not baptize them himself, but commands them to be baptized. No more than his beloved brother Paul, does Peter seem to have been anxious about the rite of baptism, provided only it was done decently and in order.* But the papists and their imitators

---

* "No passage can be produced from the New Testament in which administration of the sacraments is, by a divine law, restricted to the apostles and their delegates, or the grace of these ordinances made dependent upon the persons of the administrators. See Acts ii 41; viii. 38; ix. 18. (Ananias, for all we know, was a layman.) The two sacraments have, in the lapse of time, experienced a very different fate. By the Donatist controversy the principle was established, that baptism, even when administered by those not in the communion with the church, if only the word and the element had been present, was so far valid as that it was not to be repeated in the case of those who, having been baptized in schism, became reconciled to the church. It was argued by Augustine, most conclusively, that the sacrament is Christ's, not his who administers it; and derives its virtue from the sacred name in which it is administered. This was in effect disconnecting the validity of the ordinance from the person of the administrator; for though it was still maintained that the recipient, so long as he continued in a state of schism, derived no benefit from his baptism, still the ordinance itself was pronounced valid, and, as such, was not to be repeated. . . . The eucharist, on the contrary, has always been most jealously guarded from the profanation of lay hands. Yet if there is any difference in the Scriptures, as regards this point, between the two sacraments, baptism is the one which has more the appearance of being restricted. (Matt. xxviii. 19.) But it is characteristic of the church system to be most peremptory and exclusive in its decisions where the Scriptures supply the slenderest foundation for them." See *Litton's Church of Christ*, p. 635.

The validity of the sacraments, therefore, does not require them to be administered by certain officers: but the great law of "decency and order" makes it necessary that the church should appoint certain persons to this office; and the ministers of the word, for obvious reasons, are the persons whom the church *has* appointed. This is the common doctrine of the Reformed theologians. See, for instance, *Turretin. De Necess. Secess. Nostra ab Eccl. Rom.*, *Disp.* 8, 18, (Vol. IV., p. 190 of Carter's Ed., N. Y., 1848). Turretin is inconsistent with himself. See his *Theolog. Elench.*, L. 19., Q. 14. He admits

must make much of it, or their apostolical succession is nothing worth. Hence they must "deny the validity of all baptism but their own, and in defiance of decency, charity, and common sense, refuse to inter an infant who has not passed under their own patent process of regeneration. The consequence is that they throw doubt (and many of them do not scruple to avow it) on the final state of the myriads of unbaptized infants. Whether they are, as some of the Fathers believed, neither happy nor miserable—consigned to a state of joyless apathy, or condemned to eternal suffering—we are all, it seems, in the dark. We may hope the best, but that is all the comfort that can be given us. To a Christian contemplating this world of sorrow, it has ever been one of the most delightful sources of consolation, that the decree which involved even infancy in the sentence of death, has converted a great part of the primeval curse into a blessing, and has peopled heaven with myriads of immortals, who, after one brief pang of unremembered sorrow, have laid down forever the burdens of humanity. It has been the dear belief of the Christian mother, that the provisions of the great spiritual economy are extended to the infant whom she brought forth in sorrow, and whom she committed to the dust with a sorrow still deeper; that it will assuredly welcome her at the gates of paradise, arrayed in celestial beauty and radiant with a cherub's smile. But all these gloriously sustaining hopes must be overcast in order to keep the mystical power of regeneration exclusively in the hands of the Episcopal clergy. All charity, all decency, all humanity, as well

that some of the Fathers approved it, in Q. 13. In case of necessity, the general calling of Christians and the law of charity take the place of any particular calling of officers, and the law of decency and order. Even the papists admit the same as to the sacrament of baptism, though upon the false ground of the *absolute necessity* of this ordinance to salvation. See *Campbell's Lect. on Eccl. History*, L. IV. (specially pp. 58-72) London, Tegg, 1840, for quotations from the Fathers on the matter of authority to administer the sacraments.

as all common sense, are to be outraged, rather than that the power of conferring some inconceivable nonentity should be abandoned." *

Third: This doctrine in its extreme form is the merest paganism, and resembles much more the magical rites and mummeries of people sunk in brutish, heathenish ignorance, than that "reasonable service" which God requires of his worshippers. It is a system of forms which does not compel men to recognize a God, any more than the laws of nature compel such a recognition. It is a system whose tendency is directly to infidelity and atheism. It supposes that God departs from his usual method of working by the laws of nature to accomplish effects which can be discerned neither by sense nor reason. The mystic regeneration, so far as can be known, leaves the person regenerated in no respect changed. He is neither wiser nor better than before; just as capable of committing mortal sin, and in as great danger of eternal damnation, as if the priest's hands had not applied the magic mixture of water, oil, spittle, and salt. It has not even the plausibility of the juggler's tricks ; for the juggler *appears* to work effects which are extraordinary. What evidence can miracles afford to a man who believes the doctrine of transubstantiation? Miracles appeal to the senses. This is the differentia by which they are discriminated from every other immediate act of God upon the creature. But in transubstantiation we are required to believe a miracle which contradicts the senses. How then can a miracle ever authenticate a divine revelation? If the reality of the change in the substance of the bread and wine is ascertained to us by the words, "This is my body," the question may be asked, how are we to know that these words were ever spoken or written? It will not do to appeal to the testimony of eye or ear, for transubstantiation pronounces the testi-

* *Edinburgh Review*, for April, 1843, p. 274, Amer. Ed.

mony of the senses untrustworthy. If God were to impress the reality of the fact upon the mind *directly*, still the revelation could never go beyond the mind that received it. It could never be authenticated to the minds of other men. So that the doctrine of sacramental grace is either nothing at all, a pure imposture, or its legitimate consequence is absolute pyrrhonism. It is substantially the philosophy of Hume under a religious guise.

III. We proceed now to the last point involved in the papal doctrine of succession. It might seem superfluous to argue the question any further. If there was no priesthood instituted by Christ, if the apostles were not priests, then of course there can be no succession of priests. Remove the facts of a priesthood and a sacrifice (in the sense before explained, the papal sense) in the apostolic age, you remove the very foundation of the apostolical succession, and the whole structure tumbles into ruins. This, we venture to think, has been very effectually done, if the Scriptures are to be the rule of judgment. But we shall undertake *ex abundanti*, as the logicians say, to prove that, even if the apostles were priests, they have had no successors, or at least that there are none who can know and prove themselves to be such, which amounts to the same thing. *De non apparentibus et de non existentibus eadem est ratio.*

1. It is a principle clearly laid down in the Scriptures, that no one may presume to undertake sacerdotal functions without a divine call or commission. "No man taketh this honor unto himself, but he that is called of God, as was Aaron." Heb. v. 4.* Every

---

* It is to be regretted that these words should generally be quoted by Protestant writers in proof of the necessity of a divine call to the ordinary officers in the church. Such a call is indeed necessary, but not a direct and immediate call, such as the call of Aaron, and of Christ, to their respective orders of priesthood. This sacerdotal call is immediate, without the intervention of the church, and in the Hebrews (chap. v.) the writer uses the words in application *only* to

attempt on the part of unauthorized persons to invade the priest's office among the Jews was visited with severe penalties. For this offence Korah and his company were destroyed, and Uzziah struck with leprosy. The papists of course apply this principle to their pretended priesthood, *a fortiori*, since the Christian priesthood as much excels the Levitical in dignity, as the new law is superior to the old. So Christ, the founder of the new priesthood, having been called of God as was Aaron, called his successors, the apostles, and the apostles their successors, the bishops, transmitting to them, along with the authority of priests, the ordinary sacerdotal grace which they themselves had received from Christ. The bishops of the apostolic age have in their turn handed down the same grace to their successors, to the present time, by consecration or ordination.*

2. The power thus transmitted is twofold—a power of *order*, and a power of *jurisdiction*. The power of order is the power of immolating and offering Christ in the eucharist, as before explained and refuted. The power of jurisdiction is the power of judicial absolution from guilt. The apostles received the first power at the institution of the supper; the last, when Christ breathed on them after his resurrection, and said, "Receive ye the Holy Ghost," etc. John xx. 22, 23. Conc. Trid. Sess. 14, c. 1. See *Litton on the Church of Christ*, pp. 531-'2.

3. The external instrument of transmission is the sacrament of orders, the administration of which belongs to the bishop alone. The visible sign of the sacrament is the laying on of hands. The inward

---

Christ and Aaron. Christ's priesthood admitted of no succession, and the words admit of no further application since his inauguration into office. In the case of the Aaronic priesthood, they were true of all his successors, because the succession was determined by *birth*. Of this more hereafter.

* See *Litton on the Church of Christ*, p. 530, et seq.

effect is twofold : first, the impressing upon a soul of spiritual *character* or stamp, which is indelible, so that he who is once made a priest can never return to the condition of a layman ; and second, grace, not sancti-fying, but ministerial (*gratia gratis data**) for the valid performance of sacerdotal functions. Conc. Trid. Sess. 23, Can. 4. *Litton*, p. 532.

This is a clear and consistent theory. If no sacra-ments and no absolution, then no church. If no law-ful priesthood, then no sacraments, at least no eucha-rist and no absolution. If no successors of the apos-tles, then no lawful priesthood. If not in communion with the bishop of Rome, no successors of the apostles. Hence, beyond the pale of Rome, no covenanted grace.

This tremendous doctrine (for if it be true, it is tre-mendously true, and if false, it is a tremendous lie) we propose to examine in the light of the Scriptures, of the papist's own principles, and of history. The re-sult of this examination will show that the *fact* of such a succession is altogether incredible, and that it is the height of audacity for any Roman priest of the present day to affirm that he *knows* himself to be a true priest. The examination will be confined to the last of the above mentioned points, as the others have been sufficiently discussed in the preceding part of this article.

1. The Scriptures make no mention anywhere of the *consecration* of any church officers, *as such*. All be-lievers are priests, and are consecrated to the worship and service of God by the indwelling of the Holy

---

* " *G. g. d.*" the extraordinary gifts or charisms, bestowed for the edification of the whole church, opposed to "*gratia gratum faciens*," the gifts bestowed upon any one for his own salvation, faith, hope, &c. An unhappy *terminology* of the schoolmen, so far as it implies that all charisms are not gratuitously given. If the phrases are used at all, the first must describe the *sovereign benevolence* of God as exhib-ited in all the charisms ; the second, the effect of this benevolence in making us "accepted" (*gratas*) in Christ. See *Turretin, L.* III., *Q.* 20, ¶ 8, of Carter's Ed. Vol. 1, p. 219.

Ghost, in any calling which the sovereign will of God may appoint for them. No word signifying consecration is used of the appointment of church officers, *as such*. We shall not waste time in proving a negative. We defy papists and prelatists to produce a single example.

2. The Scriptures make no mention of any *ceremony* of consecration to be used by church officers in consecrating their successors. The papists will hardly insist on the imposition of hands, since the first instance of that we meet with in the New Testament in connection with the ordination of church officers is in Acts vi., the case of the deacons. This was a case in which the hands of the apostles were laid on officers whom the people had *elected;* and what a horror the papists have of the people's electing their own officers everybody knows. Besides, the imposition of hands was so common among the Jews that nobody pretends that it *always* meant consecration; and the papists themselves use it in cases where it is designed to have no such meaning. It would seem certain, at least, that they attach no great importance to this ceremony in the sacrament of confirmation, though it be one of the three sacraments in which an indelible character is imparted. The Tridentine Catechism gives minute directions for the celebration of this sacrament: the unction of the forehead, the sign of the cross, the kiss of peace, and even the slap on the cheek, but says not a word about the imposition of hands. This is all the more strange, because the catechism refers to Acts viii. 14–17, in proof that the bishop alone has the power to administer this sacrament; and yet in that passage it is expressly said that "the apostles laid their hands on them and they received the Holy Ghost."*

---

* The Episcopal Church is here a little more consistent. It not only *alleges* the example of the apostles, but *follows* it. Of course we do not admit that Acts viii. 14–17 has anything to do with "confirmation," either sacrament or mere ceremony.

3. The Scriptures make no mention of an *indelible character* in orders, any more than in baptism and confirmation. That the papal body attaches some consequence to it would seem to be the case, from the fact that the Trent Council curses everybody who ventures, to deny it. Sess. 23, Can. 4. Certain we are that any pious and intelligent man might read the New Testament (and for that matter the Old too) without ever thinking of any indelible character.* Still, not thinking about it is a different thing from denying it. Let us therefore examine Gabriel Biel, who flourished less than a century before the Trent Council, and was a great light in the Church of Rome. He expended a great deal of thought and of research upon this mystery, and his conclusion is thus summed up by Chemnitz : † "That the word character, in this sense, is found neither in the Scriptures, nor in the ancient ecclesiastical writers; that it is not found in the 'Master of the Sentences' himself (Lombard); that as to the thing itself, neither the authority of the Fathers nor reason compels us to posit any such character; that the passages adduced from Dionysius, Augustine, Damascenus, and Lombard in favor of the ' character,' are to be expounded rather of the sacrament of baptism itself, or of the sacramental form, than of any impress or stamp made in fact upon the soul; that all the effects ascribed to the character may be explained as well without the character as with it; that the sacraments themselves work these effects without the character; that the things attributed to the character are found in

---

* We beg pardon ; the *Roman character* is referred to in several places of the Revelation. See xiii. 16–17 ; xiv. 9, 11 ; xv. 2 ; xvi. 2, et al. The word is χάραγμα. Heb. i. 3 is the only place in which the word χαρακτήρ occurs.

† Examen Concilii Tridentini, Sess. 7, p 28. This great work is a storehouse of argument and history against the leading dogmas of Rome. See also Fra *Paolo's Hist. C. of Trent*, (Courayer French Trans.) Vol. I. pp. 438–'9, B. 2, § 86.

the eucharist, and in other sacraments, which are not supposed to imprint it; that the chief reason which weighed with the schoolmen for positing the character has little force; that the unreiterableness of some of the sacraments does not depend upon the character, but upon the nature of these sacraments and the divine institution; that it is less clear what the character is, than that baptism is not to be reiterated; that the sole authority for it is a passage in the writings of Pope Innocent III. (A. D. 1198–1216); that the passage is susceptible of another interpretation: that a theologian ought not to lay down anything to be believed which is not necessary *ex fide, et cet.*" So far this great champion of Rome. It would appear, then, to use the language of the *Edinburgh Review*, that this character is "a nonentity inscribed with a very formidable name—a very substantial shadow." "As to the *ubi* of the character," says Dr. Campbell, "there was no less variety of sentiments—some placing it in the essence of the soul, others in the understanding; some in the will, and others *more plausibly* in the imagination; others even in the hand and tongue; but by the general voice the body was excluded. So that the whole of what they agreed in amounts to this: that in the unreiterable sacraments, as they call them, something, they know not *what*, is imprinted, they know not *how*, on something in the soul of the recipient, they know not *where*, which never can be delected." And yet we are adjudged to the everlasting pains of hell for not believing it. We are willing to share the damnatoin of Gabriel if he has been damned for not believing *this*.

But what was the motive for postulating this mysterious nonentity and the transmission of sacerdotal grace? In answer, we quote the words of Litton (in the *Ch. of Christ*, pp. 534–537): "Christianity [according to Rome], being the new law of Christ, must present the same general characteristics which its prede-

cessor, the law of Moses, did.   Now every legal system
of religion being necessarily of an artificial and arbitrary character in its appointments, inasmuch as it intended to work from without inwards, and to produce
the disposition which it does not find present, a law
from without will regulate in detail all matters connected with divine worship, and especially will determine the functions and persons of the sacerdotal order.
The permanency of the external mould in which the
worshipper is to be fashioned to religion being a principal object in every such system, the institution of the
priestly order will be positive rather than natural : it
will come from without, not spring from within. *Moral*
qualifications for the ministerial office—such as wisdom, or knowledge, or personal piety—will, under such
a system, occupy a subordinate place, or rather, may
be altogether dispensed with ; the great object being
to make provision for a visible succession of sacerdotal
persons, who, whatever they may be inwardly, shall at
least possess an official sanctity. Besides, it is obvious
that no one can guarantee the transmission of moral
endowments, natural or spiritual. This object, the ancient systems of religion— the Jewish among the number—aimed at securing, and did in fact secure, by in-
corporating in themselves the principle of *caste ;* that
is, by attaching the priestly function to a certain tribe
or family, separated for the purpose from the rest of
the nation, and making it pass from father to son in
the way of natural descent, irrespectively of moral
qualifications.   By this means the perpetual existence
of a visible priesthood was secured; the only contingency, and that not a probable one, which could destroy the succession, being the extinction of the sacerdotal tribe or family.   An hereditary priesthood, the
basis of the sacerdotal character being not the *fitness*
of the individual, but the consecration of the caste,
is the natural accompaniment of every system of religion which aims at moulding men, by means of law

and discipline, into a specific type of religious sentiment.

"The Jewish priesthood was instituted on the principle just mentioned. The tribe of Levi was set apart to the ministry of the tabernacle, and out of it the family of Aaron to sacerdotal functions; and nothing more was necessary to qualify men for the priesthood than the legitimacy of birth and investiture with the sacred garments. It is obvious, that if anything analogous to this was to reäppear under the Christian dispensation, it must undergo considerable modifications to render it less strikingly inconsistent with the general principles of the gospel; it must put on a more spiritual form, and one capable of greater expansiveness. Particularly in one point a change was indispensable: a priesthood propagating itself by natural descent would manifestly be unfitted for the purposes of a religion, the professed aim of which is not, like Judaism, to be a training school for one nation only, but to embrace all nations within its pale. The transmission therefore must be independent of race or tribe. It is in fact by thus modifying its aspect that Romanism is enabled to introduce the ministry of the law into the gospel. The principle of caste is retained; but it appears under a new form better suited to Christianity. The powers which belonged to the sacred office are transmitted only in one line, and in that line they are transmitted independently of any moral qualification on the part of the recipient: only instead of priests by natural, we have priests by spiritual descent, the existing body of bishops possessing the power, in and by the sacrament of orders, of spiritually generating pastors for the church. As of old, so now, the legitimacy of the ministerial commission depends exclusively upon the legitimacy of the external succession, for the want of which no fulness of natural and spiritual endowment can compensate. Yet we are not to suppose that no internal grace accompanies the transmission of orders; that a

priest becomes a priest solely by the visible imposition of hands. Some concession must, as-regards this
point, be made to the general spirit of Christianity,
and therefore it is added, that by the sacrament of orders, working like all the others *ex opere operato*, grace
is conferred; not, however, sanctifying grace, but the
mystical grace of priesthood, grace for the valid performance of holy functions, which may exist equally
in those who have saving faith in Christ, and in those
who have not. Thus a degree of *inwardness* is imparted to what otherwise would be as purely external
a matter as the succession of Eleazer to Aaron. Finally, as the ancient priests were always priests, no
one having it in his power to reverse his natural birth,
so the spiritual stamp or impressed character, which is
a consequence of ordination, forever distinguishes him
who receives it from his brethren in Christ."

The papal idea of ordination, as thus described, receives no sanction from the word of God; none from
the Old Testament, much less from the New. Under
the Old Testament the call of God determined the
whole matter without the will of man. According to
the papists, the will of man determines everything; for
the "*intention*"* of the officiating bishop or priest determines the question, whether the grace belonging to
any sacrament shall be actually conferred or not. The
external forms may be strictly canonical; but who can
tell, whether the licentious, cock-fighting, gambling
priest intends to do the act which the church intends?
The notorious want of reverence in papal priests—and
the nearer Rome the more notorious the want of reverence—makes it very probable that in thousands of
instances of apparent baptism, or confirmation, or
ordination, the sacrament was a practical jest: meant
nothing and did nothing. The current of spiritual
electricity met with an obstinate non-conductor, was

* Concil. Trident., Sess. 7, Can. 11; and Chemnitz's Examen.

arrested and dissipated. Under the Old Testament, the extraordinary providence which was a leading feature of that dispensation, secured the family of Aaron from extinction; and the genealogical registers secured the people from the imposture of pretenders. In Rome no man can be sure that his priest is not an imposter or intruder.

Under the Old Testament there was no transmission of sacerdotal grace; and although the right of any man to be a priest was easily ascertained, no man's spiritual relations or spiritual state was made to depend upon the doings of the priest. The utmost wrong that could be done him was external, affecting his outward relations to the church. But these cruel religion-mongers boast that one grand difference between the sacraments of the law and theirs, is, that the latter *confer* the grace which the former only *signify*.* If, therefore, a poor soul goes to a priest who is no priest; or if a true priest does not happen (through ignorance, or malice, or drunkenness, or the spirit of jesting) to intend to do what the church intends, the salvation of that soul is put in extreme jeopardy! How different this hideous and cruel abomination from the merciful spirit of the gospel, which says, "Believe in the Lord Jesus Christ, and thou shalt be saved." Blessed be God, who brought our fathers out of this "pitchy cloud of infernal darkness" into the sunlight of divine truth, where we can "hear the bird of morning sing." Righteous will be our doom if we allow ourselves to be "reinvolved" in that cloud again.

When we compare this doctrine of sacerdotal grace with the teachings of the New Testament, the contra-

---

* The Tridentine Catechism says that "the sacraments of the old law were instituted as signs only of those things which were to be accomplished by the sacraments of the new law." (On the Sacraments.) Let it be remembered that Rome holds that the sacraments not only confer grace, but that *nothing* can confer it without them, that they are necessary to salvation; and the statements of the text are fully sustained and justified.

diction becomes glaring. *First*: Neither the term *or-ders* nor the term *ordination* * occurs in the New Testa-ment. It is a little remarkable that a sacrament should have been instituted without a name and without a re-cord. We find there neither name nor thing. "The word *ordination* is of all ecclesiastical terms the most purely secular in derivation. The word *ordo*, from which the Latin verb *ordinare* is derived, was the tech-nical term for the senate or council to which, in the colonies and municipal towns of the Roman empire, the administration of local affairs was committed, and the members of which were called *Decuriones*. The correlative, therefore, to the *ordo* was not the laity as distinguished from the priesthood, but the *plebs* or pri-vate citizens as distinguished from the magistracy. And in fact, the word *ordinare* is never used by the classical writers to signify consecration to a sacred of-fice. From the state it passed into the church, whence the frequent use in the early Latin fathers of the word *plebs*, to denote the Christian people or laity, in contrast with the clergy. It is reasonable to suppose that when first introduced its ecclesiastical corresponded to its civil meaning, and that to be ordained, or to be in-vested with 'holy orders,' signified merely to be chosen a member of the governing body or presbytery in a

---

* It is hardly necessary to say that we do not refer to the *English* words *ordain* or *ordination*, or to the idea of ordination in the general sense of *appointing, constituting* (see Titus i. 5); but to the *ceremony* of set-ting apart a man to an office or a work. The word *ordain* occurs again in Acts xiv. 23 in our version, but there the Greek is different, χειροτονεῖν, a verb which afterwards became a technical one in the Greek church to express ordination. But in the only other place where it occurs in the New Testament, 2 Cor. viii. 19, it is rendered by our translators "chosen." Comp. 1 Cor. xvi. 3; and this is a meaning, and apparently the chief meaning, assigned to it by Suidas, Hesychius, and Suicer. See Suicer's *Thesaurus* under the word. No doubt it came to be used of the act of ordaining because the election of officers preceded their ordination—election and ordination constituting vo-cation to office. So in the same way χειροθεσία signified blessing (εὐλογία) on account of the benediction which accompanied the lay-ing on of hands in certain cases. See Suicer *sub verb*.

Christian society; no reference being intended to a specific grade of religious standing supposed to be thereby acquired. To transfer the notions which in later times became connected with 'ordination' into the apostolic age, or the sacred narrative, is the ready way to fall into serious errors of scriptural interpretation."*

Second: This account of the origin of the word falls in with the view of ordination as given in the New Testament. In every free commonwealth citizens are elevated to office because they have, or are supposed to have, a larger measure of the endowments which qualify for office than the body of their fellow-citizens. They are not elevated to a *caste* or *rank* because they possess gifts which have been *altogether* denied to their fellow-citizens; nor are they selected out of the mass as persons upon whom certain gifts *are to be* conferred in order to qualify them for office.† They are not subjected to a manipulation by which any indelible character is to be imprinted, or any political grace imparted. They are simply put into office, with or without solemn ceremonies, by the will of the body in which all political power resides, and to which all the political gifts and capacities of its members belong. The power resides in the body as to its *being;* in the officers as to its *exercise.*‡ In the human body the power

---

* See Litton's *Church of Christ*, p. 567, foot-note. Similar confusion and error have resulted from the like use of the terms *heresy* and *schism*, the scriptural terms differing very widely in signification from the ecclesiastical. The Church of Rome, for example, has been remarkably free from the *ecclesiastical* sin of schism; no community has been more guilty of the sin of schism in the scriptural sense. How fatal has been the force and imposture of *words!*

† Hence Paul lays down in the pastoral epistles (1 Tim. iii. and Titus i.) the qualifications (the gifts) which are to *guide the electors and the ordainers*. The gifts, therefore, *already exist before the ordination*, and of course cannot be imparted by ordination. This one fact is fatal to the whole theory of orders as held by papists—and their apists.

‡ This distinction was expressed in the schools by the terms *in primo actu*, or *quoad esse*, and *in actu secundo*, or *quoad operari*.

of vision may be said to belong, as to its *being*, to the body, but as to its *actual exercise*, to the eye. The body is the *principium quod*, the eye is the *principium quo*. The body sees, but sees by the eye. The life of the body is in every part and organ, and the life of the body controls the life in every part. The eye sees by the life of the body, and sees under the control of the life of the body, and for the good of the body. The eye represents the body *quoad* seeing; is *in*, not *over*, the body for that purpose. So the commonwealth makes and administers the laws by the organs instituted for that purpose. Its life is in the legislature, in the judiciary, in the executive, for the discharge of their respective functions. The civil officers in these various departments are *in* the commonwealth, not *over* it; they represent the commonwealth *quoad* these various functions, and the functions being performed by the life of the commonwealth are performed for its interests. Further, in every such commonwealth there are solemn ceremonies by which the fact of such representation is formally recognized and published; and when the officer ceases to hold the office and relinquishes its duties, he ceases to be a representative, and falls back into the mass.

Now, this is an exact account of what occurs in the church, *mutato nomine*, if only we allow for the difference between a free commonwealth which makes a constitution for itself and a free commonwealth which has its constitution made for it by Christ.* It is in substance the view given by Paul in 1 Cor. xii., where

---

*The difference here signalized may be made plain by an illustration. The constitution of a free commonwealth is "ordained" and established by the "*sovereign people*" assembled in convention. The election of persons to fill the offices created and defined by the constitution belongs to the *people* in a very different sense, in the sense of "constituents." Hence an officer holding the office created by the constitution, or the *sovereign* people, is responsible to the people in *this* sense, and not in the sense of his constituency. The old doctrine, therefore, of "instructions" was inconsistent with the very nature of

his avowed object is to state the relations of gifts in the church to the offices and functions discharged in it. He presents the same view also in Rom. xii. The gifts are given to the church as a body; the life is hers, the life of the Holy Ghost; these gifts are given to be manifested and exercised for the profit of the whole body. The movement is *from within outwardly;* the organism effloresces in apostles, prophets, evangelists, pastors, teachers, deacons, etc. Compare Eph. iv. 4–16, in which exquisite description of the gifts and calling of the church, the introduction of the idea of priestly caste would be felt to be an intolerable impertinence.* It is plain that the gifts and offices and officers are all given to the church by her glorious Bridegroom; that in the order of nature, and even of *time,* she exists before them. She is the end, and they are the means. The powers of teaching, ruling, distribut-

a representative, as Burke told the electors of Bristol. Now, the constitution of the church comes in *no sense* from the church. There is no sovereignty but in Christ her head. He ordains and establishes her constitution; creates her offices; and her officers, though elected and "ordained" by the church, are not responsible to those who elected them, but to the Head, and to those courts which he has appointed to govern. The rulers in the church are rulers *in* her, not *over* her, as Paul hints to the elders at Ephesus. Acts xx. 28; in the Greek ἐυ ᾧ, not ᾧ. The eye is *in* the body for seeing, not *over* it. It is in a *high* place, much higher than the foot, but still it is *in* the body, as the foot is, and both eye and foot have *identically the same life.* In Rome, the priesthood is *over* the body, and has a life of its own, different from the life of the laity (or people of God), as the life of a shepherd is different from the life of the sheep whom he governs and *shears.* We may add, that it follows from the view given above, that both election and ordination, while they express the judgment of the church, express the judgment of the church that Christ, the Head, has called the persons elected and ordained, by giving them the gifts of his Spirit.

* "All office-bearers, and especially all such as are ordinary and perpetual, are given by Christ to his church; and the church is not in any conceivable sense given to them. The personal ministry of Christ was surely not utterly barren. He had disciples before he had apostles; he had many, perhaps multitudes of followers, before the descent of the Holy Ghost had fully anointed the apostles for their office and work; and we are told that after his resurrection, and before his ascent into

ing, are *her* powers; the gifts necessary for the exercise
of these powers are *her* gifts; the officers through whom
she exercises them are *her* officers; they are her eyes
and ears and hands and feet. The life is the same in
all: there is *one spirit* as well as *one body*. There is
no room here for the distinction of *clergy* and *laity* (if
those terms mean nothing more than the distinction
between office-bearers and private members); every
laic is a clergyman, because he belongs to the inheritance of God; and every clergyman is a laic, because
he belongs to the people of God. The simple statement of Paul is an overwhelming refutation of the pu-
trid figment of sacerdotal orders and sacerdotal grace.
The officers of the church are simply her representatives and organs *quoad* teaching, ruling, distributing,
etc.; and "ordination" is simply a solemn ceremony
by which the fact is recognized and authenticated.

---

heaven, He was seen of above five hundred brethren at once. 1
Cor. xv. 6. And of the vast crowds that followed him, and gladly
heard him who spake as never man spake, who shall presume to say
that multitudes did not believe on him? To those already united with
him by faith, and to his elect throughout the earth and throughout all
generations, he gave, after he had singly triumphed over death and
hell, the inestimable gift of a living and permanent ministry. But he
had a church in the world before there was either apostle, or prophet,
or evangelist, or pastor, or teacher; and he will have a church around
him throughout eternal ages, after all his saints are gathered and perfected, and whose oracles, ordinances, and ministry shall all have fulfilled their work His bride was equally his undefiled, his only one.
before any ordinance was established, or any oracle given, or any
ministry constituted, as she is now that we enjoy all these proofs of
his care and love; and if there had never been an office-bearer of the
race of Adam given as a servant to minister unto her—if angels had
been her only ministers forever, or the divine Spirit had disdained all
secondary agencies, or were now to reject the whole body of sinful
men, who are nothing but as he enables them—still that spotless bride
would be the Lamb's wife by a covenant reaching from the depths of
eternity, steadfast as the oath of God can make it, and sacred by the
blood of Jesus with which it is sealed. No, no; there is no lordship,
no headship in Christ's church but that of Christ himself; there are
but servants in the church for Christ's sake; and their Master's rule
is this: 'Whosoever will be chief among you, let him be your servant;
he that is greatest among you shall be your servant.' "—*R. J. Breckenridge's Sermon on Eph.* iv. 8.

Here is no grace transmitted from man to man in a line of priests *over* the church and *above* it; the propagation of a life separate and independent from that of the laity; but the very same grace, gifts, and *life* in the officers and in the body.*

As Christ is the head of the church, is the author of its constitution, and rules in it by his Spirit, no member of the church can be made an officer except by a call from him, any more than that member could be a member except by his calling. It is Christ who confers the gifts which qualify for office, and this is done by the Holy Ghost who dwells in the whole church. It is Christ who creates the office and defines its functions and prescribes the qualifications for it. And yet, according to the will of the same Lord and Head, the call to be an officer is not complete without the action of the church, any more than the call to be a member is complete without the action of the church. Hence vocation is both inward and outward; and the outward consists of election † and ordination. Election is the

---

* Since writing the above I have met with a passage in F. W. Krummacher's autobiography (pages 159–168) which expresses the above views. See particularly pages 164–'5.

† That the people in the ancient church had the right of electing their bishops is so notorious that we are not aware of its being seriously denied by any respectable writer. Hooker (*Ch. Polity*, B. 7, c. 14), after conceding the fact, goes on to vindicate the Church of England in denying this right to her people, upon the ground that changes of this sort must occur in the social development of a people, and appeals to the *civil history of Rome*, and the changes that took place first in the republic and afterwards in the empire! What is this but virtually asserting that the church is a natural institution like the state, and that its life is merely natural? Such a doctrine is natural in the minister of a church which was created by the state and is governed by it; but will be rejected with horror by every one who believes that Christ is the only King in his church, and that her constitution comes from him. The truth is, the dogma of apostolical succession is utterly incompatible with any election of ministers by the people; and one or the other *must* be abandoned. If anybody doubts that bishops were elected by the suffrages of the people in the ancient church, he may have his doubts fully removed by consulting Suicer's *Thesaurus Ecclesiasticus*, under the words Ἐπίσκοπος, χειροτονέω, and χειροτονία. Down to the time of Nicolaus II., who was made pontiff in 1058, the

act of the body; ordination the act of the rulers already existing, who have themselves been chosen in like manner; but both election and ordination are acts of the church, making the person chosen and ordained her representative or organ as to the particular functions to be performed. Election and ordination are therefore simply modes in which the divine calling is manifested and ascertained. The Spirit of Christ dwells in the man called, in the congregation electing, in the court ordaining; and when the presence and working of the Spirit is manifested in all these modes, the calling is as complete, and as completely authenticated as the present imperfect condition of the church will allow. Ordination imparts no authority, it only recognizes and authenticates it. The solemn ceremonies used in the inauguration of a president of the United States do not make him president (that has been already done), but only recognize and authenticate the fact. It is not necessary that the oath of office should be administered by the outgoing president (upon the principle of like begetting like); it is sufficient that it be administered by an accredited organ and representative of the commonwealth.

If this be a just view of the nature of ordination, it follows that ordination is *not unreiterable*. The occasions for a reiteration of the ceremony may be, and commonly will be, very rare, but there is nothing in the nature of the thing to hinder its being reiterated. Paul and Barnabas were separated for the special work

---

people of Rome still took part in electing the bishop of Rome. Nicolaus ordered that the cardinal bishops and the cardinal presbyters should elect the pontiff; yet without infringing the established rights of the Roman [German] emperors in this business. At the same time he did not exclude the rest of the clergy, nor the citizens and people from all part in the election; for he required that the assent of all these should be asked and obtained. It was not until the reign of Alexander III., more than a century afterwards, that the election of the pope was given exclusively to the college of cardinals. *Mosheim*, Vol II. p 233. So long did this relic of the primitive doctrine linger after the ministry had been converted into a priesthood!

to which the Holy Ghost had called them, by prayer and fasting, and the laying on of the hands of the Presbytery at Antioch. And yet Barnabas had been a distinguished teacher before in that very church, and Saul had been made "a chosen vessel to bear the name of Christ before kings, and the Gentiles, and the people of Israel," some time, according to some chronologers many years, before. If it be said that this was not a case of "ordination," of setting apart to an office, but only of setting apart to a special work; we answer, show us an instance of any separation to an office as contradistinguished from a work in the New Testament. If John xx. 22, 23, be adduced as an instance, we answer that this was an ordination by the Lord himself, and not by the church. It is true that Rome directs the bishop in the consecration of a priest to say, "Receive the Holy Ghost;" and the Episcopal church imitates Rome in one of its forms in the "ordaining of priests" (at the same time mercifully proposing another form for men whose consciences are too tender to allow them to use the first); but this is done without any warrant from Christ, and, as it appears to us, is near akin to blasphemy. We hold that the ordination of the apostles was extraordinary, as their office was extraordinary; and yet here is a case of the greatest of all the apostles having the hands of the ordinary teachers in Antioch laid upon him. He takes his place along with Barnabas, Stephen the deacon, Timothy the evangelist or bishop, or legate *a latere*, or whatever he was; Barnabas the teacher; Saul the apostle; all alike had hands laid on them, and were commended to the Lord for the *work* which he had for them to do. And if any of these illustrious men had quit their work and gone to money-making, and then returned to their work again, there could be no good reason why the hands of the Presbytery should not have been laid upon them again. Or if Timothy had become a pastor of a congregation, there was no

reason why he should not have been commended to the
Lord to that new work, by prayer, fasting, and the imposition of hands.   These things constitute the ceremonies of ordination; and Saul and Barnabas, who had
been preaching for years, had these things done to
them.   Call it ordination or anything you please, it was
a solemn act of obedience to the Holy Ghost, recognizing his sovereign will in the choice of these men for a
particular ecclesiastical work of preaching and ruling.
And if there be anything more in "ordination" than
this, we have been unable to find it.

Again, according to Rome, the bishop alone has the
power to communicate this mysterious sacerdotal grace
in orders.   Now the New Testament knows nothing of
the bishop as different in rank or order from the presbyter or priest.   The papal bishop is a pure invention
of man or—the devil.   The sacrament of orders therefore falls to the ground, being founded on the bishop.

Once more.   There is no instance in the New Testament, in which the act of ordaining was performed by
one man.   The college of apostles ordained the deacons; the prophets and teachers laid hands on Barnabas and Saul; the Presbytery laid hands on Timothy.   No doubt the apostles and evangelists did sometimes appoint or ordain elders, acting singly, when
there was no existing presbytery to do the act.   But
the record makes it very clear that they preferred the
other method where it was practicable; just as in
other acts of government, the apostles, though competent to act each one by himself, preferred, when practicable, to act jointly, or as an assembly.   They did
this, no doubt, to indicate the mode in which Christ
would have his church to be governed in all time, "by
the common counsel of the presbyters," to use Jerome's
expression.

The papists sometimes condescend to quote the
Scriptures in proof of their peculiar doctrines.   Their
quotations generally have as little to do in fact

with their doctrines as the passage cited by a simple monk in proof of the scripturalness of the two orders of clergy, the regular and the secular,—"the oxen were ploughing and the asses feeding beside them." But they find a passage (2 Tim. i. 6) which looks as if it might support their doctrine of ordination; for here is ordination by one man, and the imparting of a gift by the imposition of his hands. Upon this passage we observe, (*a*), That if this was a case of ordination, then it was either the same with that mentioned in 1 Tim. iv. 14, or a different one. If it was a *different* case, then Timothy was ordained at least *twice;* and what becomes of the indelible character, and the doctrine of the unreiterability of ordination? If it was the *same* case, then what becomes of ordination by bishops alone (for the ordination here was by presbyters)? Or if the Presbytery consisted of prelates, what becomes of the plenary authority of the apostle Paul? Was not *his* ordination sufficient to make Timothy a presbyter, or an evangelist, or even a prelatical bishop? If it is said that Paul condescended to be a bishop for the nonce; we answer that he might have condescended still further (as his brother Peter did, 1 Pet. v. 1), to be a fellow-presbyter with his brethren, and act for and with them in the presbytery in laying hands on Timothy. This, we have little doubt, is what actually occurred. (*b*), The gift that Timothy received by the laying on of the hands of Paul and the presbytery was the gift described by Paul in Eph. iii. 7, 8, as having been given to himself (perhaps by the laying on of the hands of the *layman* Ananias, Acts ix. 17–20). That it was no indelible character is evident from the fact that Timothy is exhorted to "stir it up"; Paul uses a word which implies that the gift had descended like fire from heaven; but that it was to be kept from going out, and to be increased by Timothy's care. It was a gift which manifested itself in "reading, exhortation, teaching" (see

1 Tim. iv. 13); was capable of being improved by these exercises, as well as by the "meditation" which was needful to perform them (vs. 15); and a gift in which "his profiting might appear unto all." None of these things can be affirmed of the sacerdotal grace of the papist. It exists alike in the laziest and most diligent, in the vilest and the purest, in a Leo the Great and a Leo the Tenth. Whatever, therefore, this mystic grace may be, it is certainly a different thing from Paul's gift, or Timothy's. The "character" in Paul or Timothy would certainly have been "deleted" by a tenth or hundredth part of the wickedness which failed to delete it in John XXII., or Alexander VI.

Having thus said what we proposed to say upon the papal doctrine of succession in the light of the Scriptures, we proceed to consider it in the light of history and of the conditions of the doctrine itself. These two views of the subject we combine, as the history will show that the doctrine as stated by the papists cuts its own throat, and if that we are to believe it, we must first abnegate our own reason. There is good reason why these people do not like an appeal to reason. We are very apt to be against that which we feel to be against us.

1. There is no such doctrine of succession as that of the Trent Council to be found in the first three centuries of the Church: we mean a doctrine involving a priesthood perpetuated by a process independent of the Christian people. Even the high-churchman Cyprian, in the middle of the third century, whose extravagant language concerning the priesthood and the episcopate, prelatists quote much oftener and with vastly more relish than they ever quote Peter or Paul, did not venture to deny the right of the people to have something to say in the creation of bishops and priests. The succession of the early fathers was a succession of *doctrine,* not of *persons,** except so far as persons were

---

* See Gerhard's Loc. Theology, Loc. 23, Chap. XI. Sec. 5, cxcii.,

involved in the doctrinal succession. They seem to have been led to assert such a succession by a claim of this sort made by the heretics, who, finding the writings of the apostles against them, pretended to have a tradition of the apostles in their favor. Thus Tertullian, in his book *De præscriptionibus adversus hæreticos*, urges the true succession against the false.[*] "Let them parade the origins of their churches, let them unroll the series of their bishops, so coming down by succession from the beginning, that the first bishop had some one of the apostles, or a disciple of the apostles, as his ordainer and predecessor. Let the heretics invent a figment of this sort, yet it will profit them nothing; for their very doctrine will convict them, when compared with the doctrine of the apostles, by its diversity and contrariety; for as the apostles did not teach contrary to one another, so apostolic men would not have taught contrary to the apostles." Tertullian's idea of the succession was not at all that of a priesthood whose function it was to offer sacrifice and pronounce authoritative absolution; but the succession of men in certain *churches* which, having been founded by the apostles or by their disciples, were called "sedes apostolicæ," or sees of the apostles, and were supposed to have a prescriptive right to say what the apostolical teaching really was.

This was indeed a very unsafe rule. It was not the rule given in the Scriptures. The spirits ought to have been tried by the Holy Spirit speaking in his word, and specially by the great fundamental doctrines of the word, as prescribed by John in his First Epistle, chap. iv.; but this rule was not deemed sufficiently easy, and yet it seems easy enough. "Whosoever transgresseth, and abideth not in the doctrine of Christ, hath no God. If there come any unto you, and *bring not this doctrine,*

Vol. XI. p. 297, ff. Note particularly the quotations from the Fathers in cxciii. and ff.

[*] Tertullian, de præs. adv. hæretic. apud. Turretin, L. 18, Q. 13.

8

receive him not into your house, neither bid him God-speed." (2 John ix. 10.) But men were wiser than God, and in order to extinguish heresy and prevent schism, invented the Catholic doctrine and made communion with the bishop the mark of orthodoxy. But in the whole business the *truth* was the thing aimed at, not sacramental grace or sacramental salvation. They inverted the proper order, and instead of judging the man or the church by the *faith*, they judged the faith by the man or the church. The results of this inversion have been deplorable; but these ancient worthies ought to be acquitted of the sin and silliness involved in the modern doctrine of the succession.

That this view of the position of the ancient church is the true one, is evident from the Donatist controversy. It is well known that there was no difference between the Donatists and "the church," either in faith or order; both were orthodox; both were episcopal. There was no question made by the church, whether the Donatist communion was *a* church, a part of the church visible on earth. Members coming to the church from the Donatists were not re-baptized; but more than this, ministers coming from them to the church were not reordained. Not only was this the case in the early stages of the great controversy, but even as late as the conference at Carthage, just one century from the death of Mensurius, which was the original occasion of the strife, the Catholics offered to acknowledge the bishops of the Donatists. Even the Synod of Rome offered to hold communion with them.* The Catholic

---

* See these positions fully established by Claude in his *Defence of the Reformation*, p. 3, chap. 4. Chillingworth takes the same view of this controversy. He quotes from an epistle of Augustine these words: "You (the Donatists) are with us in baptism, in the creed, and the other sacraments"; and again: "Thou hast proved to me that thou hast faith : prove to me likewise that thou hast charity." Parallel to which words are those of Optatus : "Amongst us and you is one ecclesiastical conversation, common lessons, the same faith, the same sacraments." Where, by the way, we may observe, that in the judg-

Church in fact stood on the defensive in this whole war, as any man can see by simply glancing over the writings of Augustine against the Donatists; it was simply defending its own right to be a church against a narrow-minded and fanatical sect which claimed to be the only church in the world ; it was occupying exactly the position in reference to the Donatists which *we* now occupy towards Rome and its imitators. The Catholics of that day had sense and charity enough *not* to follow the example of the Donatists, and unchurch all other communions but their own. It is very evident that they did not have, or did not know that they had, the apostolical succession. Otherwise, the argument would have been short, sharp and decisive. In that case the church which had defied the power of the Roman emperors for three hundred years, might have been saved the disgrace of invoking the authority of the emperors to decide the controversy by arbitration and by the sword.

ment of these fathers, even Donatists, though heretics and schismatics, gave true *ordination*, the true sacrament of matrimony, the sacramental absolution, confirmation, the true sacrament of the eucharist, true extreme unction ; or else (choose you whether) some of these were not then esteemed sacraments. But for *ordination*, whether he (Augustine) held it a sacrament or no, certainly he held that it remained with them entire ; for so he says in express terms in his book against Parmenianus's Epistle. Which doctrine, if you can reconcile with the present doctrine of the Roman church, *eris mihi magnus Apollo."* (*Chillingworth's Works*, p. 506, 507 of Phila. Ed., 1840.)

The learned Witsius (*De Schism. Donatistarum*, Chap. 7) says that he had read, "*non sine magno tædio*," the *Breviculum* of Augustine and the Acts of the Conference of Carthage (A. D. 411), and gives this as the main question disputed between the two hundred and eighty-six Catholic bishops and the two hundred and seventy-nine Donatist bishops assembled at the conference (held, be it remembered, a century after the breaking out of the schism), viz. : "Whether the church which held communion with Cæcilian, the Traditor, had not thereby lost the dignity and privileges of a church? The controversy, therefore, was two-fold : 1, First, of *fact* ; whether C. was a traditor, and on that account unworthy of the episcopate ? 2, Second, of *law* ; whether a church is so vitiated by an admixture of the wicked, as to cease to be a church?" This is a very different question from that which would have been discussed, if they had been disputing about the *succession*. It was indeed the same question which was afterwards debated between the Anabaptists and their antagonists, both Romanist and Protestant.

2. The papists are in the habit of imposing upon
people, by saying that the salvation of Protestants, like
their faith, rests upon fallible and uncertain grounds,
and that certainty can be found only within their
pale.   Now, not to say that this assertion comes with a
bad grace from a community which teaches in its creed
that no man can be certain of his salvation in this life;
it has been shown, over and over again, that their own
doctrine of the priesthood and the sacraments makes it
impossible for any man to know that he has ever been
truly absolved from his sins ; and this because of the
uncertainty of the succession as a fact.   That the sacrament of penance has ever been duly administered to
him, depends upon the minister's being a true priest.
" That such or such man is a priest," says Chillingworth,
" not himself, much less any other, can have any possible certainty ; for it depends upon a great many con-
tingent and uncertain supposals.   He that will pretend
to be certain of it, must undertake to know for certain
all these things that follow :

" *First*, that he was baptized with due matter.
Secondly, with the due form of words, which he cannot know, unless he were both present and attentive.
Thirdly, he must know that he was baptized with due
intention,* and that is, that the minister of his baptism
was not a secret Jew, nor a Moor, nor an atheist (of all
which kinds, I fear, experience gives you a just cause
to fear that Italy and Spain have priests not a few),
but a Christian, in heart as well as profession (otherwise, believing the sacrament to be nothing, in giving
it he could intend to give nothing), nor a Samosatanian,
nor an Arian, but one that was capable of having due
intention, from which they that believe not the doctrine of the Trinity are excluded by you.   And lastly,
that he was neither drunk nor distracted at the administration of the sacrament, nor, out of negligence or

---

* See the speech in the Council of Trent, of Catharine, bishop of Mi-
nori, in F. Paolo's Hist. (Courayer's French Trans.), Vol. I. pp. 441–'2.

malice, omitted his intention. *Fourthly*, he must undertake to know that the bishop which ordained him priest ordained him completely, with due matter, form, and intention; and, consequently, that he again was neither Jew, Moor, nor atheist, nor liable to any such exception as is inconsistent with due intention of giving the sacrament of orders. *Fifthly*, he must undertake to know that the bishop which made him priest was a priest himself; for your rule is *nihil dat quod non habet*; and, consequently, that there were again none of the former nullities in his baptism, which might make him incapable of ordination, nor any invalidity in his ordination, but a true priest, to ordain him again, the requisite matter and form and due intention all concurring. *Lastly*, he must pretend to know the same of him that made him priest, and him that made him priest even until he comes to the very fountain of priesthood. For, take any one in the whole train and succession of ordainers, and suppose him, by reason of any defect, only a supposed and not a true priest, then, according to your doctrine, he could not give a true, but only a supposed priesthood; and they that receive it of him, and again they that derive it from them, can give no better than they received; receiving nothing but a name and shadow, can give nothing but a name and shadow; and so from age to age, from generation to generation, being equivocal fathers beget only equivocal sons; no principle in geometry being more certain than this, that the unsuppliable defect of any necessary antecedent, must needs cause a nullity of all those consequences which depend upon it. In fine, to know this one thing, you must first know ten thousand others, whereof not any one is a thing that can be known, there being no necessity that it should be true, which necessity alone can qualify any thing to be an object of science, but only, at the best, a high degree of probability that it is so. But then, that of ten thousand probables no one should be false; that of ten thousand requisites, whereof any one may fail, not one should be wanting; this to me is extremely improbable, and even cousin-german to impossible. So that the assurance hereof is like a machine composed of an innumerable multitude of pieces, of which it is strangely unlikely, but some will be out of order, and yet if any one be so, the whole fabric of necessity falls to the ground; and he that shall put them together, and maturely consider all the possible ways of lapsing and nullifying a priesthood in the church of Rome, I believe will be very inclinable to think, that it is a hundred to one, that amongst a hundred seeming priests, there is not one true one—nay, that it is not a thing very improbable, that amongst those many millions which make up the Roman hierarchy, there are not twenty true." (*Chillingworth's Works*, p. 130–'2; Hooker, Phila., 1840.)

"Whether," says Macaulay in his review of Gladstone's "*Church and State*" (*Miscellanies*, Vol. III. p. 300), "a clergyman be really a successor of the apostles depends on an immense number of such contingencies as these: Whether under King Ethelwolf, a stupid priest might not, while baptizing several scores of Danish prisoners, who had just made their option between the font and the gallows, inadvertently omit to perform the rite on one of these graceless proselytes?—whether, in the seventh century, an impostor, who had never received consecration, might not have passed himself off as a bishop on a rude tribe of Scots?—whether a lad of twelve did really, by a ceremony huddled over when he was too drunk to know what he was about, convey the episcopal character to a lad of ten?"

Mr. Gladstone proposes to remove doubts which may arise from the *historic* difficulties against the doctrine of succession, by nothing else than mathematical evidence. "By a novel application of the theory of ratios and proportion, he endeavors to show that, on the least favorable computation, the chances for the true consecration of any bishop are 8,000 to 1. . . . Be it so ; this only diminishes the probability that, in any given case, the suspicion of invalidity is unfounded. What is wanted is a criterion which shall distinguish the *genuine* orders from the *spurious*. Alas! who knows but *he* may be the unhappy eighth-thousandth? According to this theory, no man in the Roman or Anglican communion has a right to say that he is commissioned to preach the gospel, but only that he has seven thousand nine hundred and ninety-nine eight-thousandth parts of certainty that he is! A felicitous mode of expression, it must be confessed. What would be the fraction for expressing the ratio of probability, on the supposition that simony, heresy, or infidelity, can invalidate *holy* orders is, considering the history of the middle ages, far beyond our arithmetic."*

"We can imagine," says the same lively writer, "the perplexity of a presbyter thus cast in doubt as to whether or not he has ever had the invaluable 'gift' of apostolical succession conferred upon him. As that gift is neither tangible nor visible, the subject neither of experience nor consciousness, as it cannot be known by any 'effects' produced by it, he may imagine—unhappy man!—that he has been 'regenerating' infants by baptism, when he has been simply sprinkling them with water. 'What is the matter?' the spectator of his distractions might ask. 'What have you lost?' 'Lost!' would be the reply, 'I fear I have lost my apostolical succession; or rather, my misery is, that I do not know and cannot tell whether I ever had it to lose.' It is of no use here to suggest the usual questions, 'When did you see it last? When were you last conscious of possessing it? What a peculiar property is that of which, though so invaluable, nay, on which the whole efficacy of the Christian ministry depends, a man has no positive evidence to show whether he ever had it or not! which, if ever conferred,

---

* *Edinburgh Review*, for April, 1843, P. 271.   Amer. Reprint.

was conferred without his knowledge; and which, if it
could be taken away, would still leave him ignorant,
not only when, where, and how the theft was committed, but whether it had ever been committed or not!
The sympathizing friend might probably remind him,
that as he was not sure he had ever had it, so *perhaps*
he still had it without knowing it. '*Perhaps!*' he
would reply, 'but it is certainty I want.' 'Well,' it
might be said, 'Mr. Gladstone assures you, that, on
the most moderate computation, your chances are as
8,000 to 1 that you have it.' 'Pish!' the distracted
man would exclaim, 'What does Mr. Gladstone know
about the matter?' And truly to *that* query we know
not well what answer the friend could make."

It thus appears that there is no historical evidence
for the succession; and that no man can be certain
that he is a presbyter or priest upon this theory. This
baseless theory is that upon which wretched men, travelling to the bar of God and the retributions of eternity, are invited to rest their hope of salvation, instead
of resting it upon Jesus Christ, the Saviour of sinners,
freely offered to them in the gospel! Blessed is he
who can say, in spite of all the cavilling of Pharisees,
cavilling about the uncanonical method of his salvation : "One thing I know, that whereas I was blind,
now I see!" Blessed is he who gets his healing directly from the Great Physician, without the manipulations of those who sit, or imagine that they sit, in
Moses' seat! No wonder that the world is infidel when
such a doctrine, without evidence and against all evidence, is preached to them. A man must denude himself of his rational nature before he can believe it.

The doctrine was invented, not for the glorifying of
Christ, but for the glorifying of the *clergy*. Great is
the contrast between the apostles and their pretended
successors. "The former are intent, almost exclusively
intent, on those great themes which render the gospel
'glad tidings;' the latter, almost as exclusively, in

magnifying their office. The former absolutely forget themselves in their flocks; the latter well nigh forget their flocks in themselves. The former, if they touch on the clerical office at all, are principally intent on its spiritual qualifications and duties; the latter, on its prerogatives and powers. To hear these men talk, one would imagine that, by a similar ὕστερον πρότερον, with that of the simple-minded monk who 'devoutly thanked God that in his wisdom he had always placed large rivers near large towns,' they supposed the church of Christ to be created for the sole use of the clergy; and the doctrine of 'apostolical succession' to be the *final cause* of Christianity."—*Edinburgh Review*, April, 1843, page 292.

The whole system to which this doctrine belongs is a substitute for Christianity, whose chief glory is its spiritual and moral character. It substitutes " for a worship founded on intelligent faith, a devotion which is a species of mechanism, and rites which operate as by magic. The doctrine of apostolical succession itself is neither more nor less respectable than that of the hereditary sanctity of the Brahminical caste; while the prayer-mills of the Tartars afford a fair illustration of the doctrine of sacramental efficacy." It is sheer heathenism.

What is Christianity if it be not a method of salvation through Jesus Christ, to be received through faith? Justification by faith alone is its fundamental article; the *"articulus stantis aut cadentis ecclesiæ."* What is heathenism but the attempt to appease an angry God by human works, or by human ordinances efficacious *ex opere operato?* The system to which the apostolical succession belongs can never consist with the doctrine of justification by faith alone in Jesus Christ. The preaching of this latter doctrine led Luther necessarily to a rejection of the papal theory of the church and the priesthood; and it was because the papal priests saw that *their craft was in danger* from

the preaching of this doctrine that they set themselves
so resolutely to overthrow it. If a sinner can lay hold
on Christ freely offered to him in the gospel, and obtain the forgiveness of sins and acceptance with God;
if he can have immediate access to Christ, the great
High Priest over the house of God, and can "draw
near with a true heart in full assurance of faith," what
need for an earthly priesthood and its sacramental
magic? *Hinc illæ lacrymæ.* The priests had no tears
to shed over the damage done to holiness by the doctrine of the reformers. They would have been "croco-
dile tears," indeed, if shed by such men, men who had
become notorious and infamous all over Europe for
their immorality.* No! they knew that their power
over men's souls, bodies, and estates was gone, if this
doctrine came to be believed.

We add something on the doctrine of succession as
held by some in the church of England, and in the
Protestant Episcopal Church in America. 1. If these
people have any "succession," they have derived it
from the Church of Rome; and as the succession in
Rome has been shown to be a grand imposture, from
the Scriptures, reason and history, and Rome, could
give no better *orders* than she had herself—of course
the succession in the Church of England is an imposture also. 2. The imposture is not grand in the last
case, for the simple reason that all that makes the fig-

---

* As to the *moral* complexion of papal councils, and especially of the
Council of Trent, the following words of a nervous writer, who was a
perfect master of the papal history, cannot be considered too strong:
"Beleaguered by strumpets, beset with fiddlers and buffoons, cursing
God's truth, and leaving tracks strewed with bastards and dead men's
bones! *Holy* councils; and above all, that of Trent! Which, by the
amazing wrath of God, cursed with judicial blindness and seared consciences, did gather into one vast monument those scattered proofs
which covered the long track of ages, and those errors and corruptions
bred in the slime and filth of the whole apostasy; and reared them up,
with patient and laborious vice, through eighteen years of God's long-
suffering, the final landmark, the last limit of his endurance with this
great, bloody, and drunken Babylon."—*Spirit of the Nineteenth Century,* 1842, page 254.

ment worth asserting or defending has been given up, to wit, the priestly character and the sacrifice. It is the play of Hamlet with the part of Hamlet left out. Without the assertion of some sacramental virtue imparted by the bishop's hands to the presbyter, and some sacramental virtue imparted by the priests' manipulations to the laity, the pretence to the apostolical succession is of all pretences the emptiest and the silliest. Hence we find that a revival of zeal for this dogma is generally followed very soon by the doctrine of sacramental grace. There is a necessary connection between the two, and they cannot long be separated. 3. We may be excused from believing the doctrine as held by Anglicans and their American imitators, so long as they show so little faith in it themselves. If they believed it, they could not help seeing that they are what Rome pronounces them to be, *schismatics,* and in no better condition than us poor "Dissenters." Let them show their faith by their works, and we shall be more disposed to consider their pretensions. 4. The advocates of this dogma in the Church of England would do well to prove that the church they belong to is a church at all. According to Rome, a bishop who is made so by the appointment *of the civil magistrate* has a very doubtful claim to the title. In the thoroughly Erastian establishment of England, the whole constitution of the church is the work of the state, and the people even pray by "Act of Parliament." The sacramental virtue, which makes bishops and priests, comes at the suggestion, at least, of the civil ministry. This accounts for the total absence of discipline in that church. It is exceedingly difficult, if not impossible, to get rid of a bishop who avows himself an infidel. It is not a very broad caricature of the "Comedy of Convocation," to represent that venerable body as debating the question, whether a member of the Church of England may deny the existence of God without losing his standing as a mem-

ber. 5. This doctrine is not taught in the formularies
of the Church of England; nor is it held by very many
of her best ministers and her highest ornaments. Chillingworth certainly did not hold it, and yet he had for
his "God-father," no less a man than William Laud,
Archbishop of Canterbury, by whose influence, in
great measure, the strayed son was brought back from
the fold of Rome into the Church of England again.
Bishop Butler, we imagine, did not hold it. It would
have been odd, indeed, if such a thinker as the author
of the "Analogy" had believed such a conglomeration
of absurdities; more especially as he had been baptized
and brought up in a Presbyterian fold. Archbishop
Whately not only did not believe it, but showed clearly,
in his *Essays on the Kingdom of Christ*, that the thing
is absurd. " There is not," says he, "in all Christen-
dom a minister who is able to trace up, with any approach to certainty his own spiritual pedigree." The
fathers and founders of the Church of England did
not believe it, as has been proved against the writers
of the Oxford Tracts.* How *could* men believe it, who
had so clear a view of the *only* priesthood and the
only sacrifice of Christ?—men, who were asking the
advice, continually, of Calvin and other Presbyterians
of the Continent? No! the really great men of the
Anglican Church, whose worth was real and conspicuous, had no need of insisting upon a sacramental
virtue which is invisible, intangible, inoperative, mani-
festing itself to no power of perception, either of the
body or mind; which, if a man has, he is none the
better; which, if he has not, he is none the worse.†

---

*See in the *Presbyterian Review* for January, 1886, testimonies and
references to to show that,. down to the time of Charles I. and Laud,
Presbyterian ordination was considered valid in the church of England.   (Pp. 119-'20 of the above number of the *Review*.)

†See *Princeton Review* for 1842, pp. 139, et seq.

Is the Church of Rome a True Church of Christ?

[Turretin, L. 18, q. 14 ; Thornwell's Writings, III. pp. 283 ff. ; Conf. of
Faith, Chapter XXV.]

1. State of the question: Not whether the church of
Rome of the apostle's time, nor of the second, third, or
fourth century, but the church of Rome since the
Trent Council, is a church of Christ. Nor is it about the
church of Rome generally considered, as contradistinguished from Mohammedanism, Judaism, Paganism, but
particularly as subject to the pope as the head thereof.

2. Proofs that it is not a church of Christ: (1), From
the design of the visible church, which is to glorify
God in the ingathering and upbuilding of the elect.
Any church whose constitution is such, or whose administration is such that the tendency, on the whole, is
not to save men, but to destroy them, is not a church
of Christ. This is conceded virtually by Rome herself, in insisting, as she does, that there is no possibility of salvation out of her communion, because she
is the only true church. Is, then, the prevailing tendency of Rome and her ordinances a tendency to salvation? I say prevailing tendency. Men may be converted within her pale, no doubt; and men may be
converted in an infidel club, or in a theatre, or in a cir-
cle of boon companions; but in spite of the tendencies, as is evident from the fact that, as soon as they
are born again, the atmosphere of such society becomes
stifling to their new life, and they quit it as soon as
possible. "Come out of her, my people," etc. Now,
that the tendency of Rome is not saving, but damning,
is evident from the fact that she has not "the ministry, oracles, and ordinances" which God has given to
the church visible for this end. Of these in their order:

(a), *Ministry.* Contrast the hierarchy with the officers of the apostolic church. The people disfranchised
and ground to pieces by the great iron wheel. The
names they have retained, those of bishop, presbyter,

9

and deacon, but how totally different the nature of the
offices.   Neither bishop nor presbyter is a preacher of
the gospel, but a priest; and, when consecrated, the
priest has given to him, not a Bible as the symbol of
his office, but the cup and paten, with authority to
offer sacrifice, and that, too, sacrifice of the body and
blood of the Son of God, for the sins of the living and
the dead : thus exercising an office totally different
from that of the minister of the word, whose commision
was, "Go ye into all the world and preach the glad tidings," etc.   The minister is no priest in the literal sense,
for Christ is the only priest ; he is not the only priest
in the tropical sense, for all God's people are priests,
a royal priesthood.   The Roman priesthood, therefore,
is at once the denial of the priesthood, both of Christ
and of his people.   The bishops are no spiritual rulers,
chosen of God, through the voice of the people, and
administering the law of Christ, but the tools of a des-
potism which consults only the demands of the lusts of
power and gold, and using heaven and hell as the
sanctions of their anti-christian tyranny.   To crown
all, the pope is antichrist, setting himself in the place
of Christ (and therefore against him), as prophet, priest
and king, and head over all things to the body, the
church—lording it over God's heritage, instead of being a helper of their joy.   Even the ambitious Pontiff,
Gregory I., in the close of the sixth century, pronounced the claim to be universal bishop blasphemous, infamous and a mark of antichrist.

(b), *Oracles.* This includes not only the Rule of
Faith, but the authorized and current interpretation of
the rule.   Under this head observe, (a), That she has
added to the rule which God has given ; (b), That in the
interpretation of the rule, she makes the part which
God has given bend to the part she herself has added ;
thus acting in contradiction to the example of the apostles who, when adding to the rules of the Old Testament
under their commission from God as inspired, still

quote everywhere the Old Testament, to show that their teaching was in harmony with the Old Testament —that their religion was not new, but as old as the garden of Eden; (c), That she denies the rule to her members, upon the pretence that the church alone has the right to interpret; thereby practically denying faith and repentance to the people, and damning them; thereby shutting out the Holy Ghost, and usurping his office as the infallible witness of Christ. Rome decrees that God shall not speak to men except through the atheists, adulterers and murderers that sit in the seat on the Seven Hills, and claiming to be gods and wor- shipped as gods; (d), That the creed thus derived, from the infallible interpretation of the church, is not a *saving* creed. Not that it formally denies all the fun- damental doctrines of the gospel, but teaches so much of error, and such kind of error, as to make the creed, as a whole, poison and not food. The sum of the teachings of Scripture, concerning the plan of salva- tion, is contained in 1 John v. 8—the three-fold record of the Spirit, the water and the blood. The two last are emblematical of the two great divisions of the Re- deemer's work—a change of state and a change of char- acter—justification and sanctification. The Spirit's tes- timony being the mode by which these blessings be- come the property of the sinner. As to the BLOOD, it can be shown that Rome is fundamentally heretical. Paul teaches that no creed which teaches salvation by works can be a saving one. But Rome teaches such a creed, resolving our justifying righteousness into per- sonal holiness, damning the doctrine of imputation, audaciously proclaiming the of figment of human merit, both of congruity and condignity, making Christ only the remote and ultimate cause of pardon and acceptance. As to the WATER, she makes holiness impossible by denying the blood. Pardon is essential to holiness, and Rome, in denying the possibility of pardon, denies the possibility of holiness. She is also *antinomian,* expunging one of the commandments of the decalogue, and making a hypocritical will-worship to take the place of holy obedience. She is an idolatrous church. As to the *Spirit,* she is a Pelagian, or, at the very best, a semi-Pelagian.

(*c*), *Ordinances.* The most of her ordinances are of her own invention; but even of those which God has ordained, she has changed utterly their *nature* and their *use,* so that they are no longer the ordinances of God. Baptism, the Lord's supper, ordination, are changed materially and formally. As to the use, her notion of the efficacy of the sacraments denies the agency of the Spirit, and makes them *causes* or *laws* of grace instead of *means.* So that no sinner believing the creed of Rome and obeying the laws of Rome, can possibly be saved. She is, therefore, no church of Christ.

The Nature and Extent of Church Power.

1. The church may be considered either as to its essence or being, or as to its power and order, when it is organized. As to its essence or being, its constituent parts are its *matter* and *form.*

2. By the *matter* of the church is meant the persons of which the church consists, with their qualifications; by the *form,* the relation among these persons, as organized into one body.

3. The *matter* of the church has been fully considered in the preceding lectures, together with some things belonging to the *form.* We come now to treat of the other questions connected with the form; and, first, as to church power—*potestas.*

4. The nature of church power must be considered before the consideration of the several modes in which it is exercised, because everything connected with these modes, offices, officers, courts, &c., is found in the grant of power to the church itself, and the institution of a polity and rule therein by Jesus Christ, her only Head and King.

5. This power comes from Christ alone. The government of the church is upon his shoulders, to order it (his kingdom), and to establish it with judgment and justice forever. All power is given to him, in heaven and earth, by the Father, and he is the head of the church, which is his body, and head over all things else for the sake of his body. (See *Westminster Assembly's Form of Government*, Preface; and our *Form of Government*, Chap. II., Sec. 1, Art. 1; Isaiah ix. 6, 7; Matthew xxviii. 18–20; Eph. i. 20–23, compared with Eph. iv. 8–11, and Psalm lxviii. 18.)

6. This power, therefore, in the church is only "ministerial and declarative," that is, the power of a minister or a servant to declare and execute the law of the Master, Christ, as revealed in his word, the statute-book of his kingdom, the Scriptures contained in the Old and New Testaments. No officer or court of the church has any legislative power. "Christ alone is Lord of the conscience, and hath left it free from the doctrine and commandments of men which are in anything contrary to the word, or beside it, in matters of faith and worship." (*Confession of Faith*, Chap. XX. Sec. 2.) Slavery to Christ alone is the true and only freedom of the human soul.

7. This statement is opposed to the theories of, 1st, Papists; 2nd, Erastians; 3rd, Latitudinarians.

8. The papists, by their claim of infallibility for the church as the *interpreter* of the Scriptures, as well as by the claim to *make* scripture (apocrypha and tradition), make the power of the church *magisterial* instead of *ministerial*, and *legislative* instead of *declarative*. Hence the brutal disregard, in that church, of the liberty of Christ's people. Antichrist has usurped the prophetic and regal as well as the priestly offices of the church's head. Hence the name *Antichrist, in the place of*, and therefore *against*, Christ.

9. The Erastians deliver the church into the hands of the civil magistrate, some of them admitting one of

the keys to belong to the church (the key of *doctrine*);
others, more consistently, denying to the church the
power of both keys, and so destroying the autonomy
of the church altogether. This is to be considered
more fully hereafter. (*Con. of Faith*, Chap. XXIII.)

10. The Latitudinarians (I use the word for want of
a better) hold a *discretionary* power in the church, limited only by the prohibitions of the word; whatever is
not prohibited, or contradicted by what is commanded,
is lawful, is a matter of Christian liberty, and the
church has power to order or not according to her
views of expediency. This theory is held, or rather
practically carried out, in various degrees. Some, as
Archbishop Whately (*Kingdom of Christ*), contend
that ecclesiastical power is ordained of God in the
sense in which the civil is ordained. (Rom. xiii. 1, 2.)
The "powers that be" are said to be "ordained of
God," because God has so constituted man that he
cannot live except in society, and society cannot be
maintained except by an organization, more or less
complete, and a government of some sort. Now, men
of different races and different histories require different forms of government. The government must be
the organic product, the outgrowth, the fruit of the
people's history; and as, consequently, it is mere political quackery to prescribe the same civil constitution
for all nations alike; so, in the society of the church,
there must be a government, and the government must
be determined by the character and circumstances of
the people; and as no form of ecclesiastical polity is
forbidden in the New Testament, the church is free to
adopt any that suits her.

Others (see Hodge's *Church Polity*, pages 121 ff.),
afraid to go so far, contend that general principles
are laid down in Scripture, but details are left to
the discretion and wisdom of the church. This is
obviously a very unsatisfactory rule. What are "general principles"? General principles may be either

"regulative" or "constitutive." Regulative principles
define only ends to be aimed at, or conditions to be
observed; constitutive determine the concrete form in
which those ends are to be realized. Regulative express the *spirit*, constitutive, the *form* of a government.
It is a regulative principle, for example, that all governments should be administered for the good of the
governed; it is a constitutive principle that the government should be lodged in the hands of such and such
officers, and dispensed by such and such courts. Regulative principles define nothing as to the mode of their
own exemplification; constitutive principles determine
the elements of an actual polity. (*Thornwell's Works,*
IV., page 252.)

Now, if Dr. Hodge's general principles are regulative only, then he is as much of a latitudinarian as
Whately. If they are constitutive, he is as much a
"strict-constructionist" as Dr. Thornwell. He uses an
illustration which in one part would seem to indicate
that his general principles are constitutive; but in the
other, regulative. "There are fixed laws," he says,
"assigned by God, according to which all healthful
development and action of the external church are determined. But, as within the limits of the laws which
control the development of the human body there is
endless diversity among different races, adapting them
to different climes and modes of living, so also in the
church. It is not tied down to one particular mode of
organization and action at all times, and under all circumstances." Now, the two parts of his illustration
do not hold together. The *organization* of the human
body is the *same* in all races, climes, and ages. Differences of complexion, stature, conformation, *et cetera,*
there doubtless are; but the *organization* is the same.
And this is the kind of unity and uniformity we claim
for the church as a divine institute. Hodge elsewhere
seems to acknowledge something like constitutive principles revealed in Scripture. He makes the three dis-

tinctive features of Presbyterianism to be: 1st, The
parity of the ministry; 2nd, The right of the people
to take part in the government; 3rd, The unity of the
church.   I do not acknowledge these to be distinctive
principles of Presbyterianism; but they look something like constitutive principles.   We shall see hereafter that the second of these principles is no principle
of Presbyterianism at all, much less a distinctive one.

In regard to this latitudinarian theory, I observe:

1st. That it differs little in effect from the Papal and
Erastian.   It makes man, and not God, to determine
the whole matter.

2d. It is contrary to the Protestant doctrine of the
sufficiency of the Scriptures as a rule of faith and
practice.   See *C. of F.*, Ch. I. Sec. 6; "the whole counsel of God," &c.   It implies that in regard to a large
sphere of human duty, and that too, concerning so
high a matter as the government of the kingdom of
Christ, men are left to walk in the light of their own
eyes.

3d. It is contrary to the liberty of the people of God.
Dr. Hodge and others speak of strict Presbyterians as
if they were bringing the church under the yoke of
bondage by insisting upon a "Thus saith the Lord"
for everything.   We answer, that the liberty of the believer does not consist in doing what he pleases, but
in being the slave of Christ.   "Be ye not the slaves of
men" is the apostle's command.   And the assumption
of this wide discretion by the church has been the
great cause of the tyranny which has been exercised by
church rulers over the poor sheep of Christ.   Liberty,
in the mouths of those who have the power in their
hands, means doing what *they* please, serving their own
lust of dominion, and lording it over the weak and de-
fenceless.   Witness the Pharisees, Papists, Anglicans,
and the free democracies.   Liberty is a mere word to
juggle with, except in the sphere of the Spirit and in
union with Christ.   Where the largest discretionary

power has been claimed and exercised in the nominal church of God, there have the people groaned under the hardest bondage; for it is the discretionary power of the rulers to impose burdens upon the people. First prelacy, then popery, with the aid of the "Catholic doctrine," grew out of the notion that the constitution of the church in the apostolic age did not suit the church in its more advanced stage, and that a form corresponding with the organization of the empire would suit the people better, and not being condemned by the Word, it might be lawfully established. Hence, as there were prefects, ex-archs, *et cet.*, in the civil, so there ought to be patriarchs, metropolitans, etc., in the ecclesiastical organization. And as the civil pyramid was capped with an emperor, so the ecclesiastical with a pope. But what became of the liberties of the people? So also in England—contest between Puritans and Anglicans. The liberty of the monarch, or the parliament, or the church, to convert the *adiaphora* into laws, was only the liberty to destroy the liberty of those whom God hath made free. The "judicious Hooker" laid the egg which was hatched by the imperious Laud. Another instance, sadder than all to us, is the history of the Old School Presbyterian Church of the North, which set up its deliverances on "doctrine, loyalty, and freedom," as terms of communion in the church. The word of God, and that word *only*, is the safe-guard of freedom.

4th. It is founded upon a false analogy between a natural, social and civil, or political development, and a supernatural, social, and ecclesiastical development. In the sphere of man's natural life, it is undoubtedly true, as has been already suggested, that the form of civil polity must be determined by the character, circumstances, or, in a word, by the history of a people; must be the *fruit* of the past, and not an arbitrary theory or utopian constitution, founded upon abstract notions of what is best. And, consequently, since the

life of every people is its own, and different from that
of every other people, the government must be different. A striking proof of this is to be found in the
present condition of this country, where two sections
of a country have had such different developments
that one must be held, by main force, as a conquered
province, *because* it adhered to the constitution of the
country, and the other has forsaken and subverted the
constitution. But the case is very different with the
church, for the simple reason that her life is not natural, but supernatural; she does not *grow* into a free
commonwealth, but is *free-born*, not of blood, nor of
the will of man, nor of the will of the flesh, but of God.
She is composed of all kindreds and tongues, and peo-
ples and nations. All the members, whether subjects
of a monarchy, or citizens of a republic, are spiritually
and ecclesiastically free: "For where the spirit of the
Lord is, there is liberty." Hence, in the early church,
the subjects of a Nero, or Caligula, or Domitian were,
at the same time, members of a free commonwealth.
In the state the soul makes for itself a body, an external organism, through which it may act; in the church
the soul, as in the old creation, has a body made for
it by God, its creator. The polity of the church, therefore, like the body of man, ought to be everywhere the
same organism essentially. It confirms this view, that
the church changed its external organization only after
she had become corrupt and had lost her internal and
spiritual freedom. After she had become worldly in
spirit, she became subject to like changes with the
world, and this liability to change became the more
marked when she became identified with the world
through her union with the state under Constantine
and his successors. In the middle ages the nominal
church had become almost natural and earthly in her
life, and, of course, lost her freedom altogether. For
a great portion of her history her true life has been
maintained in small bodies of witnesses, whom she

disowned and persecuted. And so in the Northern States of this country, she identified herself with the civil power, and exhibited more of the spirit of the harlot upon the scarlet-colored beast, than of the spirit of the spouse of Christ.

5th. It is contrary to the plain teachings of God's word and of our constitution, in regard to the nature of church power. According to those standards all church power is "ministerial and declarative." The officers of the church are, collectively, a ministry, and each officer is a minister or servant. Christ himself condescended to be a minister, and in that memorable rebuke which he administered to the ambition of his disciples, he informs them that the power which they are to exercise in the church is unlike that of civil rulers, even of those civil rulers whose administration has entitled them to the denomination of "benefactors"; for it is a power of *service*, of obedience to him for the sake of his church, and not a power of lordship or dominion. The only honor in the church is the honor of hard work for the church. The power of a preacher is the power of a minister or servant to declare his Master's will, both in reference to the *credenda* and *agenda* in preaching. The power of a ruling elder is the power to do the like in ruling, and especially to apply that will in the actual exercise of discipline. A presbytery, whether congregational, provincial or general, is a body of servants or ministers to declare the law and find the facts and render a verdict, such as is authorized by the word of Christ, who has established the court, created the judges, and defined their functions. A deacon, as his very name signifies, is a servant to do his master's will in regard to the collection, custody and distribution of the revenues of his kingdom.

6th. Lastly, it is contrary to the nature of the believer's *life*, which is a life of faith and of obedience, implying a divine testimony and a divine command. If the church officers, then, have power to make institutions and create officers which God has not ordained, then the people have the right to refuse obedience, and there is a dead lock in the machinery. There is no power to enforce obedience, for all church power is moral and spiritual, and no man can be required to promise or render obedience except in the Lord.

11. All church power then is simply "ministerial or declarative." The Bible is a positive charter—a definite constitution—and what is not granted is, for that reason, held to be forbidden. A constitution, from the nature of the case, can only prescribe what *must be.* If it should attempt, explicitly, to forbid everything which human ingenuity, malice, or audacity, might invent, the world could scarcely contain the things that should be written. The whole function of the church, therefore, is confined to interpretation and obedience of the *word.* All additions to the word, if not *explicitly* prohibited, are at least prohibited *implicitly* in the general command that *nothing be added.*

12. The ministerial and declarative power of the church has been distributed in the books into several classes. For instance, in the Second Book of Discipline of the Kirk of Scotland, Andrew Melville says: "The whole policy of the Kirk consisteth in three things, viz.: in *doctrine, discipline* and *distribution,*" where the alliteration is used for a mnemonic purpose. "Discipline" is used in the wise sense of government and "distribution" for everything pertaining to the office of deacon. Others (See *Turretin,* L. 18, Q. 29, ¶ 5), divide church power into *dogmatic* and *judicial,* or *disciplinary,* corresponding with the symbol of the "keys"—the key of knowledge and the key of discipline or government; or where the figure is that of a pastor or shepherd instead of a steward—the *staff* "Beauty," and the staff "Bands." Zech. xi. 7. There is a distribution of this power better still (see *Turretin ut supra*) into *dogmatic, diatactic* and *diacritic.* The

first relating to doctrine, the second to polity and administration, the third to the judicial exercise of discipline. Another distribution of the *potestas ecclesiastica* is into *potestas ordinis* and *potestas regiminis* or *jurisdictionis*. (Note the sense in which these terms are used by papal writers, p. 49 *supra*. See Second Book of Discipline, chapter I.; also Gillespie's Assertion of the Government of the Kirk of Scotland, in *Presbyterian Armory*, Vol. I. p. 12; of Gillespie's Treatise, Chap. II.) This distinction signalizes the mode in which power is exercised, whether by church officers *severally*, or church officers *jointly*; the *potestas ordinis* being a *several* power; the *potestas regiminis*, a *joint* power. Teaching may be either. The preacher exercises the power of order when he preaches the gospel; a church court exercises the power of government when it composes or issues a creed, or when it testifies for the doctrine or precepts of Christ, and against errors and immoralities. It is teaching, and that jointly, the word of Christ, either in regard to what we are to believe concerning God or what God requires of us. The *dogmatic* power, therefore, may be either jointly or severally exercised. The *diatactic* and the *diacritic* must be exercised *jointly*, and, therefore, belong to the *potestas regiminis* or *jurisdictionis*. The Westminster standards are composed and arranged according to this division. The Confession of Faith and the Catechisms belong to the *potestas dogmatica*; the Form of Government, the Directory for Worship, and the Rules of Order mainly to the *potestas diatactica*; the Canons of Discipline *mainly* to the *potestas diacritica*.

13. Proof that this power belongs to the church. 1st, From the gift of the keys. Matthew xvi. 19, 20; xviii. 18; John xx. 22, 23. 2d, From the nature of society. This power constitutes the bands and joints by which it is at once able to live and to act. 3d, From the existence of offices in the church; but office implies power. 4th, From the titles given to these

10

offices in 1 Tim. v. 17, 1 Thess. v. 12, Heb. xiii. 17,
Acts xx. 28, 1 Cor. iv. 1, 2; Tit. i. 7, 1 Cor. xii. 28.
5th, From passages of Scripture in which the exercise
of this power is mentioned, such as 2 Cor. x. 8, also
as 1 Cor. ix. 4, 5, 6; 2 Cor. xiii. 10, where "power"
corresponds with *potestas*. Also 1 Cor. v. 3, 4, 5. 6th,
From the fact that a distinction was made, even in the
Old Testament, between the civil and the ecclesiastical
power; but of this more hereafter.

14. As to the *diatactic* power of the church something must be said more particularly, for it is here that
the greatest controversies have arisen. How far does
this arranging, ordering power of the church extend?

According to the view we have taken of church
power, as "ministerial and declarative," this question
amounts to the same as the question, "How far, and
in what sense, has the church discretionary power over
details of order, worship, etc.?" We have seen that
there is no legislative power in the church, properly so
called, but only a *judicial* and administrative power.
The law is in the Bible and nowhere else, and Christ
is the only lawgiver. But all the details of the application of the law are not given, and could not have
been given without swelling the book to dimensions
utterly incompatible with its ready use as a rule.
Voluminous as human law is, it cannot enter into min-
utiae, *e. g.*, Congress by law establishes the Department of War, or of State, in the executive administration of the government; but it leaves the making of
"regulations" in circumstantial matters, or matters of
detail, to the head of the department or of a particular
bureau; and this officer, therefore, does not exercise
legislative power in making such "regulations," but a
diatactic power, the power of arranging and ordering
under the law. So in the church, the *doctrine* of the
church and its *government* and *worship* are laid down
in Scripture, and the declaration of this doctrine belongs to the *potestas dogmatica*. But there are "cir-

cumstances in the worship of God and the government of the church common to human actions and societies, which are to be ordered by the light of nature and Christian prudence, according to the general rules of the word, which are always to be observed." See C. of F., Chap. I. Sec. 6, and 1 Cor. xi. 13, 14; xiv. 26–40. The acts of church courts in reference to these "circumstances," are executive, or administrative, or diatactic "*regulations.*" "Circumstances," in the sense of our Confession, are those concomitants of an action, without which it can either not be done at all, or cannot be done with decency and decorum. Public worship, for example, requires public assemblies, and in public assemblies people must agree upon a time and a place for the meeting, and must appear in some costume and assume some posture. Whether they shall shock common sentiment in their attire, or conform to common practice; whether they shall stand, or sit, or lie, or whether each shall be at liberty to determine his own attitude—these are circumstances. They are necessary concomitants of the actions, and the church is at liberty to regulate them. Parliamentary assemblies cannot transact their business with decorum, efficiency and dispatch without moderators, rules of order, committees, etc.; and the parliamentary assembly, and, therefore, the church, may appoint moderators, committees, etc. All the details in reference to the distribution of courts, the definition of a quorum, the times of their meeting, the manner in which they shall be opened, details which occupy so large a space in our Book of Order, are "circumstances" which the church, in the exercise of her diatactic power, has a perfect right to arrange. We must carefully distinguish between those circumstances which attend "human actions" as such, *i. e.*, without which the actions could not be, and those circumstances which, though not essential, are added as appendages. These last do not fall within the jurisdiction of the church.

She has no right to appoint them. They are circumstances in the sense that they do not belong to the substance of the act. They are *not* circumstances in the sense that they so surround it (*circumstant*) that they cannot be separated from it. (See *Turretin*, L. 18, Q. 31, specially ¶ 3, p. 242–'3, of Vol. III. Carter's ed., 1847.)

A liturgy is a circumstance of this kind, as also bowing at the name of Jesus, the sign of the cross in baptism, instrumental music and clerical robes, *et cet.* (See Owen's *Discourse on Liturgies* and *Thornwell's Works*, IV. p. 247.) With this view agrees Calvin. (See Instit. B. 4, ch. 10, pp. 28–31.) The notion of Calvin and our Confession is briefly this: In public worship, indeed in all commanded external actions, there are two elements, a fixed and a variable. The fixed element, involving the essence or the thing, is beyond the discretion of the church. The variable, involving only the "circumstances" of the action, its separable accidents, may be changed, modified or altered, according to the exigencies of the case. The rules of social intercourse and of grave assemblies in different countries vary. The church accommodates her arrangements so as not to revolt the public sense of propriety. Where people recline at the meals she would administer the Lord's supper to communicants in a reclining attitude; where they sit she would change the mode. (*Thornwell's Works*, IV. pp. 246–7. See also Cunningham's *Reformers and Theologians of the Reformation*, p. 31, "Of the views," &c., to the bottom of p. 32. Also his essay on *Church Power*, ch. 9, of his *Church Principles* p. 235 and ff. Also Gillespie's *Dispute against the English Popish Ceremonies*, pt. 3, ch. 7, in *Presbyterian Armory*, Vol. I.

Laws bind the conscience *per se* or *simpliciter*. *Regulations* bind it *secundum quid*, *i. e.*, indirectly and mediately in case of scandal and contempt. In the first, we regard the authority of God alone; in the second, we regard the good of our neighbors. In the first, the *auctoritas mandantis*; in the second, the *mandati causa* (the avoiding of offence.)   See *Turretin*, L. 18, Q. 31, Vol. III., p. 255, *Carter's ed.*

XIII.

THE POWER ECCLESIASTICAL CONTRASTED WITH THE POWER CIVIL. RELATION OF THE CHURCH TO THE STATE.

We may obtain a still clearer view of the nature and extent of church power (the topic of the last lecture), by comparing it with the civil power, and considering the relations of the two organizations to which these powers belong.   In addition to this reason for a careful consideration of this topic, the history of this country furnishes a very weighty one.   The providence of God has, in the loudest tones, recalled the attention of the church to its own nature, as constituted and defined by himself, to the nature and functions of the state (which is also his ordinance) and to the relations between the two.

1. The fundamental relations implied in the distinction between the power civil and the power ecclesiastical have been recognized, more or less clearly, from the beginning of the history of our race.   These relations are that of man to man in a state of society, on the one hand, and, on the other hand, that of man to God, the Creator, the Moral Governor, the Judge and Sovereign Proprietor of man.   They have been designated by different names, and have been the objects of divers kinds of legislation, according to the diversities of age and country; but whether known by this name or that; whether, in practice, partially separated or totally confounded, the relations themselves have been, and could not but be, apprehended.   The relation of man to God would be developed in the operations of conscience arraigning the offender before an invisible tribunal, and pointing him to a coming retribution;

the relation of man to man would force itself upon the
notice by the necessities of every day's existence. Yet
it cannot be denied that in reference to few objects of
human thought have attempts at articulate exposition
been more unsuccessful than in reference to this; or
that the wisdom of the wisest men has still more signally failed, by any kind of political machinery, to realize perfectly the theories which make the most plausible approximation to the truth. The sources and
occasions of this failure will be better understood by a
rapid historical review.

2. It is not strange that these relations should have
been confounded, since, in the beginning, they existed
together in the bosom of the family. The family is
the social unit under the constitution of God, and not
the individual, as an infidel socialistic philosophy asserts. It is the germ out of which grows the great tree
of organized society, with its far-reaching and mul-
tiplied ramifications. In this germ the rudimental
forms of both church and state existed; but they
existed after the manner of all organic rudimental
forms, so undeveloped and so mingled that their differences could not be perceived. The head of the family
was both king and priest, governing and ordering his
household in regard to the things of this life, and in-
structing and leading them in the knowledge and worship of God. The child grew up with a reverence for
his father as the disposer of all his affairs, the director,
the authoritative director of all his thoughts and acts
in every part of the sphere of his natural life, in all his
spiritual, as in all his temporal relations. The father
prescribed the faith and duty of his children in relation to God, as well as their duty to himself and to the
other members of the family. In a word, he was the
representative of God in all things to his household.
When the child grew up, he did not pass, as he does
now, from a government of this sort into an organized
political or ecclesiastical community, into a church or

state, for there was then neither church nor state in the modern sense of these terms; but became himself the head of another family, and was invested with powers like those which his father before him had possessed, both temporal and spiritual.

3. This state of society, in which it would have been next to impossible to decide the question still mooted, whether the fifth commandment belongs to the first or second table of the law, continued in the line of Abraham, Isaac and Jacob, down to the organization of the *nation* of Israel, when the distinction between the civil or temporal power and the ecclesiastical begins to be visibly developed. Before proceeding to consider this, however, let us look for a moment at the history of other lines.

4. The patriarchal or family constitution of society seems to have been lost, and political communities to have been formed, sooner in these lines. The posterity of Cain seem to have made more *progress*, in the modern or popular sense of the word, than the posterity of Seth. In the organization of society, as well as in invention and use of the mechanical and fine arts, they seem to have been greatly in the advance. We are told in Genesis iv. 17, that Cain himself, after he went out from the presence of the Lord, "builded a *city*." He and his family, therefore, may be regarded as the founders of the state, and of that complex material and worldly civilization which the state embodies and represents. They were the sons of *men*, acknowledging nothing higher than *human* wisdom and *human* power, and bending all their energies to the one end of concentrating the forces of humanity, and of securing in this way a worldly *summum bonum*, an all-comprehending good, which might compensate for the loss of the favor and communion of God, which they had deliberately repudiated. They thus prepared the way for the Babel-builders and for heathenism, which is a worship of nature and its forces, and particularly of

the wisdom and power of the highest part of nature, *man*. It is worthy of note that over against this organization of society, and continuation of its forces in the line of the apostate Cain (the sons of men), occurs the record of something like the organization of the true worshippers of God in the line of Enos : "Then began men to call themselves by the name of Jehovah"* (Genesis iv. 26); that is, began to call themselves the children or people of God. But the time had not yet fully come for the organization of the church visible in correspondence with the state. The church thus formed united itself with the state; the sons of God intermarried with the daughters of men, and the progeny which resulted from that union was so gigantic and monstrous in its wickedness, so "violent," so regardless of everything but mere *force*, that God swept the earth with the besom of destruction, and reduced the race to its original dimensions of a single family.

5. After the flood, appears Noah as a new federal head of the human race, and as the king and priest of his household, and the development begins again. But with the like results. The spirit of the beastly serpent shows itself in the builders of "Babel" (a name which, from that time forward, becomes a symbol of the power of *man* in opposition to the power of God, and, therefore, of man as abdicating the dignity of his nature and becoming a "beast"), who renew the experiment of their forerunners, the posterity of Cain, the experiment of living without God by combining the individual forces of man. (See Genesis xi. 1, 4.) They built a city and a tower, to make themselves a *name*. They became worshippers of men instead of God; not man as an individual, weak and mortal, but *associated* man. And though God confounded the project of the city and tower, yet Nimrod, "the mighty hunter before the Lord" (that is, in the very face and in defiance of the

---

* The rendering in the margin of E. V.

Lord; compare Genesis vi. 11; xiii. 13; 2 Chronicles xxviii. 22; Psa. lii. 7), the mighty hunter of mankind, appears upon the stage as the founder of the kingdom of Babylon, or Assyria (Genesis x. 9, &c.), the first of those beastly kingdoms, the series of which Daniel gives us in his vision (Daniel, vii.), from a point of view of a worshipper of God, and which Nebuchadnezzar, from his point of view, saw as a splendid *human* image, representing the dominion and glory of *man*.

6. Here, then, we have the state in a colossal form, and from the circumstances of its origin we can expect nothing but an identification of the civil and the spiritual relations of mankind. If we read carefully the first seven chapters of the prophecy of Daniel, we cannot fail to see that the great subject is the contest between the supremacy of God and the supremacy of man; between the supremacy of God in man and the supremacy of man without God and against God. This is the real "conflict of ages," revealed in the garden of Eden (Genesis iii. 15), and ending in the triumph of the "Saviour of man," as recorded in the closing chapters of the Apocalypse. "The seed of the woman" (the "Saviour of man," God-man), and the "seed of the serpent," the beast, these are the parties which divide the world and convulse it. These are the parties which are contending for the mastery upon the territory of the United States. Nebuchadnezzar refused to listen to anything from the God of heaven, who ruled among the inhabitants of the earth, until he became a beast of the field. See the remarkable narrative in Daniel, ch. iv. Taught by this acted symbol, he acknowledged that his view of his empire as supreme, and as demanding the homage of the heart as well as the external obedience of the subject, was false, and that there was a God in heaven, who ruled supreme, and was, therefore, alone entitled to be worshipped. He became wiser than some rulers now are.

7. We need not trace the history of apostate man any further at present. In all heathen governments the result is the same. The state, the world, is τοπαν. Religion is obedience to the powers that be, and this obedience, whether rendered to an oriental or an occidental despot, or to a Grecian or Roman democracy or republic, is the whole of religion, because there is no higher God than man in "humanity," or than man chooses to allow to be worshipped.

8. We return now to the line of the chosen seed, and to the institute of Moses. What was the relation of the ecclesiastical and civil power in the nation of Israel? I answer, that they were not entirely separated nor entirely confounded. They were in that relation to each other which we might have anticipated from the *peculiar* calling of the Jewish nation, and from their position with respect to the other nations of the world. We are expressly told in Ex. xix. 5, 6, that the Hebrews were called to be a "*peculiar* treasure unto God above all people, and a kingdom of priests and a *holy* nation." If this language means anything, it means that the Israelitish nation should differ from all other nations in this, that it should be a holy, consecrated nation—a nation of worshippers of the true God, in covenant with God, ruled by his word, and his word only, and not by the light of their own reason. When other nations, therefore, call themselves Christians, and as nations make covenants with God and *consecrate* themselves to his service as worshippers, they *usurp* privileges which God has made *peculiar* to Israel. Any nation which boasts that it is a "kingdom of priests," is *pro tanto* in rebellion against God. Israel was not, in this respect, a model or pattern for civil communities, but a type of the church of God under the gospel. The relation it sustained to God is the relation that the spiritual body of Christ sustains to him. The alliances which it was forbidden to form with other nations were types of the alliances which the church is

forbidden to form with civil governments ; and the dis-
astrous results of those alliances, the slavery, degradation and misery of Israel, were types of the slavery,
degradation and misery of the church's alliances with
powers foreign to herself in nature, origin, government
and destiny.   God was the sovereign of Israel in the
sense of being their lawgiver, which he is of no other
nation.   He was their husband, and the husband of
no other.   Transgression in them was adultery as well
as treason.   They were the inheritance of God, and he
was their inheritance.   He was their landlord and they
were his tenants.   Their taxes were acknowledgments
of his goodness and of his proprietorship in the land
and in its fruits.   Nor was he an absent proprietor.
He dwelt among them.   When they dwelt in tents, he
dwelt in a tent with them.   When they lived in houses,
he dwelt in a house among them.   They were his family, and he the father and head.   None of these things
are true of any other nation, nor can they be.   They
are all true of the Christian church, the body of Christ,
and eminently true of her as the substance of which
Israel was the shadow. This being the case, there was
of necessity a commingling of the civil and the spiritual. Hence, we find the kings (whom God gave to them
reluctantly, if we may use the expression, because it
sprang from a desire to be *like other nations*,) sometimes exercising powers "*circa sacra*,"—about sacred
things.   We are not, however, to consider the king as
taking the place of God, as his vicar in the theocracy.
In the provisions of the law concerning the king
(Deut. xvii. 14–20), we find no authority given to him to
intermeddle with the faith, government or worship of the
church. He is required to have a copy of the law, made
from the standard text in custody of the priests and Levites, and to read it, and keep it, that his heart be not
lifted up above his brethren. When Uzziah undertook
to burn incense, a function belonging to the priesthood, he was smitten with leprosy, a punishment almost

as severe as that inflicted upon Uzzah, a private man,
for taking hold of the ark of God when the oxen shook
it. 2 Chron. xxvi. 16–23; 2 Sam. vi. 6, 7. There was
no king-priest, no Melchisedek, in Israel. See also 1
Sam. xiii. 9–14. David meditated building a temple,
and Solomon built it. David was prevented from building and Solomon encouraged to build by a prophet
speaking in the name of God; that is, by special direction, and not in the legal exercise of his royal functions. It is further to be noted that both David and
Solomon were themselves prophets in a general sense,
and acted and wrote under inspiration. Further still,
they were eminent types of Christ as king—the one of
Christ as warring and conquering, the other of Christ
as a peacefully reigning king. But did not Hezekiah,
Josiah and other kings destroy idolatrous worship and
reform the nation? Certainly; they could not do
otherwise and be faithful to the constitution of the theocracy, the fundamental principle of which was the
unity of God. And no civil magistrate can *now* afford
to dispense with religion altogether. The primary doctrines of natural religion, the being of a God and a
moral government, are implied in every oath of office
and in every oath of testimony. Hezekiah and Josiah
also ordered the keeping of the passover; but this fes-
tival bore a national as well as a religious character.
Still it must be confessed that the kings of Israel exercised a power about sacred things, which we contend
that no king or government has a right now to exercise. They were kings of "a *peculiar* people, a holy
nation, a kingdom of priests."

Again, let it be considered that the rise of the royal
dignity in Israel was contemporary with the rise of the
prophetical office, both growing out of the typical
character of the nation. Considering the nation as a
moral person, having an organic life and a conscience,
the prophet and not the king, unless he was also a
prophet, was the exponent of that conscience—Ex. iv.

16. It was not accidental, but necessary, that when
God had, so to speak, given way to a visible king, he
should have the prophet as his representative and
mouth-piece. Otherwise, the whole constitution must
have been subverted. The king was subject to the
prophet, because the government was a theocracy, and
all civil and social arrangements were subordinate to
the religious, as the shell is subordinate to the kernel,
or the body to the soul. Judaism was a religious
state, as Paganism is a political religion, and, it may
be added, a political religion is Paganism and a religious state is Judaism. We find, moreover, that the
prophetic office rose in importance as the tendency to
apostasy, both in king and people, increased. As men
and as citizens, priests and prophets were under obligation to obey the king; but as priests and prophets,
they were subject to God alone, the head of the theocracy; a foreshadowing of the precise relations of the
office-bearers of the church under the gospel to the
civil power.

Upon the whole it is a very striking fact, that in an
oriental nation, and in a theocracy, public forms should
recognize, to so great an extent, the distinction and
separation between civil and sacred functions. See
2 Chron. xix. 8–11, especially vs. 11.) We find the
sacerdotal functions given to a separate order of officers, and the whole ministry of the tabernacle to a
particular tribe; while the elders, the representatives
of the patriarchal system, seem to have continued the
exercise of civil functions. We do not pretend that
there was an entire separation of the secular and the
spiritual. It is possible that the synagogue, with its
mingled jurisdiction over civil and ecclesiastical affairs,
may even then have existed, as that jurisdiction was
based on the patriarchal principle upon which the
whole Hebrew commonwealth was organized. But we
assert that we have in the books of Moses what we
find nowhere else in the East, a class of high and hon-

11

orable functions in the matter of divine worship with
which the highest officer in the state dared not intermeddle; and further, that where the two classes of
functions came together the spiritual was supreme.   If
any argument, therefore, be drawn from Judaism in
support of the union of church and state, it is in favor
rather of the Ultramontane than of the Erastian theory.   In this respect, as we have seen, Paganism presents a strong contrast to Judaism in giving supremacy
to the civil power.   But in both, as also in Mahome-
tanism, the two powers are so combined that their
history cannot be separately written.   There is no history of the synagogue, or the mosque, or the pagan
temple, as there is of the church.   See Gillespie's
Assertion of the Goverment of the Kirk of Scotland, Pt.
II., ch. 7 (in *Pres. Armory*, Vol. I.), for some ingenious
arguments to prove that there was a separation of civil
and ecclesiastical courts among the Jews.   Also Pt. I.,
ch. 11.

9. We come now to the era at which the church was
to escape from the trammels of the Hebrew state and
to assume a separate and independent existence. This,
of course, could not be done without a struggle.   But
to make the transition less abrupt and difficult, Christ
so ordered it that the old dispensation was allowed to
overlap the new for forty years, during which period
the church was gradually but rapidly obtaining a foot-
hold among the Gentiles and dissolving its connections with perverted and petrified Judaism, which assumed, more and more, an attitude of bitter hostility
to it.   The woman who gave birth to the man-child
was preparing for her flight into the wilderness of the
pagan nations.   The "Acts of the Apostles," after describing this process of loosening and transition, closes
with Paul at Rome, the great representative of the free
church of the Gentiles at the metropolis of heathen-
dom and of worldly power.

10. The first issue which was formally made between

this worldly power and the church was made by the
Emperor Domitian. The persecution under Nero (A.
D. 54–68) was partial and local, and it is by no means
clear that the Christians were not persecuted as
Jews; but Domitian (A. D. 81–96) claimed to be
God, made statues of himself, to which he insisted
divine honors should be paid. He was the legitimate successor of Nebuchadnezzar and of Nimrod.
It is his persecution of the church which constitutes the historical basis or starting point of the
Apocalypse, as the persecution of the ancient church
by Nebuchadnezzar was the historical basis of the
prophecies of Daniel, the Apocalypse of the Old Testament. The question became again a practical one:
"Is there any god higher than the head of a world empire? is there any god in heaven who rules the gods on
earth, and is able to deliver his servants?" The "conflict of ages" is resumed between the seed of the serpent and the seed of the woman, between man without
God and man with God. One of the sufferers in the
conflict on the side of the woman's seed is chosen (cir.
96 A. D.) to sketch its outlines and leading characteristics, until it shall be ended in the victory of the Son
of man, and the final judgment upon "the whore," "the
beast," and "the false prophet," which are, respectively, symbols of the church visible leaning upon the
strength of the civil power, and glorifying it instead
of Christ; of that civil power usurping the prerogatives of Christ, and making war upon all who assert
the supremacy of Christ; and of the wisdom of the
world giving its support to the civil power as supreme,
as the all-disposing Lord and the all-comprehending
Good. (See Hobbes's [b. 1588, d. 1679] *Leviathan*, a
happily-chosen name, in which this view of the civil
government is audaciously advocated.) If this view of
the symbols be correct, it seems that one of the great
lessons which this wondrous book was designed to impress upon the church was the certain pollution and

misery resulting from the union of church and state;
the certain corruption of both, and the infliction of
mutual wrong and outrage; the certain supremacy of
the state over the adulterous church, and the final destruction of the adulterous church by the very power
upon which she leaned. Rev. xvii. The kings commit fornication with her (vs. 2), and then, when God's
time comes for judgment, they burn her with fire. Vs.
16; Lev. xxi. 9.

11. It was God's mercy which exposed the Christian church, almost from the beginning of its existence
and for the first three hundred years of its career, to
the bitter persecution of the civil power. The line was
thus clearly drawn between Christ and Cæsar, and it
was demonstrated that the church could live, not only
without alliance with the state, but in spite of all its
power and hate. The church was taught that the
world is enmity against God, and that any conformity
to it, or alliance with it, could only end in the corruption and slavery of the church, as the Israelites of old
were taught as to Egypt, Assyria, etc.

12. The seer in Patmos saw (Rev. xiii. 3) one of the
heads of the beast "as it were wounded to death, and
his deadly wound was healed." If the civil power is
symbolized as a beast, only so far as it is opposed to
the church of God, then the deadly wound signified its
dropping for a season its wonted appearance of hostility to the cause and kingdom of God, to cease for a
time to act as a beast; the which it could only do by
assuming either a truly religious or a professedly religious character. That this character was only professedly religious seems to be indicated by the words
"as it were," and by the healing of the wound. This
characteristic is intended to apply, probably, to the
whole period of the seventh head. In the corresponding passage in chap. xvii. 8, 11, the revealing angel
says to John: "The beast that thou sawest *was* and *is
not;*" and again he calls it "the beast that was, and is
not, and yet is;" and again, in vs. 11, "the beast that

was, and is not," is said to be the eighth and of the seven. These expressions seem to indicate the paradoxical character of the beast, a beast passing into the form of the woman, or, in unsymbolical language, the world-power, which is essentially the enemy of God, becoming or pretending to be Christian. The healing of the deadly wound indicates the reässumption, or the breaking forth again, of its hostility to the cause and kingdom of Christ. Its profession of Christ's religion has not changed its nature. It is still possessed of the spirit of a beast; it shows itself to be a part of the kingdom of darkness, of which the old serpent, the dragon, the devil, Satan, is the head and prince (Rev. xii. 9; xiii. 2, 4); the true successor of Cain, Nimrod, Nebuchadnezzar, and the Edomite Herods. Whether Nebuchadnezzar, or Cyrus, or Antiochus Epiphanes, or Domitian, or Constantine is the reigning monarch, the *spirit* of the power is the same, the spirit of the world, which is enmity against God. Hence all these powers were seen by Nebuchadnezzar in *one* image; and in Revelation xiii. John sees the first three beasts of Daniel (chap. vii.) combined in the fourth and last. (See Auberlen's *Daniel and the Revelation*, and Fairbairn *on Prophecy*.)

13. This deadly wound of the beast, this apparent change in the character of the civil power in its relation to the church, took place, or was first exemplified, in the conversion of Constantine the Great, and in his patronage of the church in the first quarter of the fourth century. The system of that emperor was only a christianized paganism, as the result showed. Religion was still considered a part of the machinery of the state. The only difference was that christianity was substituted for paganism, and the God of the Christians for Jupiter and the whole herd of divinities in the Pantheon. It was the old theory of the first centuries of the Roman republic with a new application. In primeval Rome everything was moulded by

religion.   Their *libri rituales* (to the Romans what the
Mosaic ritual was to the Hebrews), according to Festus
(See *Legare's Essay on Roman Legislation*), "taught the
rites with which cities are to be founded and altars and
temples dedicated; the holiness of the walls of towns;
the law relating to their gates; how tribes, wards and
centuries are to be distributed; armies organized and
arrayed, and other like things relating to peace and
war.   The same influence extended itself over the very
soil of the Roman territory, and made it, in the technical language of their augury, one vast temple.   It
was consecrated by the auspices; it could become the
property only of one who had the auspices, that is, a
patrician, a *Roman*, properly so called; once set apart
and conveyed away, it was irrevocably alienated, so
that sales of the domain were guaranteed by religion,
and it was sacreligious to establish a second colony on
the place dedicated to a first.   The city, by its original inauguration was also a temple; its gates and
walls were holy; its pomoerium was unchangeable until
higher auspices had suspended those under which it
was first marked out.   Every spot of ground might
become, by the different uses to which it was applied,
sacred (*sacer*), holy (*sanctus*), religious (*religiosus*).
The first *agrimensor*, says Niebuhr, was an augur, accompanied by Tuscan priests or their scholars.   From
the foundation of the city the sacredness of the property was shadowed forth in the god Terminus, and that
of contracts protected by an apotheosis of faith (*fides*).
In short, the worthy Roman lived, moved and had his
being, as the Greek writers observe, in religion." How
striking the resemblance, in this description, of many
things to corresponding features in Judaism.   The
grand difference is, that Judaism was a theocracy and
Romanism an anthropocracy.   In the one there was a
real consecration to God; in the other a real consecration only to the glory of man.   But here we find
the germ of the Erastianism of Constantine.   So far is

it from being true, that the union of the church and
the state was the work of Christian priests. It was the
work, remotely, of the "lawyer priests" of primeval
Rome, an oriental *caste* transmitted to the Romans
through Tuscany, at once by inheritance and by education (See Legare *ut sup.*), and proximately of the
jurisconsults of Constantine. Subsequently the system
was reduced to a more formal shape, and hardened by
the lawyers of Theodosius (A. D. 379–'95) and Justinian,
(A. D. 527–'65.)

14. Its Pagan origin and character was soon be-
trayed. The church began to be moulded by the
state in government, worship, and even in faith. It is
necessary that the inferior should be moulded by the
superior. Hence the ecclesiastical hierarchy corresponding with the civil hierarchy of the empire. Hence
the temples, altars, festivals, images, lustrations, sacrifices, incense; in a word, the pomp and pageantry and
hollowness of the paganized Christian worship. (See
Middleton's Letter from Rome, b. 1683, d. 1750.) Hence
the persecutions of the faithful who refused to recognize
this paganized Christianity as the religion of the crucified
Nazarene. The autonomy of the church disappeared,
and she became the slave of the civil power. The
nature of the beast passed into the woman and the
woman became the adulteress riding upon the beast.

15. In the course of time a reaction came, and the
human mind, refusing to rest in the center of truth,
swung to the opposite extreme, still holding to the
union of the spiritual and the temporal, but asserting
the supremacy of the spiritual. The woman would not
only ride upon the beast and be carried by it, but
would govern and guide it according to her own will.
This change began with the policy of the Carlovingian
line of monarchs (began 752 A. D.) and their ambitious attempts to revive the Roman empire in the
West. In order to secure the patronage and assistance
of the church, they conferred civil authority and terri-

tory upon ecclesiastics, and the pope himself became a
feudatory of Pepin (A. D. 752–'58), Charlemagne (A. D.
768-814), and their successors in the holy German Roman
empire. And here did vaulting ambition overleap itself.
This very policy was the occasion of the wars between
the popes and the emperors, which kept the world in
an uproar during the middle ages; the church gain-
ing more and more power as a temporal and civil institute under the direction of Hildebrand (A. D. 1073–
1085) and Innocent III. (A. D. 1198–1216), and others,
reaching the summit of its audacity under Boniface
VIII. (A. D. 1294–1303), and then gradually yielding
again to the temporal power. Thus the popery of
the middle ages became the Nemesis of the Erastianism or Paganism of Constantine, Theodosius and Justinian. But both popes and emperors united in per-
secuting the witnesses of Christ's supremacy.

16. Then came the earthquake of the Reformation.
But this did not dissolve the union of church and state.
"Luther had some glimpses of the grand truth that the
spiritual kingdom of Jesus Christ is something separate from and independent of the civil government ordained of God the Creator in the hands of Cæsar; but,
driven to shelter himself under the protection of the
monarch who was ambitious to rid himself of the authority of the pope, yet equally jealous of such an *imperium in imperio* as a completely organized spiritual
government in the hands of the church, Luther was
obliged, as he thought, to sacrifice a part of the spiritual prerogatives of the church for protection against
the power of the pope." (Robinson's speech at Cincinnati, November 8th, 1866.) Calvin had a much
clearer conception of the church's autonomy than Luther, and would allow no interference on the part of
the state with the discipline of the church. Yet he was
bred a lawyer; he had studied the Pandects, and allowed the authority of Tribonian (A. D. 545) to obscure
the interpretation of that word of God, to which he ad-

hered with a tenacity and fidelity unsurpassed by man. If Calvin had been a German instead of a Frenchman, he probably would not have seen so much of the truth as he did see, for Ultramontanism had the ascendency in Germany. But even his imperial mind could not emancipate itself from the thraldom of "the spirit of the age."

17. His influence, however, is seen in the original Puritan party of England, in the struggle for religious and civil liberty in Holland and the other states of the Netherlands, and especially in Scotland. The Reformation in Scotland from the first, more than any of the movements of the sixteenth century, rested upon the theory of the autonomy of the spiritual commonwealth, and it seemed to be the special mission of its martyrs to testify for "Christ's crown and covenant," against the lofty claims of the temporal sovereign. But after all the testimonies of its martyrs, and a hundred years of suffering, the seductive strategy of Carstairs[*] and the political Protestantism of William and Mary, and the settlement of the Scottish kingdom under Queen Anne, proved more powerful than the testimony of the martyrs, and at last subjugated the Scottish, as well as the English churches, under the yoke of Cæsar, leaving the piety and earnest love of the truth, which might afterward be generated by her doctors, to fly off in secession after secession till the present day." (*Robinson ut supra.* See also his lecture on *The American Theory of Church and State* before the Maryland Institue, Baltimore.) The fundamental defect in the position of the Scotch church (a defect to which the Free Church, notwithstanding its noble testimony, still clings), is the doctrine that the state ought to support the church by its revenues ; as if it were possible for the church, thus supported by the state, to be independent.

---

[*] On Carstairs, see *Macaulay's History of England*, III., p. 269, and *Hetherington's Hist of the Church of Scotland*, chap. viii. (pp. 300 and 304, Vol. V. of Carter's Ed., New York, 1844.)

18. The Confession of the Westminster Assembly being composed under the influence of the Scotch commissioners and of Englishmen brought up in the Erastian establishment, could not of course be expected to teach the truth more purely, on this subject, than the Scotch. Hence it was changed *before it was adopted* by the Presbyterian Church of the United States of America (1788), as you have been informed in a previous lecture.

19. Such being the history of this subject in other countries and ages, we come now to notice, very briefly, its history in the United States. Most of the colonists who came to this country, came of course with the ideas of church and state which prevailed in the lands from which they came. They had learned something from persecution, but they had much still to learn. The New England Puritans established a sort of theocracy, thus rushing to the other extreme from the Erastian paganism from which they had suffered so much ; the pulpit became the expounder of public policy and of the law of the land ; and the church was filled with hypocrites and pretenders to godliness. Roger Williams and the Baptists suffering persecution in Massachusetts, betook themselves, after the manner of minorities when oppressed by majorities, to the ramparts of sound principles, and founded the settlement of Rhode Island (1635) in which they proclaimed not only religious toleration, but religious liberty. The Huguenots were quiet; the Dutch were liberal; the Scotch and Scotch-Irish, who were the chief instruments in moulding the Presbyterian Church in this country, were the next, after Roger Williams, to proclaim the true theory of the relations of church and and state. Waddell, "the blind preacher," William Graham, Stanhope Smith, and the old Hanover Presbytery in Virginia, on the ecclesiastical side, with Thomas Jefferson on the civil side, who, first of all the statesmen in history, caught the true idea, co-operated

in establishing what is sometimes called the Virginia doctrine, which Mr. Stuart Robinson (accommodating the language of Melville) expresses thus : "There be two republics in this nation, one the civil republic of the United States, of which the man in the White House is the head; the other the spiritual commonwealth, of which Jesus Christ is the head, with which the man in the White House has nothing to do, but to protect the persons and property of its subjects, as that of other citizens." (Cincinnati speech.) This is the theory which was supposed to be the theory of the United States, as well as of Virginia, up to the period of the war. It was found, explicitly or implicitly, in all the constitutions and bills of rights of the States (with the exception, perhaps, of North Carolina), and is recognized by that provision of the constitution which prohibits the passage of any law infringing upon the rights of conscience. It is the clear teaching of the Confession of Faith of the Presbyterian Church of the United States of America, and, I suppose, was universally received by all other denominations, if not expressly taught in their public formularies and symbols. It is the Scotch theory, without the feature of state support, and with the voluntary principle instead.

20. But the history of this country has demonstrated that a refined and exalted worldly civilization makes no change in the heart of man; that he is an incorrigible sinner, and incurably disposed to walk in the light of his own eyes; that the kingdom of Christ is of no account to him, except so far as it can be made to subserve his own lusts. We stand amazed, notwithstanding the faithful warnings of prophets and apostles, at the reappearance of the beast, and the revival of the maxims of Roman civilians and mediæval canonists in the nineteenth century, and in "the freest and most enlightened nation of the globe." We are confounded when we see the owls and bats of the dark ages flying about in the blaze of this boasted period of

illumination, and statesmen and churchmen, in an age of boasted liberty, forging over again the chains and fetters of the ages of slavery and blood. Saddest of all, we see a church which has been accustomed to pride itself upon an ancestry martyred for Christ's crown, voluntarily pulling down his ensign and running up the ensign of Cæsar; a church which has testified "repentance" towards God and "faith towards the Lord Jesus Christ," as the burden of its commission, now drivelling about "loyalty and freedom," and outlawing men who are as good as themselves, for no other cause than the holding of a theory of the government which has been held by many of the best and wisest Americans from the beginning. Once more, then, the church is called to testify for he rights of her only head and king, Jesus Christ, and for the freedom and independence which he has conferred upon herself as the purchase of his most precious blood. Once more has she been compelled by the assaults of her adversaries to study her own nature and to define her relation to that other ordinance of God, the state. These relations we come now to consider dogmatically, as we have already considered them historically.

21. The church and the state agree in these three points: 1st, That they are ordained of God; 2nd, That they are ordained for his glory; 3rd, That they are ordained for the good of mankind.

22. They differ in the following points: 1st, In the aspects and relations in which God is contemplated by them respectively as the *source* of power; 2nd, In the aspects in which man is contemplated by them respectively as the *object* of power; 3rd, In the rule by which they are to be respectively guided in the exercise of power. Of these, in their order, we now proceed to treat more particularly.

23. First, as to the aspects and relations in which God as the *source of power* is contemplated by church

and state respectively. I observe that the state is the ordinance of God, considered as Creator, and, therefore, the moral governor of mankind, while the church is an ordinance of God, considered as the Saviour and Restorer of mankind. We need not dwell upon this point here, as the illustration and proof of it are necessarily involved in the proof and illustration of the next, which is *second*, as to the aspects and relations in which church and state, respectively, contemplate man as the *object of power*, where it is to be noted, (*a*), that the state is ordained for man as man, the church for man as a sinner, under a dispensation of restoration and salvation. The state is for the whole race of man, the church consists of that portion of the race which is really, or by credible profession, the mediatorial body of Christ. The state is a government of natural justice; the church, a government of grace.

24. The state is ordained for man as man, and is ordained to realize the idea of justice. We find it existing in the germ when the race consisted of one man and one woman. The woman was in a state of subordination to the man. This subordination was not the penal consequence of transgression, as is evident from 1 Timothy ii. 11–14, where Paul argues that the transgression was the consequence of the violation by the woman of the order established by heaven, of her ambitiously forsaking her condition of subordination, and acting as if she were the superior or the equal of the man. If it should be asked, where was the necessity or the propriety of an order implying subordination in beings who were created in the image of God, in knowledge, righteousness, and true holiness? the answer is, that the propriety was founded upon the diversity of capacity in intellect and other endowments of human nature, which it pleased God should exist in the man and the woman. If man had not fallen, it would still have been his duty to bring up his children in the knowledge of God, and to *direct*

12

them in the way in which they should glorify God; albeit these children, by the terms of the supposition, would all have been holy and without inclination to go astray; nay, more, in no danger at all of going astray, as they would have been confirmed in the possession of eternal life by the covenant with their father. In other words, if all creatures, because they are creatures, need direction from God as to the mode in which they are to glorify and enjoy him, why might not this direction be given through the instrumentality of others as well as immediately by God himself? There is not only no absurdity in such an arrangement, but there are traces of the wonderful wisdom and goodness of the Creator in it. Society is not an unison, but an exquisite harmony, a grand instrument of various chords for the harping of hymns and hallelujahs to the God and Father of all. Even among the unfallen angels, we have reason to believe, there are thrones, dominions, principalities, and powers—order in the form of a celestial hierarchy. Man having fallen, however, and the love which constituted the very spirit and temper of his mind having given place to enmity, something more than direction was now necessary. He needed *restraint;* his appetites must be bridled and coerced. The law of the two tables, which, in his state of innocence and uprightness, had been written upon his heart summarily, in the *positive* and *preceptive* form of *love*, must now be written externally, in detail, upon tablets of stone, and in a prohibitory form, "thou shalt *not*;" and in reference to the second table, which prescribes the duties growing out of the relations of man to man, it became necessary that overt acts of transgression which were not only morally wrong, but injurious to society, should not only be discountenanced by prohibition, but restrained and prevented by punishment. Hence arose a government of *force*.

25. The case, then, stands thus: In any condition of our race, the social nature of man must have given

rise to the secular power. In a state of innocence it would have been simply a directing power, a constitution designed merely to carry out and fulfil, without confusion, the blind instincts or impulses of love, love of self and love of neighbor. In a fallen state, it has become, of necessity, a restraining and punishing, as well as a directing power. But in both conditions and in both forms it is an ordinance of God, "the author of the constitution and course of nature." It is the nature of man to exist in society, and society is necessary to his existence. But society cannot exist without law and order of some sort. Therefore government is as necessary to man as society, and for this reason is as natural to man as society. It may not be an original endowment of man, but it is natural, and, if natural, then the ordinance of God. The perception of distance by the eye is not an original endowment of man, but the organ is so constituted by God, that, in the course of time, it necessarily acquires it, and it is, therefore, natural to man, and therefore the ordinance of God. Civil government, then, is a branch or department of the moral government of God, the Creator and Ruler over man. God governs man by mechanical laws, by chemical laws, by vital laws, and he governs him by civil laws. He who leaps from a precipice or drinks a glass of poison, and dies, dies under a law of God, which *executes itself*. He who murders his brother, and dies on the gallows, dies under a law of God, which is *executed by the hand* of the civil magistrate, the minister of God. In all such cases death is a penalty inflicted by God for a violation of a rule of his government, physical or moral.

26. If this be a just view of the subject, civil government is a great *moral* institute, not a mere expedient of human wisdom and sagacity for the prevention of evil. It is this low, wretched, utilitarian view which has contributed its full share to the crimes and miseries of this country, in which the criminal

law was fast becoming as pure an affair of expediency as the civil. But the government of God, as Creator, is a government of *justice*, and crime is punishable for its *ill-desert;* and the civil magistrate, who is the minister of God (Roman xiii.), while he has no right, from any view of expediency, to inflict any punishment which justice does not sanction, is bound to inflict the punishment which justice requires and crime deserves. This remark is needed for the sake of one important inference, and that is, that every civil government on earth is bound explicitly to recognize its responsibility to God as the moral governor of mankind. It is perfectly monstrous that the power which bears the sword and exercises the awful prerogative of taking human life, either in peace or war, should not acknowledge itself to be the servant of the sovereign Lord of life and death ; that the power which represents the majesty of justice, should not recognize its responsibility to him who is the eternal foundation and standard of all righteousness. So much for civil government as the ordinance of God. It regards man as man, and, therefore, regards *all* men.

27. The church, on the other hand, is the ordinance of God, considered as the Saviour of men in the person of Jesus Christ, his only begotten Son. It contemplates man, not simply as man, nor as upright in his original condition of innocence, nor simply as a fallen creature, but as "the prisoner of hope," or more strictly still, as "the heir of salvation," really or by credible profession. It, therefore, does not contemplate all men, but only those who enjoy a dispensation of grace, or more strictly (as to its government) those who profess and call themselves Christians.

28. We note again, (*b*), that the state considers man only as to his *outward* being. It protects the citizen or the subject in his person, his property, his liberty, by punishing illegal assaults upon either. Its punishments affect the body and outward condition of the

transgressor. It compels obedience and punishes disobedience by brute force. This is the sanction of its law. Its symbol is the sword. It can have nothing to do, therefore, with the faith of its subjects; for faith lies in the domain of the spirit, and cannot be compelled. The state does not, and cannot, aim at holiness, it aims only at social order. It has nothing to do with the religion of the citizen, or the loyalty of the heart, but only with his obedience to the laws, affecting the body and the outward estate. It cannot require the citizen to approve and love the laws, but only not to violate them.

29. The church, on the other hand, moves in the sphere of the spirit. It has nothing to do with the bodies, the estates, the outward condition of mankind. Its sanctions are not corporeal, involving the exercise of brute force, but only moral and spiritual, appealing to the judgment, the faith, the conscience of its members. It knows nothing of the sword, the dungeon, the lash, pecuniary fines, etc., etc., but only of argument, exhortation, admonition, censure, etc., etc. Its great function is to teach, to convince, to persuade, "to bear witness of the truth." Its triumphs are the triumphs of *love;* it drags no reluctant captives at the wheels of its chariot; the design of its ordinances, oracles, ministry, is through the efficacious operation of the Holy Ghost to bring its captives into hearty sympathy with its king, and so to give them a share in the glory and exultation of the triumphs of the king. Its symbol is the "keys," by which it opens and shuts the kingdom of heaven, according as men are believers or impenitent. Its only sword is the sword of the Spirit, which is the word of God. Its discipline is not the punishment of an avenging judge, asserting the unbending majesty of the law, but the discipline of a tender mother, whose bowels yearn over the wayward child, and who inflicts no pain, except for the child's reformation and salvation. The authority of his king-

dom is spiritual. His sword is a sword "coming out of his *mouth*." His voice, is "Son, give me thy *heart*"; "Repent for the kingdom of heaven is at hand"; and by the power of his Spirit, he sweetly constrains those whom he chooses for members of his kingdom to call him "Lord." He makes them *willing* in the day of his power. They are his, or profess to be his; have, or make a credible profession of having, the great law of love written upon their hearts, and, therefore, need more the directing than the restraining power of the law. The whole discipline of the church is based upon the supposition of faith in its members, so that what is of no account in the eye of the state, is primary and fundamental in the eyes of the church. It is so perfectly obvious, that the employment of force is abhorrent, from the whole nature and genius of the church, that even the fiends of the "holy office" were compelled to profess the greatest horror of shedding the blood of heretics, and piously turned them over to the secular arm. The Inquisition was always, in theory at least, what every court of the church is, a "penitentiary tribunal," a tribunal whose function is not punishment, but discipline, not the destruction, but the edification of the offender, brought about through his personal repentance.

30. *Third.* The state and the church differ in the rule by which they are respectively guided in the exercise of power. The constitution of the church is a divine revelation; the constitution of the state must be determined by human reason and the course of providential events. (Assembly of 1861.) The Bible is the statute-book of the church, the visible kingdom of Christ; the light of nature is the guide of the state. The church has no legislative power, properly so-called, but only a power to declare and obey the law of Christ's kingdom. The church is only a witness, and she cannot go beyond the divine testimony of the Word; she has no commission to open her lips, but

with a "Thus saith the Lord." All her acts of government are acts of obedience to Christ, her only king. As a church, she owes no allegiance to any authority but that of Christ ; as his bride, she owes no loyalty to any person but him.   Her members, as citizens or subjects, owe allegiance to the civil power, and are subject to it in their bodies and estates ; but as Christians, they know no authority but Christ's; and if the church itself should enact laws against her divine constitution, her members must appeal from her to Christ, the king.   The state may adopt any form of government it pleases—its power is magisterial and imperative.   The power of the church being only "ministerial and declarative," she must adopt the form of government whose regulative and constitutive principles are revealed in the Scriptures, her constitution and charter. The life of the state is natural, and it is left to create an organization for itself.   The life of the church is supernatural, and God prescribes an organization for it.

31. When we say that the Bible is not the rule for the state, we do not mean that the state is at liberty to disregard its teachings.   We mean to affirm that God has given no commission to the state to testify to the truth of Christ's revelation, or to interpret it.   *It is to the church that the lively oracles have been committed by her divine Head*.   The church alone is founded upon the prophets and apostles, Jesus Christ himself being the chief corner stone.   The church alone is the pillar and ground of the truth.   She is the woman, clothed with the sun, with the moon under her feet, and upon her head a crown of twelve stars.   She is the system of candlesticks, in the midst of which the King of the kingdom walks, and in his hand alone are the stars, the teachers and the rulers of the church.   Christ is the *lumen illuminans*, the church is the *lumen illuminatum*.   It is the kingdom of the Son of Man, and not the kingdom of the leviathan of the state, which is the light of the world.   This

is the case under the present dispensation, whatever
may be the case when kingdoms of this world shall become the kingdoms of our Lord and of his Christ.
Hence the change which has been proposed from time
to time in the constitution of the United States, so as
to make that instrument acknowledge the divine
authority of the Scriptures and the kingly office of
Christ, proceeds upon a totally false conception of the
sphere and functions of the state. As the state is the
ordinance of God, as creator and moral governor, and
is designed for man as man, it has nothing to do with
any principles of religion but those which belong to
man as man : to wit, the being of God and a moral
government. To give it any power over the truths of
revealed religion, and over the records which contain
those truths, is to confound it with the church, or what
is practically the same thing, to abolish the church, except as an auxiliary of the state, in preserving order.
It becomes then, what infidel philosophers have represented it to be, a mere temporary "crutch."

32. The definition of the church visible in our Confession (Chap. XXV. Sec. 5, 2), makes it to consist of
those "who profess the true religion, together with their
children." Now, if the proposed change in the constitution of the United States were made, the state would
answer to this definition. It would profess the "true
religion." If it should be said that it is but a single
doctrine, which the state professes, we answer again,
(a), that it is a confession fully as comprehensive as
that which the church itself made for centuries under
its patriarchal form ; (b), that in itself it includes the
whole plan of salvation ; for Christ's kingly office is
based upon his priestly. It is certainly no narrower
than the confession in Acts viii. 37, and 1 Corinthians,
xii. 3. It is the very substance of the teaching of the
whole gospel history, specially of the first three Gos-
pels. The burden of this history is the "kingdom of
heaven" and the "Son of Man," the king. (c), That

the principle upon which the advocates of this amendment proceed does not hinder the state from enlarging its confession at any time, or from finally enlarging it to the dimensions of the Westminster standards. Upon the whole, then, it appears that these brethren would *logically* confound church and state, by making the same definition answer to both; and *really* confound them by making the state and church both witnesses of Christ.

33. The only safety for liberty and religion is in rigidly enforcing the maxim that the Bible is the *positive* rule for the church, a *negative* rule for the state. The state may do whatever the Bible does not *forbid*. The church may do only what the Bible directs or permits; and where the Bible is silent, the church must be silent. Whatever the Bible does not grant is *eo-ipso* to the church prohibited. This distinction is almost certain to be overlooked when civil and ecclesiastical functions are mingled, as in England in the days of Hooker and Cartwright—Hooker and the court party contending that matters not expressly prohibited in the Scriptures were matters of lawful legislation on the part of the church. This approval of the principle, that whatever is not forbidden is lawful, was natural enough to these men, because the church had been subject, and continued to be subject, to the civil power; and the principle is justly applicable to the state. Cartwright and the Puritans contending, on the other hand, that the principle was false in its application to the church; that the Bible was the *constitution* and *charter* of the church, and consequently the silence was prohibition, or, in other words, that all additions to the things in the Bible, if not contrary to any particular command, were contrary to the general command that "nothing be added." So, also, in the United States, when the church, forgetting her exclusive relation to Christ, committed fornication with the civil power, and abdicated her high dignity and

glory as the free woman, voluntarily enslaved herself
to the state. We find the church, on the one hand,
leaving her testimony and prescribing terms of communion not revealed in the Scriptures; and the state,
on the other hand, transcending its sphere and usurping the privileges of the church and of Christ. The
state, and even a party in the state, dictates (virtually
at least) the testimony of the church; and the church
(or its doctors) insist that the state also testify for a
doctrine, which she herself had practically denied, the
royal authority and headship of Christ. How re-
morseless is that unconscious logic which governs men
who have forsaken, or who are ignorant of, a conscious
logic. The church *feels* that there is no great difference
between her and the state, and, therefore, on the one
hand, acts upon the rule, that whatever is not prohibited is lawful; and, on the other hand, insists that the
state shall adopt her lip-service, and confess that Jesus
is the king. She feels that Christ is no more her king
than he is the state's king, and therefore the confession and the legislation ought to be the same in both.
How else can we account for the remarkable fact, that
in the very midst of all the shameful subserviency of
the church to the civil power, and its superserviceable
zeal on behalf of the government in the midst of its
apostasy from true allegiance to Christ, it should insist upon the state amending its constitution, so as to
confess Christ to be a king. True, a like proposition was
made in the Southern church, and in the midst of great
political excitement, when the state loomed out in pro-
portions vast enough to fill nearly the whole field of
vision. But it has been buried effectually, and that,
too, because deemed inconsistent with the Scriptural
doctrine of church and state.

34. This view of the relation of the Scriptures and
of the truth they reveal to church and state respectively, is, we think, clearly taught in John xviii. 36, 37.
Jesus answered, "My kingdom is not of this world; if

my kingdom were of this world, then would my servants fight that I should not be delivered to the Jews; but now is my kingdom not from hence.   Pilate, therefore, said unto him, Art thou a king, then? Jesus answered, Thou sayest that I am a king.   To this end was I born, and for this cause came I into the world, that I should bear witness unto the truth. Every one that is of the truth heareth my voice."   1. Jesus teaches us that his kingdom is not of this world, either as to its origin or its nature.   2. That it is not, therefore, a kingdom of *force*, but of persuasion, founded upon the conviction of the truth.   Its great glory is internal, the possession of the truth; its great external feature is "bearing witness to the truth."   The truth is the means by which this kingdom is established and extended, and the only subjects it recognizes are those who are "of the truth," and all *such* are its subjects.   3. That this opposition between his kingdom and the kingdom of this world (which Pilate represented), should last during the dispensation of the calling of a people out from among the Gentiles.   "*Now* is my kingdom not from hence."   Now, if a commission has been given to civil governments to profess the truth of Christ, how could Christ say that his kingdom differed from the kingdoms of the world in this very respect? The ideas of "the truth" and "the sword" are set over against each other.   A kingdom of force is not a kingdom of truth, and *vice versa*.   This is the very point of the contrast between the two kingdoms, as Christ presents it.   And the question of Pilate, "What is truth?" taken in connection with the following declaration to the Jews, "I find no fault in him," shows that he understood this much, that Christ's kingdom was a totally different thing from that of Cæsar.   He understood the difference better than many Christian kings, and even Christian churches, have understood it in later times.   Bearing witness to the truth, therefore, is the function of Christ's kingdom, not the function of the kingdom of this world. It may do very well for a Saracen to talk of propagating the truth by the sword, but it is a shame for a Christian to think of *force* in connection with the *truth*. Only they who are "born of the truth" and "of the spirit of the truth" can "obey the truth" and "hear the king's voice." The sword has often silenced, but never convinced men.

35. The idea of a Christian nation, which is associated with this amendment of the constitution, is, as has been already suggested, a false and impracticable idea during the present condition of trial, testimony, and conflict. The Jews were a *"peculiar* people" in this respect, and were, therein, a type of the Christian church. The conception of the state which prophecy generally gives us is that of an organism operating by brute force, and it is generally represented in an attitude of opposition to the church of Christ. Hence we find those civil governments which have undertaken to "bear witness to the truth" have usually denied the truth and persecuted its professors. And even where civil governments make no such pretensions, their policy, both domestic and foreign, demonstrates that they are "of the earth, earthy," "kingdoms of this world," and not of the Lord and of his Christ. We must wait for the sounding of the seventh trumpet, in order to see a Christian nation or a Christian government. Till then civil government will be, in the main, what Hobbes, its worshipper, represents it, a leviathan.

36. It may not be amiss to add a word or two more upon the use which may be legitimately made of the Scriptures by the state. 1. In the *first* place, the light of nature and reason, which is the guide of the state, is made clear by the revealed will of God. The true statesman will seek light from every possible quarter. As he will enlarge his views by the study of the political writings of Plato, Aristotle and Cicero, and by the study of the great historians of Greece and Rome, as well as those of modern states, so he will not neglect

the laws of Moses, nor the striking biblical histories in which the operation of those laws is exemplified. And upon many points of civil regulation he will find that the Bible sustains the conclusions of reason and experience. For example, in respect to the justice and expediency of capital punishment for the crime of murder, the Bible not only gives its sanction to this penalty, but makes it the duty of the civil magistrate, as the sword-bearer, to inflict it. It represents the land in which murder is not thus punished, as " polluted with blood," and thereby provoking the judgment of heaven. So also as to the lawfulness of war, and of the profession of a soldier. The sword-bearer is bound to wage defensive war; to punish the invader, and to protect the lives and property of the people, upon the same principle upon which he punishes the individual murderer. According to the light of nature, interpreted by the Scriptures, the Quaker theory of war is not merely a sickly sentimentalism, but a rebellion against the organized law of society and government. The law of marriage is another example. The Bible gives us, in the account of the creation of man, as male and female (one man and one woman, the one sex as the complement of the other), the true idea which should govern all civil legislation concerning this relation. It shows the inexpediency of polygamy. In assuming, further, a community of life between the husband and the wife, it makes the promiscuous intercourse of the sexes a *monstrous* crime against nature, and so confirms a physiological law, which has been established by observation and experience. It settles, also, the question of independent, marital rights.

37. In the *second* place, the Bible rectifies the teachings of the light of nature. In the case of a weekly rest, for example, it teaches that such a rest, like the institution of marriage, belongs to man as man, was ordained before his fall, and is necessary to his well being. Reason and experience have amply demon-

13

strated the same truth, that the " Sabbath was made
for man"; but it is doubtful whether the fact would
have been recognized by the light of nature alone; and
Christian governments, so-called, habitually violate
reason and experience in their legislation concerning a
weekly rest. The French, at the close of the last century, abolished it altogether, and with what results all
the world knows.

38. In the *third* place, every man who has received
this revelation is bound to accept it as a revelation
from God, and to regulate his faith and practice by its
authority, either in a positive or negative way. Touching the whole matter of the method of salvation, the
whole question as to what is necessary to be believed
or done, and *all* that is necessary to be believed or
done, in order to salvation and eternal life, the Scriptures are a full, complete and *positive* guide. Touching the life that now is, the conditions necessary to
sustain the being or promote the well-being of society,
agriculture, commerce, manufactures, civil and criminal laws, the man, if he be a civil magistrate, or whatever else, is to be governed by the negative authority
of the Bible. He can do anything which the Bible
does not *forbid*.

39. It may be said that this cannot be the theory
received by the church and people of this country before the war; for it had become the settled policy of
the Federal government to have chaplains of Congress
and chaplains of the army and navy, and of the army
and navy schools; and of the State governments, as
well as the Federal, to recognize the Sabbath as the
law of the land; to prescribe the reading of the Bible
in the public schools, etc. We answer: 1. In reference to the chaplains, that the government was bound
to provide religious ordinances for those whom its service prevented from procuring them for themselves,
but the choice of religious teachers ought to have been
left to the men who were to be placed under their in-

struction; and, in respect to the chaplains of Congress, the compensation ought to be paid by the members themselves, not out of the government treasury; or, in other words, they ought to act as men or citizens, not as legislators—in like manner as the President of the United States, or a Governor of a State, can *invite* the people to observe a day of prayer or thanksgiving, only as a distinguished citizen. If the chief magistrate should issue a proclamation of this sort, as of authority, without the action of the legislative department of the government, he would be guilty of usurping the powers of that department; and if the legislative and executive departments together should *ordain* such a day, both would be guilty of usurping the powers of the church. 2. In regard to the use of the Bible in the public schools, the state has no power to ordain anything about the Bible in the public schools, either in the way of prescribing or proscribing its use as the word of God. It might ordain the use of the English Bible as a classic of the English language, but, in my judgment, it would not be expedient to do so. The public schools are not designed to teach revealed religion, but the branches of secular learning. The teaching of religion must be left to the family and the church. 3. In regard to the Sabbath, we have already alluded to one ground upon which it is recognized in civil law.* It may be added, that the state has no right to violate liberty of conscience; and by disregarding the Sabbath as it does in some of its laws (in the post-office department, for example), it *does* violate the liberty of conscience by excluding from offices those who regard the Sabbath as a rest divinely ordained. On the other hand, it is absurd to contend, as Jews and infidels contend, that their rights are violated by the state's prohibiting buying and selling on the Sabbath, unless they take the position that the state has no right to put any restriction whatever upon trade. If they take this po-

---

* See *Southern Presb. Review* for Jan. 1880, pp. 101 ff.

sition, they make civil government an impossibility. Illustrate the relation of church and state further by reference to the provision contained in the constitution of some of the States, forbidding ministers to be chosen to certain civil offices.

40. One more question of great importance, as recent events have shown it to be, demands a brief notice. The respective jurisdictions of church and state seem to meet in the idea of *duty*. In many things, in the majority of things, this is the occasion of no difficulty. The church enjoins duty as obedience to God, and the state enforces it as the safeguard of social order. But there can be no collision unless the one or the other blunders as to the things that are *materially* right. When the state makes wicked laws, contradicting the eternal principles of rectitude, the church is at liberty to testify against them, and humbly to petition that they may be repealed. In like manner, if the church becomes seditious and a disturber of the peace, the state has the right to abate the nuisance. In ordinary cases, however, there is not likely to be a collision. The only serious danger is where moral duty is conditioned upon a political question.* Under the pretext of inculcating duty, the church may usurp the power to determine the question which conditions it, and that is precisely what she is debarred from doing. The condition must be given. She must accept it from the state, and then her own course is clear. If Cæsar is your master, then pay tribute to him; but whether the "if" holds, whether Cæsar is your master or not, whether he ever had any just authority, whether he now retains it, or has forfeited it, these are points which the church has no commission to adjudicate. (Letter of Assembly of 1861 to the churches throughout the world.) This was the view also of Dr. Hodge and others who protested against the "Spring Resolutions"

---

* On the tactics of Erastians and Ultramontanists as to these *mixed* questions, see *Cunningham's Church Principles*, page 152.

adopted by the Northern Assembly of 1861. They say: "We deny the *right* of the General Assembly to decide the political question, to what government the allegiance of Presbyterians, as citizens, is due, and its right to make that decision a condition of membership in our church." . . . "The General Assembly in this decided a political question, and in making that decision practically a condition of membership in the church has, in our judgment, violated the constitution of the church, and *usurped the prerogative of its* divine Master." (See the paper quoted in Bullock's address, page 10.) The Synod of Kentucky of the same year, under the lead of Dr. R. J. Breckinridge and Dr. Humphrey, adopted a similar testimony against the action of the Assembly. In this they followed the example of the Master, who, though head over all things to the church, refused to decide the question of civil allegiance, or to exercise any other secular function. In this they followed the example of the church for many generations, which recognized no political questions, as questions of allegiance to this or that emperor. It was only after the establishment of the Christian religion under Constantine, that church questions became complicated with questions of allegiance and of support to this or that government.

41. It is a question, as the protestants of the Assembly of 1861 (Northern) say, about which Christians may honestly differ. In this country it is a question about the interpretation of the constitution. The Federalist ministers of the North, before the war, often exchanged views with States-rights ministers of the North and South upon this question, and no one of them thought of denouncing the States-rights theory, either as a *heresy* or as an *immorality;* nay, not a few of them, who are now foremost in denouncing us as rebels, unworthy to sit with them at the Lord's table, asserted and defended the right of the South to seek redress against the tyranny of a majority, and one of them went so far as to defend the right of the South

to make war for her own protection. (See Breckinridge in *Presbyterial Critic* for July, 1855.) Surely it is an astounding spectacle to see this church fall so suddenly, headlong, down from the very battlements of heaven into the boiling abyss of partisan political passion, hatred, and excess. A solemn warning to us all to "watch and pray, lest we enter into temptation."

42. The foregoing views of the relations of church and state, of the indispensable necessity of each moving in its own orbit and attending to its own concerns, have been fully vindicated by the history of this country. The church in the North became corrupt; the glory of Christ was sacrificed to the interests of Cæsar; the lovely fruits of charity perished in the storm of political prejudice and passion; the unclean spirit of the world took possession of the temple of the Holy Ghost, and the church, instead of being a sequestered and quiet retreat for the heart weary of strife and turmoil, became itself the scene of strife and turmoil. As its great type, the nation of Israel, dwelt in peace, while the surrounding nations were convulsed, so long as Israel was true to its vocation as a peculiar people and separate from the nations, but became subject to the dangers and calamities of those nations, even in a higher degree, when it formed entangling alliances with them, so also the church in this land, by renouncing her dignity and safety as an organism entirely separate from the state, became subject to the miseries of her ally. Better, a thousand times better, would it be for her to be wasted by the fire and sword of the beast, than to ride upon it and be carried hither and thither by it, or, in other wards, to renounce her allegiance to her royal spouse and become a harlot.

XIV.

OTHER THEORIES OF CHURCH AND STATE.

1st, That of *alliance*. The great expounder of this theory is Bishop Warburton (in his treatise entitled

Alliance between Church and State. It is briefly as
follows (see *Southern Presbyterian Review*, Vol. III., p.
214, October, 1849): "Church and state are originally
both independent and sovereign societies, having different ends in view, and hence not clashing, although
the same persons may be under the jurisdiction of
both. The office of the state is to provide for the *temporal* interests of man. That of the church, for his
eternal interests. The care of the one is confined to
the *body*, that of the other is directed to the *soul*. The
one looks upon offences as *crimes*, the other takes cog-
nizance of them as *vices* and as *sins*. Now, as civil
society can only restrain from open transgression, nor
always from this without opening the way to crimes
still more flagitious; as it cannot enforce the duties of
imperfect obligation; and further, often inflames the
appetites it proposes to correct; and as religion, having the sanction of rewards (while civil government
has only that of punishment), exactly supplies these
defects; so the church becomes necessary as a complement to the state. The state, therefore, proposes
to the church a union for their mutual benefit, and
this union is called an 'alliance,' to indicate the original sovereignty of the parties. By this alliance the
state pledges itself to endow, protect, and extend the
church, and the church to lend her whole influence to
the state. The reciprocal concessions are, that the
church resigns her supremacy by constituting the civil
ruler her supreme head, and by submitting her laws to
the state's approval; and the state, in compensation,
gives to the church a coäctive power for the reformation of manners, and secures her a seat and representation in the national council. By this alliance the
civil magistrate gets additional reverence, and the
church a power which does not belong to her."

In reference to this theory it is sufficient to say: 1st,
That the church has no "sovereignty," and, therefore,
could form no such "alliance." 2nd, That while it is
true that she supplies the deficiencies of civil govern-

ment, it is also true that she does this most effectually when she is untrammelled and uncorrupted by any such *mesalliance,* as all history shows. 3rd, That the "coërcive" power she gets from the state is a power which does not belong to her, a power which tends to destroy that moral and spiritual power which does belong to her, and to nullify her vocation as a witness for the truth. She must be like her Master (John xviii. 36, 37). 4th, The theory is inconsistent with itself. The church and state are represented as sovereign and independent, having each a life, a sphere, an aim, etc., etc., of its own; and yet the alliance is made necessary to the life of both.

II. *The Church of Scotland Theory.*—The most illustrious defender of this theory is Dr. Chalmers, in his *Lectures on the Establishment and Extension of National Churches.* This is, in sum, that the church has a right to a "legal provision for the expenses of its ministrations." The church does not, however, resign any portion of her independence. She receives from the state the maintenance of her clergy, and the clergy in return give to the subjects of the state a Christian education; but they may and do reserve to themselves the whole power and privilege of determining what that education shall be. For their food and raiment, and their sacred, or even their private edifices, they may be indebted to the state; but their creed, discipline, ritual, articles of faith, formularias, whether of doctrine or devotion," etc., etc.

Answer: (1), Such an establishment is as purely utopian as Plato's republic. (2), The history of the church of Scotland refutes it all. (3), No state will, or ought to, support a church without holding the church accountable for the mode in which the funds are expended. If the state pays for "education," she has a right to say what sort of education she is willing to pay for, and to enquire whether she is getting it. (4), Then the civil magistrate must be the judge as to matters of faith, which is the principle of all the persecutions which have cursed the earth, and of which the kingdom of Scotland has had its full share. (5), The spirituality of the church impaired. Moderatism in the kirk of Scotland.

III. *Gladstone's Theory.*—(*The State in its Relation with the Church*, by W. E. Gladstone, Esq., M. P. See also Macaulay's review of this work in his *Miscellanies*.) The theory, in sum, is the same as that of Vattel and other old civilians, that civil government is instituted for the highest good of the whole in every concern, and is bound to do all in its power for this end in every department; that a commonwealth is a *moral person*, having judgment, responsibility, etc., etc. (compare *Theory of Territorial Jurisdiction*, page 162, below), and is, therefore, bound as a corporate person to recognize and obey the true religion. Hence the state, as a state, must have its religion. It must profess this religion by state acts. It must have a religious test for office, because otherwise the religious character of the state would be lost; and it must use its state power to propagate this state religion. Macaulay's review showing that, upon these principles of Mr. Gladstone, every army, bank, railroad corporation, would be bound to have its own religion, the author, it is said, in his second edition modified his statement so as to make moral personality, etc., etc., the attributes only of those associations which have these three characteristics, viz.: (1), That they are of divine institution; (2), That they are perpetual; (3), That they are universal, that is, embracing everybody. These marks are found in two natural associations of men, as well as in the supernatural society of the church, the family and the state. Now, as all admit that the family must have a religion, so also must the state, for the same reasons.

The simple answer to all this is: (1), That it makes the state $\tau o \ \pi a \nu$, in the moral world, and it absorbs all other relations, both of the family and the church; a Lacedæmonian theory of the state, and an Erastian annihilation of the church. (2), It contradicts plain definitions of the several spheres of the church, state, and family, as laid down in the Scriptures. (3), It is the parent of tyranny in the state, of formalism and hypocrisy in the church.

IV. *Dr. Arnold's Theory.*—(*The Principles of Church Reform, The State and the Church,* with other Essays, by Thomas Arnold.) This theory is expressed in the following extract (see *Southern Presbyterian Review,* Vol. III. p. 227): "Where a state chooses for itself the true religion, it declares itself Christian. But by so doing it becomes a part of Christ's holy catholic church, not allied with it, which implies distinctness from it, but transformed into it. But as for the particular portion of this church which may have existed before within the limits of the state's sovereignty, the actual society of Christian men there subsisting, the state does not ally itself with such a society, for alliance supposes two parties equally sovereign; nor yet does it become the church as to its outward form and organization; neither does the church, on the other hand, become so lost in the state as to become, in the offensive sense of the term, secularized. The spirit of the church is transfused into a more perfect body, and and its former organization dies away. The form is that of the state, the spirit is that of the church; what was the kingdom of the world has become a kingdom of Christ, a portion of the church in the high and spiritual sense of the term; but in that sense in which church denotes the outward and social organization of Christians in any one particular place, it is no longer a Christian church, but what is far better and brighter, a Christian kingdom." Same thing, substantially, as that of the rationalists. (See Hertzog's *Encyclopædia sub voc.* "Church.") The answer to all this is contained in the last sentence, that the church ceases to exist

altogether.   It is Erastianism in its boldest and
extremest form.   The same theory really with that
of Hobbes, only Dr. Arnold's leviathan is a pious
beast.

V. *The Popish Theory.—(Ultramontane).*—The different stages of its development may be seen in the
claims of Hildebrand (1073–1085), Innocent III. (1198
–1216), Boniface VIII. (1294–1303).   The doctrine, in
brief, is that the pope is vicar of Christ; and as Christ
is the head of the church and head of all things
besides, for the sake of his church, so the pope is the
visible head of the church on earth, and all civil powers are subject to his direction and power whenever the interests of the church require it, of which the
pope, and not the civil power, is the judge.   The
claim, in its extremest form, is contained in the *Bull*
"*clericis laicos,*" and in the message of Boniface VIII.
to Philip the Fair, King of France (1296) *Scire te volu-
mus quod in spiritualibus, et temporalibus nobis subes.
Alind credentes, hæreticos reputamus.*   And a sufficient
answer to the claim is contained in the reply of Philip:
*Sciat maxina tua fatuitas, in temporalibus nos alicui
non subesse.   Secus credentes futuos et dementes reputamus.*   (See Kurtz's *Church History*, Sect. 140–'1.)   It
must be acknowledged, however, that as between *Ultramontanism* and *Gallicanism*, the former has the best
of the argument from papal premises, accepted by
both.   (See Thornwell on the *Apocrypha, Collected
Writings*, Vol. III., pp. 540 ff., for a full discussion
and refutation of this abominable theory.   (See also,
for some concessions in regard to the effect of such
claims upon the causes of civil freedom, p. 44 of the
memoir of Dr. Muller, prefixed to Robertson's translation of his *Symbolic.*)   The legitimate fruits of this
Ultramontanism are seen in the Albigensian Crusades
and the Inquisition.   No surer evidence is needed to
prove that the liar-murderer was the author of the
theory.   (See Gillespie's *Assertion of the Government*

of the Church of Scotland, Part II., Ch. I. See on the
Gallican Liberties, Gregorie—French papal bishop—
Les Liberties de l'Eglise Gallicane. *)

XV.

SUBJECT OF CHURCH POWER.—*Materia in qua.*

See *Confession of Faith*, Chap. XXX. Sec. 1. All
church power (of which Christ, the head, is, as we
have seen, the only source) is in *secundo actu*, in the
officers; in *primo actu*, in the whole body. The life
of the church is one; officers are but the organs through
which it is manifested, in acts of jurisdiction and instruction; and the acts of all officers, in consequence of
this organic relation, are the acts of the church. They
are the *principium quo;* she is the *principium quod.*
The power resides in her; it is exercised by them.
Ministers are her mouth as elders are her hands.
Both equally represent her, and both are nothing, except as they represent her. All lawful acts of all lawful officers, are acts of the church, and they who hear

---

* By way of *addendum* attention may be called to the three theories held in the Lutheran Church:

1. The "Episcopal system," originated by Constantine the Great, in
which the chief magistrate is head of the church (*circa sacra*), in virtue of his being the *præcipuum membrum ecclesiæ*, in Constantine's case
as *Pontifex Maximus.*

2. The system of "territorial jurisdiction" (*cujus regio, ejus religio*)
according to which the chief magistrate is regarded as the head of the
church, not as its chief member, but as the "father of his people," and
bound to look after all their interests. (Compare Vattel and Puffen-
dorf, and Gladstone, as above.)

3. The "collegiate system," according to which the three estates,
which constitute the *Ecclesia synthetica,* (to wit: "Economic," "political," and "ecclesiastical") are all represented, differs from the first
(the Episcopal system) in that it gives much greater prominence to the
people (*status economicus*), while the "Episcopal" does not go behind
the ministers (the *stat. ecclesiasticus*). It made the power to reside in
all the three estates, but primarily, in the *status economicus*, which
could transfer its authority to the civil ruler. It was called the "collegiate" system, because it made the "*jura in sacris*" (doctrine, worship, appointment to ministry, etc. *Jura collegialia* (collective rights).
See Kurtz's *Church History*, Vol. II. pp. 246-'7. Hase's *Dogmatic Evan-
gel.* (Protestant), p. 438, and Quenstedt, as quoted there.

the preacher or the presbytery, hear the church. The case is analogous to the motions of the human body. Vital power is not in the hands or the feet, it is in the whole body. But the exercise of that power in walking, or in writing, is confined to particular organs. The power is one, but its functions are manifold, and it has an organ appropriate to every function. This makes it an organic whole. So the church has functions; these functions require appropriate organs; these organs are created by Christ, and the church becomes an organic whole. (*Thornwell's Writings*, IV. pp. 272-'3.) This theory is opposed to the popish and prelatic assumption, that the power resides in the clergy, and is transmitted in a certain line of succession. The history of the very terms "clergy and laity" is the history of the growth of this grievous error in regard to the subject of church power. The terms are derived from two Greek words, κλῆρος, lot or inheritance, and λαος, people. When it became fashionable for the pastors of the church to widen the distance between their own order and the condition of their Christian brethren, the Christian commonwealth was by them divided into clergy and laity; the former term was appropriated to themselves as selected and contradistinguished from the multitude, as being in the present world by way of eminence, God's *peculium* or special inheritance. (See Campbell's Lect. on Eccle. History, 9, p. 151.) This usage was derived, as was pretended, from the Old Testament, in which the tribe of Levi was called the inheritance of the Lord. But it so happens that the tribe of Levi is never called the inheritence of the Lord, as distinguished from the people, but only as a part included in the whole.—Moses, himself a Levite, says in an address to God (Deut. ix. 29), "They (*i. e.* the whole nation), are thy people (λαος), and thine inheritance (κλῆρος)." In the LXX. version of this passage, the same persons are in the same sentence declared to be both λ and κ. In

14

the New Testament the term *κ* is applied to persons but in one passage (1 Pet. v. 3), and in that the term is applied not to the shepherds but to the flock, in opposition to the pastors. The Lord is said to be the inheritance of Levi (because that tribe had no landed possessions, but lived by the temple), but not *vice versa*. Strange the confusion about so simple a matter. Clemens Romanus, indeed, uses the term "*λαικοι*" to distinguish the mass of the Jews from the Levites (including the priests);* and on this account, the use of the terms "clergy and laity" is thought to be as old as his day. But, as Dr. Campbell observes (*loc. sup. cit.*), he is speaking of the *Jewish priesthood*, not of the *Christian ministry;* and he does not use it in opposition to any one general term, such as *clericoi*, but, after mentioning three different orders, he uses the term *laicoi*, to include under one comprehensive name all that were not specially comprised under any of the former—corresponding to the application sometimes made of the Latin word *popularis* (*e. g.* a citizen, one that is not a *soldier*). In this view it might be contrasted with men in office of any kind whatever; thus, in civil government, with "rulers," to distinguish the people from the magistrate; in an army with "generals," the soldiers from the commander. In this sense like *idiotes*. (See *Horsley's Tracts against Priestly; Alexander on Acts* iv. 13.) Even in its application to the Levitical economy, Clemens (as Dr. C. maintains) does not use it so as to imply that it was in itself exclusive of the priesthood and of the tribe of Levi. They are indeed excluded, because separately named, but not from the import of the word. Take an example from the New Testament (Acts xv. 22): "Apostles and elders with the whole church." Here are three orders plainly mentioned and distinguished (compare the phrase, "the law, the prophets and the scriptures"; see Alexander's Isaiah, p. xix.), the apostles or extraordinary ministers,

---

* Clement's words are "The High Priest, the Priests, the Levites and the laics."

the elders or fixed pastors, and the church or Christian people.* But does this imply that the name *church* does not properly comprehend the pastors as well as people? By no means. They are not, indeed, in this passage comprised under the term, not because it does not extend so far (which is not the fact), but because they are separately named. The import of the expression is no more than this : the apostles and elders, with all the Christian brethren who come not under either of these denominations. So also 1 Pet. v., the presbyters are opposed to the *cleroi*, not as though the former constituted no part of God's heritage or clergy ; they only do not constitute that part of which they are here commanded to take the charge. So Clement's *laicoi* is " all the Jewish people."

I have said that the history of these words is the history of the grievous error of popery and prelacy, which lodges church power in the ministry or clergy. The distinction of clergy and laity took its rise in the church about the same time with the rise of the doctrine of a sacerdotal character in the ministry. Churches became temples, ministers, priests, and worship, sacrifice. Now, under the law, the priesthood was a separate caste, the succession depending not upon election by the people, but upon birth ; and so also with the Levitical ministry in general. It was all a matter of birth. Consequently, although the whole nation of the Jews was called a " kingdom of priests," in a figurative sense, yet the power of the priesthood was not in the people, but in the family of Aaron alone. Hence the terrible judgment upon Korah and his followers. When, therefore, the sacerdotal theory of the ministry began to prevail, and the Levitical priesthood was considered the type of the Christian ministry, it was inevitable that the ministry should become a *caste*, and the people become a flock of sheep only to be fleeced.

---

* This is the division found in the Hebrew Scriptures, in Josephus and Philo. and alluded to in Luke xxiv. 44, where the "Psalms" are mentioned as representing the Hagiographa (or Scriptures.)

Hence the privileges of the people began to be abridged, in the matter of electing their own church officers, until the settled doctrine of the church of Rome was thus expressed in the words of Bellarmine (See *Clericis*, Chap. vii., cited by Cunningham; see *Thornwell's Writings*, IV. p. 271): "The election of pastors pertains to the government of the church. The people, therefore, ought not to elect their pastors." So long as they had the power of election it might appear as if the people was the body in which the vital force resided, and that the officers were merely the mouth, or hands, or feet.

The same leaven of prelacy is manifested in the use of the terms "clergy and laity" by some in our own church. (See *Thornwell's Writings*, IV. p. 277.) Important, therefore, to point out in what sense these terms may be used in harmony with the doctrine that all church power is, as to its *being*, in the whole church. (See *Thornwell's Writings, ut supra.*) Clergy and laity are terms which in the New Testament are indiscriminately applied to all the *people* of God. About this there can be no question. In the New Testament sense, therefore, every minister is a layman and every layman is a clergyman. In the common Protestant sense, the origin of which it is useless to trace (it is given above from Campbell), the terms express the distinction between the office-bearers of the church and the people in their private capacity. A clergyman is a man clothed with the office of a Presbyter. Now, an office in a free government is not a *rank* or a *caste*. It is not an estate of the realm. It is simply a public trust. A man, therefore, does not cease to belong to the people by being chosen to office. The president of the United States is still one of the people. The representatives in Congress are still among the people. Our judges and senators are still a part of the people. Office makes a distinction in relations—the distinction between a private and a public man, but makes no distinction in person or in rank. Office-bearers are not an order in the legal sense.* * * To convey the idea that the distinctions induced by ordination are official, and not personal, our standards have studiously avoided the word clergy, which had been so much abused in the papacy, and substituted the more correct expressions, offices and office-bearers. See Acts xx. 28, where bishops are said to be *"in* the flock" † (a part of the flock), not over it, as in our version. Power, then, is *in primo actu*, in the church as a body, an organic whole; the people and the rulers are the organ of election. The officers elected are the organs by which the functions of teaching, government, and distribution of revenues are exercised. And as the organs are, in a truer sense, given to the body than the body to the organs, so it is more proper to say that the ministry is given to the church than the church to the ministry. The former is Paul's mode of stating the case (Eph. iv. Cor. xii., Rom. xii.); the latter is the mode of the prelatists.

II. Power *in actu secundo*, or as to its exercise, is in the officers of the church. This is opposed to the Congregational theory of church power, which makes it to reside in the people, both in *actu primo* and in *actu secundo*. When I say the Congregational theory, I do not mean that it was the accepted theory of the English Independents as a body, for John Owen held the true doctrine upon this point, as you may see by referring to his *True Nature of a Gospel Church*. So far as a particular church is concerned, he was a Presbyterian; but he was an Independent in denying that the church visible was one in any such sense as to warrant classical, synodical, or general assemblies. The Congregational theory to which I refer was defended by John Robinson, a portion of whose congregation

---

*Compare the terms, "*ordo* and *plebs*"—which are very different from clergy and laity.

† Revised New Testament.

in Holland constituted the colony of the Mayflower in
1620. He was opposed, and his theory refuted, by
the famous Samuel Rutherford, in a treatise entitled
The Due Right of Presbyteries, etc., London, 1644.
The theory is called by Rutherford, "The way of our
New England brethren," and we may call it, therefore,
the "New England Congregational theory." It is
briefly this: that all power resides in church-members,
in the brotherhood, and that they delegate this power
to those whom they elect to bear office; these office-
bearers being deputies or proxies of the people, and
doing only in the matter of government what the people themselves might of right do; or, as it is given by
Rutherford (I suppose from Robinson): "The church
which Christ, in his gospel, hath instituted, and to
which he hath committed the keys of his kingdom;
the power of binding and loosing the tables and seals
of the covenant; the offices and censures of his church;
the administration of all his public worship and ordinances, is a company of believers meeting in one place
every Lord's day for the administration of the holy
ordinances of God to public edification." (*Right of
Presbyteries*, ch. 1, sec. 1, prop. 1.) In answer to this,
Rutherford contends that "the keys," the power of
binding and loosing, are not given to a company of
believers, considered as an unorganized assembly, but
to the organized church, an assembly under officers of
their own choice; and that this organized body is the
"subject" of ecclesiastical power in *actu primo*, and
that the presbyters are the "subject" of the power of
government in *actu secundo*, or, as our *Confession of
Faith* (xxx. 1) expresses it, the Lord Jesus is king and
head of his church, and hath therein *appointed a government in the hands of church officers*, distinct from
the civil magistrate. The rulers of the church, therefore, although the representatives of the people, are
not their deputies or proxies; are not responsible to
them, though elected by them; but are responsible to

Jesus Christ, who has ordained the constitution of the church, created these offices, and defined their functions. The difference between the Presbyterian and the New England Congregational theories may be illustrated by the difference between the true theory of our civil constitution and the false, though popular, theory of it. Our civil government is a representative republic. The source of all political power is the people, who ordain and establish a constitution, a fundamental law, by which the exercise of the various departments of government is given to certain officers or bodies of officers, legislative, judicial, and executive, chosen or appointed in a certain way prescribed by the people in the constitution. Now, all these officers, whether in this department or in that, whether acting singly or jointly, represent the people, because they were chosen by the people, directly or indirectly. But they are, when chosen or appointed in a constitutional manner, not responsible to the people (that is, in the sense of "constituents" or "electors"), but to the law. The representatives in the legislature, and the executive, and all other officers chosen by the popular vote, are responsible, not to their constituents, but to the constitution—"that is to say, not to the people who elected them, but to the people (sovereign) whose will is expressed in the constitution." So that, as Burke said to the electors of Bristol he had done, the representative is often compelled to maintain the *interests* of his constituents against their *wishes*. (Thornwell, Vol. IV., page 100.)

The popular theory, on the other hand, is that the will of the people, through the ballot-box, is the law; that is, that our government is a democracy like that of ancient Greece, with this difference, that while in the old democracies the people assembled *en masse*, in ours they assemble by proxies or deputies. So in the church, Presbyterians hold that the rulers are representatives, deriving their authority, when once chosen

to office by the people, not from the people, but from
Jesus Christ, who ordained and established the constitution; that the people have no share in the government, but only the right of choosing their governors;
while the New England theory is that the people govern themselves, are themselves rulers, either *en masse*,
or by proxies or deputies. The error upon which the
New England theory is founded is that contained in
the sentence already quoted from Bellarmine, that the
election of pastors is a function pertaining to the government of the church. Bellarmine, as we have seen,
draws from this principle the conclusion that the people have no right to elect their pastors. The Independents in the Westminster Assembly, on the other
hand, accepting the principle, drew the conclusion that
the people have *some* share in the government of the
church, and consequently that the Presbyterian doctrine, which excludes them altogether from government, must be false. The true way of meeting both
extremes, papists and Independents, is by denying the
principle and asserting with Ames, in his answer to
Bellarmine, "*Electio quamvis*," etc. "Although election pertains to the constituting of government, it is,
nevertheless, not an act of government." Dr. Hodge
holds the same erroneous view, laying it down among
the fundamental principles of Presbyterianism that
the people "have a right to a substantive part in the
government of the church." (See *Discourse on Presbyterianism*, published by the Board of Publication,
Princeton Review, July number, page 547; *Thornwell*,
Vol. IV. p. 274–'5 ff.) Hence he makes the ruling elder
a mere expedient by which the people appear in church
courts; and the people appear, not as the church, considered as a whole, but as a separate class or party,
opposed to the clergy; hence, again, the ruling elder is
not a representative, but a deputy, a mere factor of the
people. (*Thornwell, ut sup.*) More will be said on
this subject when we come to consider the meaning of

the term presbyter as an official designation, and the nature of Presbyterian government as representative.

XVI.

OFFICERS OF THE CHURCH.

I. Officers in the apostolic church were of two kinds, extraordinary and ordinary. See Eph. iv. 11; 1 Cor. xii. 28, and compare, for the grounds upon which the extraordinary are defined to be temporary, 1 Cor. xiii. 10, etc., with Warburton's exposition of the passage in his "*Doctrine of Grace.*" We shall consider the ordinary officers first, as those in which we have a practical concern in the administration of the affairs of the church. (See *Form of Government.*)

1. Bishops, or pastors, and elders. I put these together because they are all designated in the New Testament by a common term, *presbyters.* Our church derives its name from *presbytery*, the government being lodged in the hands of courts consisting of presbyters. See the definition of Presbyterianism on page 194 *et seq.* Our book uses the terms in the popular acceptation "bishops or pastors," denoting the presbyters who "labor in the word and doctrine;" "ruling elders" denoting the presbyters who rule only. In the New Testament all these terms are used interchangeably. Take one example in which they all occur (or their equivalents) Acts xx. 17–28: "Take heed therefore unto yourselves, and to all the flock, over the which the Holy Ghost hath made you ("presbyters" vs. 17) overseers (episcopos), to feed (perform the office of a *shepherd* or *pastor*) the church of God," etc. "Presbyter" is the title of honor or respect, "bishop" the name designating the function, "pastor" the poetical name, and expressive chiefly of affection.

There are three leading opinions as to the use of the term "presbyter" in the New Testament. *First,* That it denotes an officer inferior in order to the "bishop," and differing in function. *Second*, That it denotes a preacher of the word, and cannot be applied to a ruling elder. *Third*, That it means a chosen ruler, and that, while it is used to denote pastors or ministers of the word, it is not so used because pastors are ministers of the word, but because they are rulers; the shepherd having two staves, the one Beauty, the other Bands (Zech. xi. 17), he is called presbyter on account of his staff Bands, his power of rule, and not on account of his staff Beauty, his power of teaching. The first of these opinions is that of the prelatists, the second is that of the Congregationalists generally, and of some leading men in our own church (Hodge, Smythe of Charleston, etc.), the third is that of our standards and of the strict constructionists, or *jure divino* men, in our own church. Instead of considering each of these opinions separately, I shall establish the last as the true view of the term, and in so doing of course the other two will be overthrown. See a very clear, full, neat presentation of the evidence from our book and from Scripture on this point. Read *Thornwell's Collected Writings*, Vol. IV. pp. 104–114: " That presbyter as a title of office, etc." See *Owen's True Nature of Gospel Church*, Ch. 7, (works) Vol. XX. pp. 472, *et ff.; Rutherford's Due Right of Presbyteries*, pp. 141, etc.; *Miller on Ruling Elders.*

The classic place of the New Testament in proof that the term presbyter is not descriptive of a preacher as such, is 1 Timothy v. 17. The obvious meaning of these words, that which would suggest itself to any unbiased reader, is, that there are two sorts of presbyters, one sort ruling only, the other laboring in the word and doctrine, as well as ruling. The term "presbyter," therefore, is applied to an officer in the Christian church who does not " labor in the word and doctrine;" and if so, the word cannot designate the function of preaching, and cannot be applied to preachers only. When applied to a preacher it must be on account of some function other than preaching, which he performs, and this function is explained to be that of ruling. The general sense of the term, therefore, is a ruler. It follows from this statement : 1. That it is a false induction to collect together a bundle of passages in which presbyters are mentioned, who were unquestionably preachers, and then, without pausing to inquire whether there may not be "negative instances" (as Bacon calls them), or whether the real ground has been discovered of the application of the term, to lay it down as an axiom that the scriptural presbyter is a minister of the word. " The negative instance is the most powerful." Compare reasoning of Baptists about *baptizo*.

To produce a thousand texts in which the words presbyter and preacher appeared to be interchangeable would signify nothing, if a single case could be alleged in which they were evidently of different import. In such a contingency, the dictate of sound philosophy and sober criticism would be to inquire whether there were not some property common to both terms, in consequence of which the affirmative and negative instances might be fairly harmonized. A definition should be sought embracing the points in which those who were and those who were not preachers agreed.

This definition would include all that is essential to the meaning of the title, and would set forth the precise ground on which it is attributed to either class. Now this common property, the essence of the presbyterate, is given in the passage in Timothy. It is the function of ruling. To affirm in the face of this scripture that all elders are teachers, is no less absurd than to affirm, in the face of experience, that all that are mortal are men. There are only two other interpretations, so far as I know, deserving of notice : 1, Vitringa's (*De Syn. Vet.*), that *all* presbyters were ordained to preach as well as rule ; but that, in fact, they did not all preach. 2, That the emphasis is on the word

κοπ (laboring to *weariness*.) According to this interpretation ministers are represented as worthy of
"double honor" who do not labor "to weariness."
According to Vitringa's, men are ordained to do that
which they are not expected to do.

2. It follows that the objection which is taken from
the use of the word *deacon* has no force. The objection is thus stated: "As the Greek word for *deacon* is
used in a general sense for all church officers, and yet
is the specific title of one particular class of officers; so
the word presbyter may be taken in a wide sense, including even apostles, and is yet the definite title of
ordinary ministers of the word, and is never applied in
its specific sense and without qualification to any who
are not ministers;" *i. e.*, presbyter, from being a generic term, susceptible originally of a larger extension,
became eventually the definite title of a particular
class. It is a universal law of classification, that what
logicians call the whole comprehension of the *genus*, or
every idea which enters into a just definition of the
name of a class, must be found in *all* the species which
are included under it. This is the only ground on
which the *genus* can be predicated of the subordinate
classes. Hence, if the word presbyter is generic, and
in its full comprehension capable of being affirmed of
other classes of men, besides ministers of the gospel,
the idea of preaching cannot enter as an element into
a definition of the *genus*. The specific differences
which distinguish the various classes under a common
name, cannot be included in the definition of that name.
If preachers, accordingly, constitute a species of the
genus presbyter, and some who are not preachers constitute another, it is intuitively obvious that the comprehension of the generic term excludes the property
of preaching. The specific difference of the classes
consists in the possession in the one case and the absence in the other, of lawful authority to preach.
Hence the authority to preach could not be the ground

of the term presbyter being applied to preachers in a restricted sense (even if such restricted sense existed), but some property belonging to the comprehension of the *genus*. And this, for all that appears to the contrary, may be the function of ruling. Illustrate by "deacon," and show how this example makes for us. (*Thornwell* IV. p. 109.)

The history of the term elder, or presbyter, or *zaken*, shows that its primary and common meaning is that of "ruler" and not "teacher." It has reference primarily to superiority in years. Now the earliest form of government being the patriarchal, the patriarch or elder being the governor, nothing was more natural than that elder should come to mean governor when used of official station; afterward, such terms came to be used in all languages as terms of respect or reverence, since respect belongs both to age and office—senior, *signore*, *seigneur*, sire (lord and father), *sieur*, *monsieur*, senator, alderman. First age; then authority; then respect—this seems to be the history of the word. So also the terms pastor and bishop, which we have seen to be used interchangeably with elder, properly denote government, not teaching.*

Pastor, or shepherd, in the Old Testament, is generally used in this sense, and where it is used of a teacher, the ground of such application is probably the tendency of teaching to regulate the life. In our version, this usage does not always appear, because the expression to "feed" is very often used to represent the word for performing the office of a shepherd. But in the following passages there can be no doubt of the meaning of the term: Ezek. xxxvii. 24, where shepherd and king are used as synonymous; Ezek. xxxiv. 24, 25, where shepherd and prince are the same; 1 Chron. xi. 2.

So in the New Testament, Rev. ii. 27, "ruling" with

---

* For a conclusive argument from the earlier *Fathers*, see *Spirit of the XIX. Century* (1843), pp. 621 ff, by Thornwell, in his "*Collected Writings*," Vol. IV., pp. 115 ff.

a rod of iron, is "shepherding" with a rod of iron; Matt. ii. 6, the governor shall shepherd my people Israel; and in Eph. iv. 11, if pastors are not rulers, there is no mention made of rulers at all. In the classic Greek writers, reference may be made to Homer, in whom "shepherd" is constantly used for "king," ποιμηνλαὸν.

Bishop, as a title of office, is properly applicable to a subordinate class of rulers, who, possessing no independent powers of their own, are appointed to see that duties enjoined upon others are faithfully discharged. They differ from the higher order of magistrates in having no original authority, and in being confined to the supervision of others in the department committed to their care. They have no power to prescribe the law, they can only see that its precept is obeyed. Their functions seem to be exactly expressed by the English word "overseer." The subordinate magistrates sent out by Athens to take care of her interests in tributary cities were styled *episcopoi*.

Homer, to inculcate the doctrine that the gods will protect the sanctity of treaties, calls them the bishops of covenants. (Il. xxii. 255.) Hector, as the guardian and defender of Troy, is lamented by Andromache, under the same title. (Il. xxiv. 729.) So in the LXX., in Numbers xxxi. 14, officers of the host are "*episcopoi*" of the host. See also Judges ix. 28, 30, where bishop and ruler of the city are the same; Nehemiah xi. 9, 14, 22, a ruler of the specified division, not a teacher. In the Apocrypha, see 1 Maccabees, i. 51. The first meaning Hesychius gives to "*episcopos*," is "king." In 1 Mac. x. 37, αρχοντες is used, bishops (overseers) appointed by Antiochus Epiphanes.

Lastly: This is the sense in which our standards explain the term "presbyter." (*Thornwell*, IV., p. 105.) It says (*Form of Government*, Ch. IV. Sec. 2, Art. 1) that the reason why the pastor (or minister) is called *presbyter* is, that it is his duty to be grave and prudent, and an example of the flock, and to govern well in the house and kingdom of Christ. Compare this now with the reasons assigned for calling him "ambassador" or "steward," and nothing can be plainer than that of set purpose, our standards define presbyter in such a way as to make the definition as applicable to a ruling elder as to a pastor (commonly so called). The preacher shares in common with the deacon the title of minister, because both are appointed to a service; and he shares, in common with the ruling elder, the title of presbyter, since both are appointed to rule. Our standards also quote 1 Tim. v. 17, in Ch. V. of the old book, in proof of the divine right of the office of ruling elder, implying a judgment that presbyter means ruler. Neither the word of God, therefore, nor our standards, countenance the notion that presbyter means preacher. See Gieseler, Vol. I. pp. 56, 57, etc., who contends that elder and bishop were the same, and that neither term had any reference to teaching. He goes too far, however, in asserting that the term is not used of those who did teach.

Here, then, we have one fundamental principle of Presbyterianism (see the traces of this doctrine even in Rome—Cunningham's *Church Principles* p. 159, and *Historical Theology*, Vol. II., p. 251), a principle by which it is distinguished from other evangelical churches, to wit: that there is one order of presbyters or chosen rulers, that in this order there are two classes, like the *genus* and its co-ordinate species: 1, Presbyters who rule only; 2, Presbyters who not only rule, but also labor in the word and doctrine ; and both these classes entering into the composition of the church's parliamentary assemblies, we have an exemplification of the same principle which is exemplified in our civil legislatures by two houses, an expedient which is as great an improvement upon the representative principle as that principle is over the principle of the old democracy.

XVII.

PRESBYTERIES—CONGREGATIONAL.—" SESSIONS." *

See Owen, Vol. XXII., pp. 481 *et seq.*, for the principle in its application to a single congregation (which is the only visible church which as an Independent he acknowledges.) See *Form of Government*, Ch. V., Sec. 3; R. J. Breckinridge's speech on " Presbyterian Government not a Hierarchy but a Commonwealth"; *Thornwell*, Vol. IV., pp. 43, ff. In opposition on one hand to prelacy, which puts the government of the church into the hands of single men, and may therefore be called the monarchical form, and on the other to Congregationalism, which puts the government into the hands of the people or brotherhood, and may, therefore, be called a democracy, Presbyterianism is distinguished by a government in representative assemblies, and may therefore be called a republic or representative commonwealth. (*Form of Government*, Chap. V., Sec. 1, Art. 1.) We agree with Congregationalists against the prelatists in holding that the power of rule is a joint and not a several power; but we differ from the Congregationalists in this, that while they put the power in the hands of the people *en masse*, or in their deputies, we put the power in the hands of presbyters assembled in presbyteries, these presbyters being the chosen representatives of the people, yet according to the principles already stated under the head of the " Subject of Church Power," deriving their authority from Christ the head of the church and the author of its constitution.

1. The first step in the proof is to show that there was a plurality of elders or bishops in every church in the times of the apostles. This is to be proved not only against the prelatists, but against the Congregationalists also. The Congregationalists of England

* See Psa. cvii. 32, and Alexander *in loc.*

and of New England, as a general if not a universal
rule, have but one elder, who is a teaching elder. (See
The Ruling Eldership, by Rev. David King of Glas-
gow; Pittsburg United Presbyterian Board of Education, 1860.) And many leading Congregationalists
have contended that this was the practice in the primitive church; but other leading Congregationalists, such
as Dr. Wardlaw in his *Congregational Independency*,
Dr. Vaughan in his *Congregationalism*, and Dr. Davidson in his *Ecclesiastic Polity*, have of late years
admitted (according to King, from whom these references are taken), that in the primitive church there
was a plurality of elders in each church. They contend, however, that these elders were all preachers,
which has been shown to be a mistake. If they will,
however, carry out their own convictions and make a
plurality of preaching elders in any church, they will
soon find that the circumstances will compel the most
of their elders to become ruling elders only, and thus
their organization will become practically the same as
ours. But to the proof. (See Acts xi. 30, xiv. 23;
xv. 2, 4, 6, 22; xvi. 4; xx. 17; 1 Tim. v. 17; Phil. i.
1; Titus i. 5; 1 Peter v. 1.) These references are
taken from *Owen's Nature of a Gospel Church: Works*,
XX., p. 481, and Owen was an Independent, and not a
Congregationalist. The argument from these passages
is this: A plurality of elders or bishops is spoken of
as existing in the church of Jerusalem, the church of
Ephesus, the church of Philippi, etc. Now the word
church in such passages means either a particular
church, a single congregation of the faithful, or it
means a church consisting of several congregations
united under one government. If it means a single
congregation, then both Congregationalists and prelatists must give up their theories; the former must assert that in every congregation, however small, there
were many preachers, and admit, consequently, that
their present practice is unscriptural in having only

one. The latter must admit there were several bishops in each congregation, and, therefore, that these bishops were not diocesan. If the word church in such passages, on the other hand, means several congregations united under one government, then the Independents must give up the distinctive principle of their sect, that a single congregation is the only visible church known to the New Testament; and the prelatists must give up their principle, that the church is governed by a single bishop instead of a presbytery. But this last point will appear more clearly hereafter. Here note that Schaff (see *Apostolic Church*, sec. 132, p. 526), although he differs from his master, Neander, as to the nature of the office denoted by the term presbyter, denying what Neander affirms, that presbyter denotes two classes of rulers—a teaching and non-teaching class—yet contends that in Acts xiv. 23, Titus i. 5, the force of *kata* is adverbial, not collective, and that the meaning, therefore, is that elders were ordained in each city (city by city, church by church), not as Baur and others assert, one presbyter in each city or church.

2. The next step in the argument is to show that these elders in each church constituted a parliament or court for the government of said church, or in other words, that they ruled jointly and not severally. We argue this: *First*, From the nature of the case. If they were all rulers of equal authority there could be no decency or order in the exercise of their power except by agreement; that is, by an agreement of the majority. There must have been deliberation, conference, interchange of views, and a vote which made the action the action of the whole governing body. (Compare Acts xv., the account of the proceedings of the council at Jerusalem.) *Second*, From 1 Tim. iv. 14, compared with Acts xxii. 5, and Luke xxii. 66. The lexicographers (see Schleusner, *in voc.*) give as the meaning of *presbyterion* a college of elders, or a

senate, implying an organized body, a corporate unit, of which the elements are presbyters.   There can be no doubt of this being the meaning of the terms in Luke xxii.* and Acts xxii., for in these places it denotes the sanhedrin, the highest court in the Jewish church and state.   But in the place of 1 Tim., so high an authority in Hebrew antiquities as Selden (*De Synedris*, L. I, c. 14, cited by Vitringa, *De Synag. Vet.* L. 2, c. 12), asserts that it means the presbyterate, the office of presbyter;† as if Paul intended to say, "Neglect not the gift that is in thee, which was given thee by prophecy, with the imposition of hands, by which imposition thou wast made a presbyter, or endowed with the presbyterate."   To this it is sufficient to reply: 1, That it is not very likely that a word which is used only in three places of the New Testament should in two of them designate, beyond all doubt, a college or council of presbyters; and in the remaining one the office of a presbyter.   So that, while it is admitted, so far as the termination of the word is concerned, no argument can be made for one meaning or the other, the prevailing usage is in favor of a council or college of persons possessing the presbyterate, and not the presbyterate itself.   2, A comparison of this passage with 2 Tim. i. 6 (as Vitringa suggests in *loc. sup. cit.*), shows that the genitive here is not the genitive of the thing conferred, but of the body conferring; *mou* in this passage standing in the same relation to "hands" as "presbytery" does in the other.   In the

---

* In Luke xxii. 66, the "$\pi\rho\varepsilon\sigma\iota\overline{\jmath}$" seems to be distinguished from the "$\sigma\nu\nu\varepsilon\overline{\delta}\rho\iota\upsilon\nu$"; but it must, in any case, denote a collection of elders. ("Estate of the elders," in Acts xxii. 5, both in A. V. and Rev.)   In the Revision of 1881, the word is rendered in this place, "Assembly of the Elders," but in 1 Tim. iv. 14, "Presbytery," as in the A. V.

† Calvin in his Institutes (B. iv. c. 3, ¶ 16) takes this view also; but in his commentary on 1 Tim. i. 14, he takes the view here defended. The commentary on 1 Tim. was published in 1556; the last edition of the Institutes in 1559   Calvin died 1564.

one, the gift is said to be conferred by the laying on of
the hands of Paul; in the other, by the laying on of
the hands of the presbytery. *Presbyterion*, therefore,
is the cause and not the effect of the imposition of
hands. 3, This use is sanctioned by the writings of
Ignatius, which the prelatists are so fond of quoting,
but which have all been proved to be forgeries.
(*Killin's Ancient Church;* see citations in Vitringa, as
above cited.)   He calls the presbyters of the Trallean
church "the sanhedrin of God." Vitringa refers also
to Theodoret, Chrysostom and Theophylact, as giving
the interpretation which we have defended.   Perhaps
words terminating like *presbuterion* belong to the same
class with such words as prætorium, originally denoting the *place* of business.   Some of this class of
words might be transferred to denote the officer or
body of officers doing business in the place.   Sometimes, again, the fact of sitting together, or the mode of
sitting, gives name to the body, as session, consistory,
sanhedrin, or even the nature of the seat, as "divan"
(cushion).   Compare the use of the word "church"
for the body of believers and for the house where they
assemble; also synagogue, etc., etc.   Jerome seems to
have had this word in his mind in that famous passage
of his commentary on Titus i. 7, which has excruciated
so much the prelatical patrolaters.   (See it in full in
Gieseler, Vol. I., p. 56, note. *Idem est*, etc.)

We have thus proved that in the apostolic church
the government of single congregations was in assemblies called presbyteries, because composed of presbyters—these presbyters being of two kinds, teaching
and ruling elders.   This is the very government which
in modern times, among free nations, has been considered the most perfect, or, to use the language of
Milton, "the noblest, the manliest, the equalest, the
justest government" on earth—a government by representatives, not by the people in *propria persona*, or by
deputies; and these representatives not all of the same

class, but of different classes, so that, as the representative principle is itself a check upon the excesses of the democratic principle, the two classes of representatives constitute a check upon the evils incident to representation by one class.

Both these principles are recognized in the civil constitutions of this country—the principle of representation, and of representation by two classes of representatives, "senators" and "representatives." The apostles seem to have put special honor on this government by sitting themselves as elders in settled churches, especially toward the close of their ministry, when the church was so far established as to be ready to pass out of the state of infancy and childhood into that of manhood. (1 Cor. xiii. 8–11; see Acts xv. 2, 4, 6, 22; 2 Tim. i. 6; compare with 1 Tim. iv. 14; 1 Peter v. 1.)

An incidental confirmation of this government by presbyteries may be derived from the concessions of Independents. These concessions are made in two ways: First, in words. (Beside the quotations from King in the beginning of this lecture, see *Miller on Ruling Elders*, Chap. 7, who quotes largely both from English and New England Independents.) Second, in practice. (See *Miller* as before, Chap. 8, p. 186; *King on the Eldership*, Part I., pp. 27–32.) Although Independents contend that the discipline of the church is in the hands of the brotherhood by divine right, yet in practice they find that a promiscuous "church-meeting" is an assembly very unhappily constituted for judicial purposes; and the tendency has been to remedy the evil in one of two ways: first, by making the pastor or elder sole ruler, that is, by converting the democracy into a monarchy;* or, second, by associating with the pastor a few of the most godly and prudent men in the congregation as an advisory commit-

---

* A Democracy always tends toward the *centralization* of power.

tee—a sort of eldership, with the disadvantage of being unordained, and unpledged to support the constitution. Dr. King gives some quotations from Independent writers, such as Davidson, James, Campbell, asserting for the pastor of a congregation a degree of power which Presbyterians would be very far from conceding to the pastors of their congregations. (See *King on the Eldership*, page 15, footnote.) The more common method, however, is the second above named, the selection of a committee. But this expedient, though a concession to our principles, is far from being as efficient or wholesome, for the very obvious reason that these *quasi* ruling elders are made by the pastor and not chosen by the people, and that they are temporary officers, not permanent, and that for the reason already assigned, they are under no engagement of faithfulness to the constitution of the church. We might argue also from the concessions, in words and in practice, of Episcopalians. But I simply refer you to *Miller on Ruling Elders*, Ch. 6, and Ch. 7, page 185, and *on the Christian Ministry*, Ch. 8. That these presbyteries must consist of two sorts of presbyters, so far as the sphere of a particular congregation is concerned, is conceded by all who admit government by presbyteries at all. The only question upon this point concerns the higher courts, "classical" presbyteries in particular. I shall reserve, therefore, the discussion of this point till we reach the subject of the manner in which the idea of the unity of the church is realized in the Presbyterian government. Meanwhile note that our inquiries have led us to two fundamental principles of Presbyterianism: 1st, The principle of representative government—of government by parliamentary courts composed of presbyters duly appointed and ordained; 2nd, That these representatives must be of two classes, belonging to the one order of *presbyters*. They all of them belong to the one order of rulers, and only as rulers, chosen rulers or representatives of the people, can they appear in any of these courts,—presbyters who rule only, and presbyters who both rule and labor in the word and doctrine. This answers to the two houses in modern legislation. Presbyteries are not divided, however, into two houses (each class of presbyters deliberating and voting separately), because presbyteries are courts, and are required to act as units. *Note* that the elders who rule only are called "representatives of the people," not because they only are representatives of the people and ministers are not, but because it is a complete description of their office.

Compare the use of the terms senator and representative. It does not imply that the Senate is not a body of representatives because the other house is called the House of Representatives. Both houses consist of representatives; the lower house of Congress is so called because the title is a complete description of their office. The Senate discharges *executive* as well as *legislative* functions.

XVIII.

PRESBYTERIES—CLASSICAL, SYNODICAL, GENERAL.

[See *Form of Government*, Ch. V., Sec. 1, Arts. 1, 2; *Confession of Faith*, Ch. XXXI, Sec. 1. See also *Divine Right of Church Government*, by the London ministers, Pt. II., Chs. XIII., XIV., XV., p. 177, etc., of the New York edition of 1844, by R. Martin & Co. *Dick's Theological Lectures*, 99, Vol. II., pp. 448, *et seq.*, of Carter's edition, New York, 1851. *Principal Hill's Theology*, B. 6, Ch. II., Sec. 2, pp. 591, *et seq.*, of Hooker's edition, Philadelphia, 1844. *Rutherford's Due Right of Presbyteries*. *Killen's Ancient Church*, p. 248, *et seq.*, New York, Scribner, 1859; also of the same, pp. 605, et seq. *Miller on Ruling Elders*, Ls. 1, 2, 3. *R. J. Breckinridge's Sermon on the Christian Pastor*, pp. 25, 26. *Thornwell*, Vol. IV., pp. 134, ff.]

All these sorts of presbyteries are named together because the same principle underlies them all. When we have once determined that two congregations (*cœtus fidelium*) can be connected together in government, we have demolished the fundamental principle of Independency, and established a fundamental principle of Presbyterianism. It is a matter of no consequence, then, how much the number of congregations may be increased, the principle upon which they are united is the same, and the arrangement of the courts, their number, extent of territory, etc., is an affair to be determined by human wisdom, accommodating its plans to the circumstances of the case, with a view to decency, order and general edification. Mountains, rivers, political divisions, language and other circumstances do and must modify our attempts to realize, in any external form, the idea of the unity of the church.

I. The principle which justifies the union of several congregations under one government has just been suggested: it is *the unity of the church*. I am aware that the idea of unity can never be perfectly realized, in an external organization, upon earth, and the attempts which have been made for that purpose, from the days of Cyprian to the present, have only served to sacrifice the substance of unity to the shadow. Still the Independent and the Presbyterian cite with equal approval (see *R. Hall's Terms of Communion, Works*, p. 289, Vol. I., Harper's edition, and *Miller on Ruling Elders*, p. 16), the splendid description by the Bishop of Carthage of the church as one. In the strict and proper sense, unity is an attribute of the church invisible, and exists in perfection only in the mystical body of Christ; yet even Independents acknowledge (see Hall, as above), that there ought to be some anxiety and some effort to exhibit it externally.

"Nothing can be more abhorrent," says this eloquent writer, "from the principles and maxims of the sacred oracles than the idea of a plurality of true churches, neither in actual communion with each other, nor in a capacity for such communion," and well may he say so. (See Eph. iv. 3–6; 1 Cor. xii. 12, etc., x. 17; John xvii., *passim*. (See *Mason on the Church*, No. 1, "Plea for Communion," P. I., pp. 9, *et seq.*) So glaring is this doctrine of the unity of the church, even as a visible church catholic, in the sacred Scriptures, that it is unconsciously recognized even by those Christians whose church organizations proceed upon a denial of it. They talk habitually of the church, the faith of the church, the worship of the church, the sufferings of the church, God's dealings with his church, and a thousand like things. Let them ask what they mean by such expressions. They will not say "a particular congregation"; and if they say "the election of grace," they will speedily contradict themselves, and fact, and the word of God too. (*Mason.*) The unhappy division of the church into sects has been the chief means of obscuring the idea of her unity; and, therefore, in this discussion we confine ourselves to one denomination, or to the church before sects existed. The question, then, is, is the visible church one in any such sense as to warrant the union of two or more congregations under the same government? I answer in the affirmative, for the following reasons:

1. From the nature and ends of church fellowship. The union of believers with Christ and each other is the source of communion with each other. This communion is involuntary, or spontaneous where the union is real. As a man cannot help feeling sympathy with his fellowmen, because he and they possess the same nature—as one member of the body cannot help sympathizing with the other members, because they possess the same life, so one believer *must* sympathize with other believers. It is the very nature of the spiritual life which they all possess in common. God has made

them so.   But as God has ordained the family and the
state that the natural fellowship of men may be expressed and strengthened, so he has ordained the
church that the fellowship he has instituted among his
people may be promoted by joining in the observance
of common ordinances of worship, and by obedience
to common rules of government.   They all have the
same end in view, the glory of God in their own salvation and in the salvation of mankind.   Every Christian
is as much interested in the consistent walk and growth
in grace of every other Christian as he is in his own ;
and is therefore as much concerned in the purity of
the faith and the holiness of the life of other congregations as he is in those of his own.   In the matter,
for example, of the character of ministers of the word,
their training, their soundness in doctrine, their godliness, they all are equally interested.   Why not then
commit the whole affair of examining, licensing, ordaining, installing, removing, and judging ministers to
a body of presbyters representing all the congregations
within a certain district, and common to them all ?
Again, in cases of conscience, in questions of doctrine
or discipline which are of common concern to all congregations, is there not the same reason for having
such matters decided by a court representing all, as
there is for Christians of a single congregation uniting
in submission to a court of their own in ordinary
cases of discipline ?   So also in the application of the
rules of discipline to particular cases.   The presbytery
in a particular church is sometimes so small, or the
members so liable to bias and prejudice by reason of
their relationship to parties in a cause, as to make it
inexpedient for the court to issue, if not to investigate
the cause ; and there ought to be a provision by which
the cause can be "referred" (*Rules of Discipline* Ch.
XIII., Sec. 2), to a court representing a larger section of
the church, or several congregations.   Or the session
of a particular church may, through ignorance or un-

faithfulness, take no steps to institute process, or in conducting process may violate the moral or legal rights of accused parties, or may, in issuing a case, violate the plainest dictates of justice. There ought to be, therefore, provisions made for "reviewing" (*Rules of Discipline*, Ch. XIII., Sec. 1), or judging by "appeal" (Sec. 3 of the same chapter), or "complaint," (Sec. 4) by some higher court, the doings of the lower. These principles are acknowledged in the constitution of the judiciary in every free commonwealth. The necessity of some such arrangement is more clearly seen in the matter of the discipline of ministers of the gospel for heresy or immorality (specially the former) than in anything else. Heresiarchs are generally plausible, and if the responsibility of judging a minister rests upon a single congregation, or upon the rulers thereof, it is not difficult to see how unequal the contest is likely to be between truth and justice on the one hand, and error, or even immorality, combined with talents and personal popularity on the other. The history of congregationalism in this country is very instructive upon this point. It has shown itself powerless either to prevent or to remedy the inroads of error. Once more, the church is not merely to maintain itself, but to extend itself. Its great vocation is to be a witness for Christ, and the sphere of its testimony is no narrower than the world. How can it accomplish its missionary work except by union? For all purposes of aggression, unity of counsel and effort is the first and fundamental prerequisite. This is signally illustrated in the history of Jesuitism and Methodism. I grant that in these instances efficiency in aggression has been purchased at too great an expense. The individuality of the laborers has been impaired and almost destroyed. Still, extreme cases illustrate best the operation of principles. An autocracy is more efficient in a war of invasion than a democracy. Popery and Methodism have gone everywhere in this country. Congregation-

alism has been established only where Congregationalists have gone before in large numbers. Congregationalism can conduct foreign missions only by *irresponsi-
ble* boards of commissions or associations. Presbyterianism conducts them through its regular courts, which
are representative bodies; and it is the only system
which combines efficiency of aggressive operations
with the full preservation and development of individual life. Its members are not mere spokes in a
wheel; they are wheels within a wheel. The missionary
work is an essential part of the calling of the church;
union under one government is essential to the proper
prosecution of this work. *Ergo*, union under one government, is essential to the church's calling.

2. From the concessions of Independents. *First*,
in words. (See *Owen's True Nature of a Gospel
Church*, Ch. XI. Works (Russell's ed. Lond. 1826),
Vol. XX., pp. 569 ff.) This whole chapter, it seems to
me, is a concession to Presbyterian principles; and is
conclusive only against the prelatical notions of the
unity of the church, and especially the papal. See
the last paragraph in the chapter, in which, after dis-
cussing the nature of the Synod at Jerusalem (Acts XV.,)
he says, p. 601, Vol. XX., last paragraph in the Treatise,
"Hence it will," etc., every word of which a Presbyterian might adopt, not excepting the words "voluntary
consent." (See *C. of F.* Ch. XXXI., § 2.) *Second*, in
universal practice: As they are compelled to imitate
Presbyterians on the scale of a single congregation (see
Lect. on Congregational Presbyteries): so also on the
larger scale of districts containing many congregations,
they have their associations, consociations, confer-
ences, etc., which practically attempt the work of Presbyteries, with the disadvantages already indicated of
putting the power in the hands of men who have no
official authority, and are under no official responsibility. It is a painful evidence of the power of prejudice that a man like Owen could lay down the princi-

ples touching church power so clearly, and contend for the divine warrant of Synods to the extent of asserting that their decrees " are to be received, owned and observed, not only on the evidence of the mind of the Holy Ghost in them," but also on the ministerial authority of the Synod itself (see place above cited), and yet hold that they have no power of censure (judicial) or excommunication, and that it belongs not to the rulers of the church, as rulers, to be members of such Synods, but to private members as well, provided they be delegated thereunto by the people.

3. From Scripture. The federal character of the government of Israel, combining unity with the full development of tribal and individual life. Force of the words "congregation of Israel." The word "church," ($εχκλησια$) has already been noticed as equivalent, in LXX., to the word rendered "congregation" in ours, and as the term "congregation," in the Old Testament, denotes the whole body of the visible people of God, so the term "church," in the New. But here the Independents join issue with us. They deny that the term, when used in the singular number, and in application to a visible body, ever denotes anything larger than a single congregation. It is necessary, therefore, to argue this point a little. I. The phrase "church" of or at "Jerusalem," occurs several times in the Acts. (See ii. 47; viii. 1; xi. 22; xv. 4.) II. The church of Jerusalem must have consisted of several congregations. Argued, (1), From the multitude of believers. Acts ii. 41, 47; iv. 4; v. 14; vi. 1, etc., vs. 7. These notices refer to the church before the dispersion, upon the persecution which arose after the death of Stephen; and the number of believers could not have been much, if any, short of 10,000. After the dispersion we have notices like the following: ix. 31; xxi. 20; "$ποσαι$ $μυριαδες$," "how many tens of thousands." (2), From the manner of meeting among the primitive Christians. This was not in spacious halls built for the purpose,

but in dwelling-houses, chambers, upper rooms, etc.[*]
Acts i. 13; ii. 46; xii. 5, with vs. 12; xix. 9; xx. 8.
Rom., xvi. 5. (*Div. Gov't*, by Lond. Ministers.) (3),
The church is represented as one body, in the New
Testament, "*fitly joined together* and *compacted* by that
which every *joint* supplieth." (Eph. iv. 16.) As this is
the church to which is given the ministry (vs. 11, etc.),
it must be the church visible; and it is just as natural
to consider these "bands" and "joints" as designating
the means by which different congregations are united
in the same confederation, as it is to consider them the
means of union to the individual members of the same
church, particular or single. (*Killen*, p. 250.) (4),
This doctrine of the visible unity of the church seems
to have been sanctioned by the practice of the apostles.
See Acts viii. 14; xi. 22; also ch. xv., where they are
represented as acting in concert, although, from the
very nature of the apostolic office, each was a governor
of the whole church.

4. A fourth general argument may be taken from the
Jewish synagogues. It is conceded, even by candid op-
ponents of the Presbyterian system, "that the church
did really derive its polity from the synagogue, and
that it is a fact, upon the proof of which, in the present state of theological learning, it is needless to ex-
pend many words" (see *Litton's Church of Christ*,
cited by Killen, p. 251); and this accounts for the fact
that in the New Testament there is no formal statement in regard to the constitution of the Christian
church, just as there is no formal explanation of the
meaning of the word Christ or Messiah. Killen gives,
out of standard authors (Selden, Lightfoot, etc.), the
following account of the government of the synagogue,
(p. 251 *et seq.*): Every Jewish congregation was gov-

---

[*] This view is confirmed by the well known fact that the synagogues
were generally not large. It is said (See Prideaux) that there were 480
of them in Jerusalem in the Saviour's time, and yet the population of
the city was probably not more than 150,000 at the outside, giving an
average of one synagogue to a little more than 300 people.

erned by a bench of elders; and in every city there was a small sanhedrin or presbytery, consisting of twenty-three members, to which the neighboring synagogues were subject. Jerusalem is said to have had two of these small sanhedrins, as it was found that the multitude of cases arising among so vast a population were more than sufficient to occupy the time of any one judicatory. Appeals lay from all these tribunals to the great sanhedrin, or "council," so frequently mentioned in the New Testament. (Luke xxii. 66; Acts v. 21; vi. 15; *Prideaux's Con.*, Part II., Book 7.) This court consisted of seventy or seventy-two members, made up, perhaps, in equal portions, of chief-priests, scribes, and elders of the people. (Matt. xvi. 21; xxvi. 59; Mark, xv. 1.) The chief-priests were probably 24 in number—each of the 24 courses into which the sacerdotal order was divided (1 Chron. xxiv. 4; vii. 18), thus furnishing one representative. The scribes were the men of learning, like Gamaliel (Acts v. 34), who had devoted themselves to the study of the Jewish law, and who possessed recondite as well as extensive information. The elders were laymen (?) of reputed wisdom and experience, who, in practical matters, might be expected to give sound advice. . . . Our Lord himself, in the Sermon on the Mount, is understood to refer to the great council and its subordinate judicatures (Matt. v. 22); and in the Old Testament, appeals from inferior tribunals to the authorities in the holy city are explicitly enjoined. (Deut. xvii. 8–10; 2 Chron. xix. 8–11; Psalms, cxxii. 5.) All the synagogues, not only in Palestine, but in foreign countries, obeyed the orders of the sanhedrin at Jerusalem, and it constituted a court of review to which all other ecclesiastical arbiters yielded submission. (See also *Miller on Ruling Elders*, Ch. II., p. 31, *et seq.*)

These principles and facts undoubtedly explain and harmonize all the notices of the New Testament in regard to elders, and the organization of the church, better than the theories of Independents or prelatists, although it may be conceded that absolute certainty cannot be reached upon these points as it can be in regard to those articles of faith which are fundamental and necessary to salvation. And, hence, while we contend for the scriptural order of Christ's house, as a matter of faith and of vast importance to the prosperity and efficiency of the church, we do not unchurch and remit to the uncovenanted mercies of God those who, holding the head, yet differ from us upon these points.

We have thus reached, in the course of our inquiries, a third distinctive feature of Presbyterian church government—the mode in which it realizes the unity of the church. It realizes this idea by the *elastictity* of its parliamentary representative system. If there was but one congregation on earth, its presbytery or " session," would constitute the parliament of the whole church ; if half-a-dozen, the representatives from each would constitute a parliament for the whole church ; if a still larger number, the same results would follow. And representatives from all the churches (or from the smaller parliaments, which is the same principle,) constitute the parliament for the whole church. Only two churches on the earth realize this idea of church unity—Rome and our own church. But these are the poles apart as to the system by which they realize it. Rome, with her infallible pope at the head, and with graded authorities extending over the whole earth, one class subservient to another and all to the pope, secures a terrible unity, binding all, abjectly, to a single throne. Our system, on the other hand, secures unity in consistency with the most perfect freedom. Presbyterianism, may, therefore, be thus defined : The government of the church by parliamentary assemblies, composed of two classes of presbyters, and of presbyters only, and so arranged as to realize the visible unity of the whole church. (*Thornwell*, Vol. IV., p. 267.)

II. In the light of these principles we recognize the

truth of the statement of the fundamental principles
of Presbyterianism contained in the note to *Form of
Gov.*, B. 1, Ch. XII., in the old book. If all the communicants in the Presbyterian Church of the United
States could meet for worship in the same place, they
might and should be under the government of the
same session; but as this is impossible, they are
broken up into single congregations, each with its own
session. But in order to preserve the unity, all these
single or local presbyteries are ultimately combined
by representation in one presbytery, which we call
the General Assembly, passing through the inter-
mediate stages of classical and synodical presbyteries.
Of this General Assembly we might say, in the language of Milton (*Reason of Church Government against
Prelaty*, Ch. VI.), "every parochial consistory is a
right homogeneous and constituting part, being in
itself a little synod, and towards a general assembly
moving upon her own basis in an even and firm pro-
gression, as those smaller squares in battle unite in
one great cube, the main phalanx, an emblem of truth
and steadfastness." It is not one order of clergy
rising above another, like the gradations in the Roman
hierarchy, but a larger square of the same order of
presbyters, including a smaller, until the "great cube"
is reached. The subordination is not that of inferior
officers to superior; but of a smaller body to a larger
body of officers of the same order—the smaller constituting a part of the larger. Now in regard to this
series of courts it is important to observe: 1, As has
already been noted, it is a matter of conventional
arrangement, founded upon expediency, how many
and how large these courts shall be, how often they
shall meet, how they shall be constituted; that is, of
what number of elders and how many of each class,
how many shall constitute a quorum, etc. 2, That
as appellate jurisdiction must belong to the courts
above the sessions, or congregational presbytery, it is

also a matter of convention or of constitutional arrangement how this appellate jurisdiction shall be distributed and regulated; subject of course to the principle of a larger reviewing the doings of the smaller part, and consequently of the highest appellate jurisdiction belonging to the highest court which is allowed appellate jurisdiction at all.   3, That in matters of original jurisdiction every court has, prior to any constitutional distribution of power, all the power that any court has. The presbytery does not derive its powers from the session, nor the synod from the presbytery, nor the general assembly from synods or presbyteries in an ascending scale, nor the synod from the general assembly, etc., in a descending scale.   But as every court is a presbytery composed of presbyters of two classes, it is clothed with all the powers of government. So that a session might ordain and send out missionaries, and the general assembly might examine and receive members into the communion of the church, if these powers had not been distributed in the constitution.   The sphere of the several courts, therefore, in matters of original jurisdiction is not determined by the places they occupy in the scale, but by the definitions of the constitution.   This is an important principle to the freedom and independence of the courts.

The dictum by which the unity of the church, the power of the parts, and the power of the whole over the particular parts, are expressed is as follows: "The power of the whole is in every part, and the power of the whole is over the *power* of every part."   The power of the Presbyterian Church of the United States is in the general assembly, the synod, the presbytery, the session, and the power of the general assembly is over the power of the synod, presbytery and session.   This last expression is intended to preserve the rights and powers belonging to the lower courts (guaranteed by the constitution).   The general assembly has no power directly *over the part*, but only over the *power* of the part, which implies that the part has a power. Compare the civil commonwealth. The Commonwealth of Virginia appears in all its parts or courts as a party and judge in every criminal cause, and as a judge only in every civil suit. This fact is the ground of the provisions for appeals, complaints (bills of exceptions), references (change of venue), etc. See the action of Assembly, 1879, on the overture of Atlanta Presbytery on worldly amusements (answer to third question).

XIX.

THE DEACON'S OFFICE.

The communion of saints is implied in the very notion of an organized church having its polity and its ordinances of worship. But this communion ($\varkappa o\iota\nu\omega\nu\iota\alpha$) is most impressively exhibited in two ordinances, both of which are emphatically denominated by the word *communion*, to wit: the Lord's supper and contributions in money, or its equivalent. (Acts ii. 42–45; 1 Cor. x. 16; 2 Cor. viii. 4; Heb. xiii. 16; Rom. xv. 26, 27.) Both of these belong to the worship of God. No definition of worship can be framed which can be justly applied to the Lord's supper, that will not apply also to these contributions. There is no more glorious act of worship described in the Bible than that in the last chapter of the First Book of the Chronicles.

This view of contributions accounts for the importance ascribed to them in both Testaments. They are the tokens, and, in some respects, the most unexceptionable tokens of the reality of the communion of saints. Considering the power of the feeling of *mine*, who can read that the primitive Christians were not accustomed to say, "that aught of the things which they possessed was their own," but that "they had all things common," can doubt that a new principle was at work in their hearts, a principle not earth-born, but descended from heaven. Still more manifest did this

become when the Gentile Christians contributed to the
relief of their Jewish brethren.   Here there was no
bond of blood to prompt the beneficence; rather was
there the bitter prejudice of race.   No wonder that the
great apostle was willing to travel all the way to Jerusalem to *seal the gift* to the recipients; that is, to expound its comprehensive spiritual meaning, and to impress upon their hearts the reality and the glory of
the communion of saints.   (Acts xi. 29, 30 ; Rom. xv.
25–28 ; 1 Cor. xvi. 1–4 ; 2 Cor. chaps. viii. ix.)

It was in this form, "in relieving each other in outward things according to their several abilities and
necessities" (*Con. of Faith*, Ch. XXVI., Art. 2.), that the
communion of saints was first and most conspicuously
exhibited in the primitive church ; and it was in connection with this form that the deacons first appeared,
(Acts vi. 1–6.)   They were the deacons of "tables," as
the apostles were deacons of "the word."   The saints
had communion with each other in the apostles' teaching and in breaking of bread and in prayers (Acts ii.
42) ; but they had also communion with each other in
"outward things"; and this form of communion is that
which the narrative enlarges upon in the succeeding
verses (44, 45), and reverts to in ch. iv. 32–37.   The
prime aspect, then, of the office of deacon is that of a
representative of the communion of saints.   The word
may be and is preached where there are no saints, and
therefore no communion; it is conceivable also that
ruling elders may exercise their authority in a dead
church ; but deacons have nothing to do, except in a
church which has life enough to show itself in a ministry to the saints.

This circumstance demonstrates the dignity and
spirituality of the deacon's office.   Albeit concerned
mainly with "outward things," it is with the outward
things of a spiritual body that the office is concerned,
and spiritual qualifications are indispensable to a right
administration of them.   Hence we find Paul, in pre-

scribing the qualifications of church officers in the third chapter of his First Epistle to Timothy, saying as much of those of the deacon as of those of the elder, if not more. It is not a little remarkable that a deacon should have been chosen rather than an apostle to see that it was God's plan to abolish the Mosaic form of the true religion, and to establish one which should be spiritual and universal. The celebrated saying of Augustine, "If Stephen had not prayed, we should not have had Paul," was perhaps more comprehensive in its scope than the great thinker supposed. The prayer of the dying martyr was perhaps the means, not only of the conversion of Saul of Tarsus, but of bringing him upon the scene as Paul the apostle of the *Gentiles*. Certain it is that the charges against Paul, by which the Jews thought themselves justified in seeking to kill him, were the very same as those which led to the murder of Stephen. (Compare Acts vi. 11–14 with xxi. 28; xxv. 8.) It is also not a little remarkable that while the account of the death of James, the brother of John, one of the three apostles who were admitted to special intimacy with the Lord, is dispatched in one short sentence (See Acts xii. 2), the account of the deacon's death is given in detail. A dozen verses would embrace all that is said of James in the New Testament; two chapters, one of them long, are occupied with Stephen, the deacon; and every reader of church history knows what a prominent part deacons have played in it. It is not a small office. Paul probably had Stephen in his mind when he wrote the sentence (1 Tim. iii. 13), "They that have served well as deacons gain to themselves a good standing and great boldness in the faith which is in Christ Jesus." But the same may be true now, if deacons will take the pains to understand their office, and seek grace from God to perform its duties and to improve its privileges.

That special condition of the early church in Jerusalem which gave occasion to the appointment of

deacons was temporary and local, and was designed to
be so. We know not how long it lasted, probably not
long. It is easy to see that a permanent condition of
that sort would have resulted in many and great evils,
unless prevented by a continued miracle, and there is
no trace of such a condition in any of the Gentile
churches. Nevertheless, "the poor were not to cease
out of the land"; they were to have the gospel preached
unto them; and to the end of time the ministry to the
necessities of the saints should continue to be needful.
The office of deacon was therefore intended to be perpetual.

But it would be taking too narrow a view of the
office to confine its exercise to this kind of ministry.
The communion of saints "in outward things" is more
extensive than can be adequately exhibited by the relief of the poor in a single congregation or in a single
city. A single congregation, or all the congregations
united in a single city, is not the church universal, or
even the church of one state or country. The communion, therefore, "is to be extended as our Confession
says, (Ch. XXVI., Art. 2) "unto all those in every place
who call upon the name of the Lord Jesus." The rule
holds still, that "by an equality the abundance of one
part should be a supply for the want of another part."
(2 Cor. viii, 14.) "Our committees of Home Missions
and Education are but great central deaconships of
charitable ministrations, by which in these things the
burdens of the church may be equalized; the richer
provided with the means of helping the poorer, and
the unity and union of the church at once manifested
and strengthened. And it is but a slight variation of
the same principle that is developed in the work of
Foreign Missions, in which the church unites in sup-
porting her sons and daughters whom she has sent forth
to the nations, and in sustaining and enlarging the
feeble churches established amid the wild wastes of
heathenism." (See Dr. Ramsay's *Essay on the Deacon-
ship*, p. 20.)

"To the deacons also may be properly committed," says our *Form of Government* (Ch. IV., Art. 2), "the management of the temporal affairs of the church." The church, like the individual Christian, has its "temporal affairs." This phrase denotes specially the *property* of the congregation, the house in which it statedly worships and the ground upon which it stands, as well as the expenses necessarily attendant upon the comfortable use of it.*

This brings up the question concerning the relation of the deacons to the trustees of the property—a relation which in many congregations, especially in the cities, is far from being satisfactorily settled. In some congregations, the trustees are allowed to determine the salary of the pastor, for the reason that the salary comes from the rent of the pews, and the pews belong to the house. If this inequitable method of raising the salary were abandoned, as it ought to be, there would be no plausible pretext left for the usurpation of the trustees. The officers who represent the property, it is argued, ought to regulate the disposal of the proceeds thereof. Now, when it is considered that these trustees are often not professing Christians, but men of the world, chosen because they are monied men and men of business, and sometimes because they have property in the neighborhood of the church building whose market value will be affected by the character of the vicinage, it needs no argument to prove that the trustees are not the persons who are most likely to seek the spiritual edification of the church in the choice of a pastor. Others propose to remedy or prevent this odious form of "patronage" by having the deacons incorporated as trustees. But the obvious objections to this scheme are, (1), That such trustees would have no more right to usurp, though there might be less temptation to usurp, the

---

*For the Scotch doctrine, see *Baird's Digest*, pp. 38, 39.

prerogative of the congregation as to the pastor's salary, than the trustees of the other sort; (2), That it would be contrary to the American theory of the relations of church and state to make ecclesiastical officers, as such, officers of the state.* The trustees, in the eye of the law, are not representatives of the church as such, but of a body of citizens who have a right to claim from the civil authority protection for their property. But deacons are ecclesiastical officers, and represent the church. The remedy of the evil is to be found in the principle that trustees of church property are intended to act only in cases of the purchase or sale of property, or of invasion of right, when litigation before the court becomes necessary. This is the principle acted upon almost invariably in the country congregations of the South. It is doubtful in most of such congregations if the trustees are known at all, or could be found in an emergency, or whether, in consequence of omission to fill vacancies, the board has not entirely expired.

That it is the official duty of the deacons to take charge of the pastor's salary would probably not have been questioned, if the salary had not been regarded as a pure affair of business, and not in any just sense as an expression of the communion of saints. In point of fact, it partakes of the nature of both; and this is enough to justify our church in inserting the article upon which the foregoing comments have been made, and to refute the notion that the pastor's salary is an affair of the civil officers called trustees. According to our constitution, the body that calls the pastor is the body that fixes the salary, and that body is the body of communicants. (See *Form of Government*,

---

*It cannot be denied, however, that our American theory is not consistently carried out. In Virginia, for example, whose traditions have been more decided and operative than perhaps those of any other state against the mingling of the two jurisdictions, a minister of the gospel is *ex officio* an officer of the state in the matter of celebrating a marriage.

Ch. VI., Sec. 3, Arts. 4 and 6.) The deacon, therefore, is the proper officer to take charge of the pastor's salary, and the trustees as such have nothing to do with it.

Another question to which importance has been given by discussions in the church is concerning the relation of the deacon to the session. How far is the deacon responsible to the session in the performance of his official duties? It is, of course, conceded on all hands that in the case of criminal conduct he is responsible to the session—the court to which, according to the constitution, all original jurisdiction, except in the trial of ministers, belongs. It must be conceded also, that money contributed for a specific purpose, say Home or Foreign Missions, cannot, in good faith, be diverted from that purpose, by either session or deacons, without the consent of the contributors. In reference to all other funds, it would seem that they are under the direction and control of the session. The public purse must be under the control of the government. In free civil commonwealths, the government is distributed into different branches; and the power of the purse, for obvious reasons, is lodged with that branch which more immediately represents the people from whom the money is derived by taxation. But it belongs to the government. So in the church. The government is not, indeed, distributed into branches as it is in the state, neither is there any taxation; but the rulers are the representatives of the people as chosen by them, and the people consent that their voluntary offerings shall be controlled by them. To give the deacons, who are not rulers, power to dispose of the revenues as against the elders, would be virtually to create an *imperium in imperio;* for the power goes with the purse. Hence we find the contributions of the primitive church laid "at the feet of the apostles." (Acts iv. 35, 37; v. 2.) It is in accordance with this view that our Form of Government

provides (Ch. IV., Sec. 4, Art. 4), that "a complete
account of collections and distributions, and a full
record of proceedings, shall be kept by the deacons,
and submitted to the session for examination and approval at least once a year."

Another question which has been debated in our
church concerns the relation of the deacon to the
courts above the session. Is he exclusively a congregational officer? Or, may he be employed also by the
presbytery, the synod, and the general assembly? Is
there anything, either in the nature of the office or its relation to the congregation, to forbid the
management by it of the Foreign Missionary or any
other of the schemes of the Assembly? If not, why
not commit such of these schemes to a board of deacons, and set free the ministers of the word for their
high calling? Did not the apostles insist upon the
appointment of deacons "to serve tables," in order that
they might give themselves to the "service of the
word"? The answer to these questions may be given
in a series of propositions:

1. It is plain that the original deacons were not confined in their ministrations to a single congregation
(Acts vi.), unless we suppose with the Independents
that there was but one congregation in Jerusalem.

2. If a deacon may extend his ministrations beyond
the bounds of his own congregation, the principle is settled, and it becomes a question merely of expediency
how many congregations may be embraced within their
scope. Their scope may embrace all the congregations represented by a general assembly.

3. There may be cases in which the collection and
disbursement of the people's offerings demand, for
their full effect, the accompaniment of instruction
which can be best given only by ministers of the
word. In such cases ministers may be associated
with, or even take the place of, deacons. Instances of
this sort we find in Acts i. 29, 30; xxx. 4, compared with

xxiv. 17; Rom. xv. 25–28; 2 Cor. viii. 16–24; and Paley's *Horæ Paulinæ*, Ch. II., No. 3. Paul seems to have attached so much importance to the contributions mentioned in these passages as to justify his leaving his work among the Gentiles and his taking laborious journeys to Jerusalem, in order to expound their spiritual significance and to seal to the recipients the precious fruit. How far these principles apply to any or all of the Assembly's schemes, it is for the wisdom of the church to decide; but it is the author's conviction that the tendency is now to excess in the employment of ministers of the word, and to a return to plans which the church, many years ago, formally repudiated as wrong in principle and injurious in results.

Touching the qualifications for the deacon's office, two places of Scripture may be compared: Acts vi. 3, 5; 1 Tim. iii. 8, 9. The differences here may be explained by the difference between a temporary condition of the church, in which gifts of the Spirit were prodigally and generally bestowed, and a condition of the church designed to be permanent, in which gifts are conferred with a more sparing hand. The proportion between the gifts generally bestowed and the special gifts for the exercise of office is in both conditions about the same. The rule for the guidance of the church in all time is, no doubt, that given in the third chapter of the First Epistle to Timothy.